EL MUNDO ZURDO 4

SELECTED WORKS FROM THE 2013 MEETING OF THE SOCIETY FOR THE STUDY OF GLORIA ANZALDÚA

EDITED BY
T. JACKIE CUEVAS,
LARISSA M. MERCADO-LÓPEZ,
AND SONIA SALDÍVAR-HULL

aunt lute books

San Francisco

Aunt Lute Books
P.O. Box 410687
San Francisco, CA 94141
www.auntlute.com

Cover design: Amy Woloszyn, Amymade Graphic Design
Cover art: "Querida Maestra: Anzalduista y Muxerista Siempre" by Dr. Anita Tijerina Revilla
Text design: Amy Woloszyn, Amymade Graphic Design
Senior Editor: Joan Pinkvoss
Managing Editor: Shay Brawn
Production: Maya Sisneros, Taylor Hodges, Erin Peterson, and Katie Seifert

Library of Congress Cataloging-in-Publication Data

El Mundo Zurdo 4 : selected works from the 2013 meeting of the society for the study of Gloria Anzaldúa / edited by T. Jackie Cuevas, Larissa M. Mercado-López, and Sonia Saldívar-Hull.
pages cm
Includes bibliographical references and index.
ISBN 978-1-879960-91-6 (acid-free paper)
1. Anzaldúa, Gloria--Criticism and interpretation. 2. Mexican Americans in literature. I. Cuevas, T. Jackqueline, editor. II. Mercado-López, Larissa, editor. III. Saldívar-Hull, Sonia, 1951- editor.
PS3551.N95Z795 2015
818'.5409--dc23
2015012577

Printed in the U.S.A. on acid-free paper

10 9 8 7 6 5 4 3 2 1

CONTENTS

TOWARD POETIC HEALINGS

CONTRIBUTORS

INTRODUCTION

THE CRITICAL WORK OF ANZALDÚAN STUDIES

T. JACKIE CUEVAS

The 2013 conference for the Society for the Study of Gloria Anzaldúa (SSGA) assembled a range of people interested in thinking together about the critical contributions of Anzaldúa as writer and theorist. Since its inception in 2007, the conference has gathered Anzaldúan thinkers, and the attendant publication has archived a selection of contributions to build up the body of written work on Anzaldúa. The finale event of Cindy Cruz's 2013 plenary keynote brought together a mixed crowd of activistas, academics, artists, creative writers, spiritual healers, and families with children. The conference's panels featured a wide range of topics, such as spirituality, pedagogy, illness, queerness, and connections between Chicana feminism and Palestinian activism. The formats included scholarly papers, roundtables, workshops, art exhibits, and poetry readings. The volume here represents a sampling from participants of the 2013 meeting.

This collection opens with Cindy Cruz's keynote talk, in which Cruz reflects on the significant role Anzaldúa's work has played in her research and teaching as she helps her students "think through the process of knowledge construction and coming to political consciousness." Cruz's work with queer youth of color who find themselves embattled in California's public education system serves as

a testament to the long and varied effect of an Anzaldúan pedagogy of resistance and the continued impact her thought has on the emerging generation. According to Cruz, "When students read Anzaldúa together, they begin to recognize the 'many-headed demon of oppression' (*Bridge*, p. 195)..." and imagine forms of resistance. As Cruz observes, "So many of us are drawn so strongly to Anzaldúa's writing when she recoups aspects of our experiences, testimonio-like, that have otherwise been denied." This echoes the sentiment expressed by Norma Alarcón in the first volume of *El Mundo Zurdo* when Alarcón says, "None of my academic training and knowledge had prepared me for the encounter with Anzaldúa's text *Borderlands*, though there was a 'structure of feeling' that linked with mine" (18). The structure of feeling so many have likened to what Anzaldúa refers to as conocimiento, a complex process of breaking open and transforming, weaves through the work here, particularly for those recalling the first time they or their students encountered Anzaldúa's writings.

In this vein, the first section on pedagogy and the academy includes contributors for whom Anzaldúa's writing has served as rupture or suture, sometimes both. As they recount aspects of an Anzaldúan feeling, they describe the coming to consciousness and challenges of implementing Anzaldúan feminist pedagogies. Rob Johnson and Deborah Cole document the contentious history of a 1960s discriminatory speech test at Pan American College, one of the schools Anzaldúa attended. Cynthia María Paccacerqua, Rufina Cortez, and others consider how Anzaldúan concepts and pedagogical practices have been received, challenged, and developed within the academy. Some use an Anzaldúan approach to their writing, mixing styles of testimonio and scholarly essay. Many of their ideas resonate with those presented in the recent anthology *Presumed Incompetent: The Intersections of Race and Class for Women in Academia,* edited by Gabriella Gutiérrez y Muhs, et al., which documents the challenges women of color face in a hostile academy and how they resist its power dynamics.

Given Anzaldúa's emphasis on rethinking the spiritual as well as how we tell stories, it makes sense that any collection on her thought would engage questions of spirituality and storytelling. AnaLouise Keating and April L. Michels each take up the question of spiritual activism. Adrianna Michelle Santos and Cristina Rose Smith explore the significance of storytelling, with Smith employing an autoethnographic approach to thinking about identity and creative knowledge production by drawing connections between Anzaldúan concepts and Filipina traditions.

Some contributors use Anzaldúan concepts as a springboard for thinking through feminist conundrums. For example, Michael Lee Gardin's essay looks at ongoing tensions between feminist and transgender studies. Magda García contends that Anzaldúa's concept of "El Mundo Zurdo" must be taken into con-

sideration as an "anti-capitalist intervention that emerges from the materiality of a specific site, namely the Rio Grande Valley." The work such contributions perform is critical in that they both drawn on and critique Anzaldúan thought and they perform a vital function in contributing to women of color feminist thought.

Just as Anzaldúa's groundshifting text *Borderlands/La Frontera* ends with poetry that serves as an opening rather than a finite ending, we close this anthology with poetry inspired by la Gloria's writings. ire'ne lara silva's poems speak to the toll that being a woman of color in this world takes on the body and the imperative to heal. As Anzaldúa's mixed genre of work reminds us, knowledge and theorizing take place in myriad sites, and poetry was such a critical site of meaning making for Anzaldúa. ire'ne lara silva, author of *furia* (Mouthfeel Press, 2010) and *flesh to bone* (Aunt Lute, 2013) helped close the 2013 conference with poetry and song. She and other volunteers led the audience in an impromptu grito, filling the auditorium with the hearty collective shout of activists, writers, and educators re-energized to carry on the legacy of Gloria E. Anzaldúa and the critical work of Anzaldúan studies. The subsequent work collected herein represents the labor of those who seek to adhere to the Anzaldúan edict and wish: "May we do work that matters."

Note: The editors would like to thank Raquel Torres and Megan Nieto for assistance with the preparation of the manuscript.

NOTES ON CROSSING DISCIPLINARY BORDERLANDS: ANZALDÚAN PEDAGOGIES AND A DEFENSE OF EXPERIENTIAL KNOWLEDGES

CINDY CRUZ

Throw away abstraction and the academic learning, the rules, the map and compass. Feel your way without blinders. To touch more people, the personal realities and the social must be evoked—not through rhetoric but through blood and pus and sweat.
—Gloria Anzaldúa, *This Bridge Called My Back: Writings by Radical Women of Color*

My whole struggle is to change the disciplines, to change the genres, to change how people look at a poem, at theory or at children's books. So I have to struggle between how many of these rules I can break and how I still can have readers read the books without getting frustrated.
—Gloria Anzaldúa, *Borderlands/La Frontera: The New Mestiza*

INTRODUCTION.

I would like to thank the organizers of the conference for inviting me to speak today. Dr. Norma Cantú and the organizing committee, thank you for this great honor to speak here and I am greatly humbled by the generosity and all the work that goes into this conference that centers a much beloved mentor and guide. Dr. Sonia Saldívar-Hull, I am honored to always be in your brilliant presence, you have been my mentor since my chingona years at UCLA and

through 1,697 miles we have remained friends and colleagues in this struggle to move U.S. Third World feminisms forward in the academy and I continue to be grateful for your words of advice and dangerous knowledge because I do think we are at a crossroads, *la encrucijada*, when it comes to making legible the project of Gloria Anzaldúa and women of color feminisms.

Let me begin here as I imagine an audience of graduate students who are working with the theories and literatures of feminists of color, scholars who are interviewing and organizing youth, immigrants, queers, advocating with and for women who have been abused, coalition building with African American and indigenous communities, teaching young people who are English language learners, working with students who are being pushed out of their schools, and standing by those same students who are trying to respond critically to the institution of schooling. Let me begin here.

When I engage with the writing of Gloria Anzaldúa, I recognize in the documentation of her experience the many moments where she refuses the management of her body, rejects the racialized and gendered behavior imposed on her by her family, and challenges the cultural values of a community that have become restrictive for certain kinds of women, men, and others. Whether through her childhood example of being corporeally punished at school by teachers for speaking Spanish, or from her refusal of the passive and obedient role of a traditional *mujer* (and I am thinking about the passage: "The concepts 'passive' and 'dutiful' raked my skin like spurs and 'marriage' and 'children' set me to bucking faster than rattlesnakes or coyotes" that is in *Bridge*, p. 202), or even in the declaration in *Borderlands* when she states that she has "made the choice to be queer," I want to think with and from Anzaldúa in these passages of testifying what it means to be contained within the multiple worlds she moves in. As a teacher and an educational researcher, I want to think about these instances of unmanageability as examples of an Anzaldúan pedagogy that are refusals to be contained on multiple registers. Anzaldúa's narratives document the many confrontations by family, community, the university, to restrict her, but she also offers a vision of what it means to transcend these imposed limits to her very being. Anzaldúa's writing forces me to think about the attempts of the field of education, in which I work, to discipline me as an assistant professor undergoing the tenure process. I am also thinking about the future projects of the students I work with who are also centering women of color thought and the preparation and socialization of feminist of color scholars. Like Anzaldúa, I also refuse this containment that happens when I cross disciplinary boundaries. There is a pedagogy implied in this refusal. But I want to be strategic in my response to the disciplining I experience as I move forward with my research agenda and to share my thoughts about my re-commitment to the field of feminist of color thought.

WE DO THIS WORK OF PRAXICAL WRITING TOGETHER

For many years, I taught writing composition for summer bridge programs that targeted low-income students of color, many of whom would be the first generation of their families to attend college. My role as a writing instructor was clear—not only was I tasked to ensure students understand what the university expects of them in terms of writing proficiency, but I also taught the course with a political urgency in the development of undergraduate writers. Teaching writing post-Proposition 209[1], where gender or racial/ethnic identity became prohibited in the admissions decisions in all California public universities and directly impacted the numbers of first generation students of color admitted to the University of California, was about developing reflexive, critical thinkers. If the university wanted students to develop into intellectuals who understood that one of the most important ways they have of making discoveries about themselves and the world around them with the strength of communicating these insights to others, then the teaching of writing and the literacy skills necessary to mediate experience in these ways needed to be developed in relation to political consciousness raising. Thus, *This Bridge Called My Back* and *Borderlands* were required readings in my classroom.

> I passed my adolescence combatting [my mother's] incessant orders to bathe my body, scrub the floors and cupboards, clean the windows and the walls. And as we'd get into the back of the "patron's" truck that would take us to the fields, she'd ask, "Where's your gorra (sunbonnet)?" La gorra—rim held firm by slats of cardboard, neck flounce flowing over my shoulders—made me feel like a horse with blinders, a member of the French Foreign Legion, or a nun bowed down by her wimple. One day in the middle of the cotton field, I threw the gorra away and donned a sombrero. Though it didn't keep out the Texas 110° sun as well as the bonnet, ***I could now see in all directions***, feel the breeze, dry the sweat on my neck. (*Bridge* 198)

When students read Anzaldúa together, they begin to recognize the "many-headed demon of oppression" that the symbol of the *gorra* represents (195). Students analyze the structure of Anzaldúa's texts and the careful move she makes in documenting her experience to provide an explanation of her world that is not part of how the institutions or the ideologies of those in power construct knowledge about Chicanas and Mexicanas. What is important to acknowledge is how Anzaldúa and the writers of *Bridge* take this documentation of lived experience, the body interrogated, and how they purposefully reclaim or revise experience on the side of resistance. Many of us are drawn so strongly to Anzaldúa's writings when she recoups aspects of our experiences, testimonio-like, that have otherwise been denied. Through this interrogation of the body, in

tandem with others who are also struggling to create alternative explanations of their experiences, Anzaldúa peoples a theoretical landscape with those who are also trying to re-vision and re-member these critical stories. It is the re-visioning that is important here, the recouping of the narratives of the lived experience of women of color not as some pure and authentic narrative for the consumption of hegemonic feminists, but one that has been carefully analyzed, interrogated, and performed. As Maria Lugones makes clear, Anzaldúa's U.S.-Texas borderlands, in whatever form, become spaces for new resistant socialities ("On Borderlands" 36).

I want to think about these off-stage spaces of sociality in multiple ways because I think they are important when sharing knowledge, or practicing new ways of thinking and being, spaces that are outside of the surveillance of those in power. Those are spaces filled with creativity and possibility. When writing students recognize that Anzaldúa's alternative construction of knowledge is often made in tandem with activism and oppositional political struggles (Mohanty 213), they sense the kinds of socialities necessary to write against the grain of power. It is knowledge mediated with other feminists of color who are also part of larger coalitional social movements. *Bridge* and *Haciendo Caras* are exemplary in these ways. Maybe we need to see these texts as the documentation of resistant socialities, as primers that help us think through the practices of coalitional relations and decolonizing ways of being in our worlds. To read Anzaldúan and feminists of color thought in ways that index oppression and categorize the layers of outrage in her stories and in the testimonies of women of color writing seems incomplete. "They would chop me up into little fragments and tag each piece with a label" ("*Bridge*" 205), writes Anzaldúa, critical of the ways the academy accounts for the limited and inadequate interrogation of the writing and theorizing of women of color thought and experience. Students may start with the interrogation of the social relations of power, but a political consciousness begins when they understand that knowledge created against the grain of power depends on their comprehending what it would take to change these relations of power (Mohanty 214). To claim alternative knowledge, students discover the aspects that make up the multiple worlds they inhabit which define their sense of self and the options they are taught to have. They recognize the plurality of their selves, the multiplicity of their experiences. A major ingredient of the consciousness raising is creating the space and openness in the writing classroom where students not only feel safe to take theoretical risks and question the multiple worlds around them, but they also learn to listen and support one another in this process. To recognize our plurality is to recognize how a dichotomous relation will always reduce our differences into that other unrecognizable being. Anger may also be part of the process—it almost always is—when students struggle to make sense of their lived experience in our racist/sexist/immigrant-bashing/

homophobic world. Anger, then, as Audre Lorde would say, becomes more than a personal response. It is also the "theoretical prism" (Mohanty 209; Lorde 54-56) through which post-Proposition 209 students help see their world and themselves in it critically.

Making this praxis explicit is vital. It does not always work, but I consider this the beginnings of thinking about how we engage student writers in the creation of new knowledge. When I re-read *Bridge* and *Borderlands* and *Haciendo Caras*, I remembered why I was so drawn to its praxis—Anzaldúa was not only asking me to write as a brown bodied, working-class, hard scrabble, Chicana dyke, she was also teaching me how to write reflexively, critically, with purpose. To teach and facilitate writing curriculums that ask questions about who is allowed to write and who is censored and what the experiences of feminists of color teach us and why, is the work of naming and making clear the pedagogies of a text such as *This Bridge Called My Back.* It is one that clarifies revolutionary thinking and offers pedagogies of disciplining against the grain of power.

When Anzaldúa throws her *gorra* away in the fields and writes, "I could now see in all directions," I think about how these narratives or *cuentos* are more than examples of her rejecting the management of her body. They are pedagogical in a way that not only helps us re-examine these cultural-political meanings and theories (that are differentially racialized, gendered, and specific to Anzaldúa's social locations) attached to *la gorra*, but also make it possible for us to detect new ones, new theories and new technologies to move our own projects forward. Anzaldúa's writing does so by guiding us to new designs and new hybrids, always pragmatic, and asking us to see in all directions, teaching us what to take seriously and what to re-interpret. When Anzaldúa states that the "past can be as malleable as the present" ("*Haciendo Caras*" xxvii), I am guided to think about queer youth narratives that show them not as victims but as survivors and resistors.

When I first compiled the testimonies of the queer street youth that center my own project, I was not able to recognize resistance, at least in the ways that resistance had been defined in the current literature. I did not see it. But I sensed it and I knew through my own experience that there must be a way of thinking about resistance that could reclaim some of the behaviors and small acts of defiance that I saw every day as a high school teacher. So when I take Anzaldúa's notion of "malleability," I think of these narratives and stories that youth tell me as clay, ready to be shaped and stretched and challenged and even bent into other truths. For positivists, whose methodology is the disciplinary way most of us in the social sciences have been trained, this must sound like blasphemy. Yet I believe that the "truth" is multiple and that maybe we need to think about how we use the notion of objectivity in very narrow ways and how we can rethink it

in our favor.

Let me offer an example how I use Anzaldúa's concept of malleability: To think about resistance in educational research is to take the stance that youth are not victims, but are often witnesses and survivors of great trauma and oppression. In the stories that students tell me, I am often forced to recognize their stories of oppression in order to later recognize their resistance. For instance, an 18-year-old Eastern European gay youth told me about his experience meeting online an older American photographer "friend" who later sends him a plane ticket to the U.S. for them to meet (the youth was 16 years old at the time of the story):

> When I got to [large East Coast city], I lived with this photographer who said that maybe I could work for him, as photography is my passion. But after a little while things weren't going to work out between us and I left him with the cash that he had given me. I stayed with new friends for a while, crashing on their couches as I looked for work. Nobody was going to hire me—young, and now illegal, as I had already overstayed my visa. I did bar back work at a bar, but I didn't make enough to really live on, and slowly I found myself at the shelters.

When this young gay man tells me that "things weren't going to work out between us," I was forced to acknowledge that I was hearing a story of youth trafficking, reframed by the youth as an ending of a (mutual) relationship. Enticed by a potential offer of a job in photography and a plane ticket that arrives in the mail, the youth leaves his home and into a short lived "relationship" with the photographer and soon finds himself homeless in a large East Coast city. But what catches my attention as an ethnographer was in the way that the young gay man framed the story to me that was important. In his telling of his story, the culmination of the relationship is mutual for both the youth and the photographer. The youth also emphasizes that he "leaves" the older man on his own terms. What is important is his generation of events, where the young gay man, caught in the traffic of youth bodies that manipulates on multiple levels this longing for a new life in the U.S., refuses to be defined as a victim. In this story, my close reading of what I now realize is the trafficking of a queer migrant youth becomes intimately tied to the recognition of his refusal to be seen as such. He refuses to be contained under the label "unaccompanied minor." He refuses to be seen as someone "trafficked."

In this world of trafficking, youth are seen as exploitable, defenseless, and utterly victimized. The young man in this story refuses that world, and instead reframes his story in a world where he is perceived as ambitious and entrepreneurial. Yet a researcher also recognizes this other space of trafficking. In these multiple and contradictory worlds and border crossings that exist in this

example, it is important that we attend to the conflict between how the youth sees himself in his reframed world as ambitious and entrepreneurial, and how a researcher might see him as a victim or as a vulnerable subject under similar circumstances. Maybe I have taken Anzaldúa's concept of "malleability" too far for some positivist researchers. But I know that I have to recognize how the researcher's role becomes so vital in this negotiation. To create different interpretations of experience, and to create new knowledges that are outside of the usual frames of the public performances of power, is a risking together and often challenging both subject and researcher to see what meaning can be made here. It is the shift I demand of my writing students. To recognize and validate the multiple narratives and plurality of this example is an important methodological move, where this queer street youth's story can be reclaimed/recouped/revisioned as resistant, agentic, and sometimes even liberatory, even under such high stakes.

The queer youth who are the subjects of much of my writing take many calculated risks, such as the youth mentioned earlier, where they may weigh the costs of certain kinds of decisions they make about their lives against a chance of immigrating to the U.S. or even for a commitment of intimacy and connection. Unlike the very public moral panics that are prominent in the US around sexuality and gendered lives that rationalize the "protection" of youth by withholding information about safe sex, contraception, and sex education, the young man here is well aware of the unequal transaction here between a 16-year-old and an older American professional. Because of the politics of disguise and anonymity in the research interview process[2], it may be that the youth testimony is designed to have multiple meanings to shield the identities of the actors in this story. If this is indeed a narrative crafted in this liminal space of constant struggle, the notion of a "malleable" narrative must also consider the sociality of these tight spaces where such resistance is developed, encouraged, and given new meanings. And this kind of revisioning of youth testimonials helps me think about the "lived experiences" of youth away from theories of change that simply reinscribe deficit and often dangerous representations of youth of color, or even the idea that with better methods we can get better data. Without these alternative constructions of knowledge, without revision on multiple levels, without an Anzaldúan notion of "malleability" or a methodology based on coalition, both the street youth and the writing students I am working with and teaching are limited to the constructions and representations authorized by the very ideologies and institutions of those in power (Harding 127). When I think about power, and youth of color, and resistance, thinking through feminist of color theory, that is but one way that I make my own refusal in the academy.

WOMEN OF COLOR SURVIVAL KIT: OR HOW NOT TO TAME A WILD TONGUE

> She has discovered that she can't hold concepts or ideas in rigid boundaries. The border and walls that are supposed to keep the undesirable ideas out are entrenched habits and patterns of behavior; these habits are the enemy within. Rigidity means death. Only by remaining flexible is she able to stretch the psyche horizontally and vertically. (*Borderlands* 101)

I have lived a long time with a passage in *Borderlands* where Anzaldúa claims a "feminist architecture," where she states that she wants the freedom to carve and chisel her own face, where if going home is denied her, she will have to stand and claim her space, making her own house with her lumber, her bricks and mortar (44). So I want to be very strategic here when I say that we, as a collective, must also take a stand and claim our theoretical space to become legible in the academy. It is no accident that *Bridge* is out of print, that women's and queer bookstores and printing houses have closed and the infrastructure that supported women of color writing, however small it was originally, is now miniscule. So I am asking for a renewed commitment to women of color thought, where we organize, support one another, create summer institutes, offer conferences, make coalition with other communities of women. Our infrastructure, through MALCS and the beautiful MALCS Journal, through the strong caucuses at NACCS, and the Society for the Study of Gloria Anzaldúa, is powerful. I am also thinking about my graduate students who are committed to the politics and pedagogies of feminists of color, and I am saying Feminists of Color as a field, and what they should expect as they enter the job market as emerging scholars. Because there is a problem with our legibility in the academy, and for those of us who are attempting to procure tenure at the university, these issues are repeatedly being reflected in evaluations and promotion and merit reviews. So there are several things I would prepare the graduate students I advise about research that centers feminist of color thought. I am trying to think of it as a Women of Color Survival Kit.

We must attend to the discussions in feminist studies and history around the notion of "lived experience." Joan Scott's 1991 article *On Experience* and Judith Butler's 1992 introduction in the edited book *Feminists Theorize the Political* are often used to discount certain kinds of empirical research that centers "lived experience," whether that was their intention or not in both essays. But both articles have greatly influenced how empirical work that centers women of color research is evaluated and I am suggesting that we be strategic in how we use experience in our own work. There are several counter-arguments in literary theory, many of them coming from multiculturalists who are invested in the literature of people of color who have taken this as a mission, such as Paula Moya, Satya Mohanty, and Ernesto Martinez. Their work is helpful in thinking

through how we defend "lived experience" in our own research. But we need to pay attention to the idea that experience is mediated by many of the ideologies/beliefs/values that surround us. Our job is making clear what those practices are and how mediation animates other alternative understandings. This task points to the interdisciplinary work we need to do to make these connections in fields other than our own disciplinary homes. It also points to a redefining of the concept of objectivity away from its narrow positivist origins (Mohanty). Maybe we also need to think about these issues coalitionally, to share strategies with other communities of women, men, and others.

I also want to help my graduate students think through the processes of knowledge construction and coming to political consciousness. In the field of Education, Paulo Freire's theory of critical consciousness is helpful here, as is new work by Vygotskian scholars such as Kris Gutierrez who are looking at the best practices for literacy and language development. Thinking through texts such as *Bridge* and *Haciendo Caras*—the body interrogated—with literacy scholars is also useful. How do we then talk about experience and knowledge production? How do we problematize the practice of mediation for our own research? If feminist of color writing is seen as unmediated experience, that is, as confessional, "pure" or authentic voice, how does this contribute to our legibility issue? And how do we reconcile this knowledge that may not be mediated in ways that are legible, in forms that are not recognizable, especially when feminist of color authors know that the traditional forms do not often work for their writing?

So I am asking for a dedication of space and time in our various infrastructures and organizations, undergraduate and graduate courses, and institutes to begin grappling with these issues of legibility in strategic ways. Part of this work is tracing genealogies, mapping schools of thought, understanding our relationship or departures from the conceptual tools that originate in women of color thought. Laura Perez's recent 2010 article in the journal *Qui Parle* reflects her (our) continuing concern that the transnational circulation of knowledges is not one-way when working with other progressive leftists and social movements, and that a feminist of color critique become part of the common basis for the critiques of Eurocentrism. New theories of race and colonization from the global south in particular are positioned in ways that overlook gender or see it only in terms of reproduction (Quijano), or have bypassed Anzaldúa's contributions to border thinking except for few citations (Mignolo). It is so telling that in Sonia Saldívar-Hull's *Feminism on the Border* that she states that so many of us find "theory" in the non-traditional spaces—the margins, the footnotes, the archives. So we must organize, time publications in various journals to make a greater impact, get on those editorial boards and book series, create the courses for graduate study, participate in the rigorous interrogation of Anzaldúan and

feminist of color thought. We are the new mestizas, and this new mestiza consciousness, like any other field, needs a method and a pedagogy!

Let me go back to why we write: Many of us write to counter the deficit and dehumanizing representations and inscriptions that have been forced onto our bodies, the ontologically inscribed notions of the culture of poverty, of eugenistic amplifications that dominate our lives and the lives of our families and communities. We write to reclaim and re-vise, remember the dead, and sometimes grieve. All of the youth who were part of my research carried huge artist journals, bound with tape and rubber bands, where they wrote on every centimeter of their paper. One student told me if she could not write she would die. I understand better this writing practice that documents street life. Youth were trying, desperately, to think through their life experiences. But in order for them to develop alternative explanations that are other than what the hegemony gives youth, their understandings of the social relations of power and privilege depend on their learning how and what their worlds require to change those relations. They write with others in socialities that helped them share knowledge and survive, on street corners and schoolyards, outside of the surveillance of power. We need to think about how feminist of color theorists have created socialities to write that also helped them share knowledge and survive. We are dependent on others to do this work of writing and teaching.

Not only is the mediation of experience that produces this writing pedagogical, it is also methodological. So when I suggest that we make a call for feminist of color thought as a field, a discipline, I wonder how Anzaldúa would react, who struggled against her own disciplining in every move. The master's tools will not dismantle the master's house, yes? Many of us are already part of the university, some of us as deans and presidents! Yet Anzaldúa carried a great discipline of her own, carving out her own intellectual spaces, creating a new mestiza culture, writing, teaching, organizing, troubling even the very languages we speak. Talk about disciplined! And yet we continue to demand our space in the academy and we demand our legibility. We have to do it ourselves.

> Why am I compelled to write? Because the writing saves me from this complacency I fear. Because I have no choice. Because I must keep the spirit of my revolt and myself alive. Because the world I create in the writing compensates for what the real world does not give me. By writing I put order in the world, give it a handle so I can grasp it. I write because life does not appease my appetites and hunger. I write to record what others erase when I speak, to rewrite the stories others have miswritten about me, about you. To become more intimate with myself and you. To discover myself, to preserve myself, to make myself, to achieve self-autonomy. To dispell the myths that I am a mad prophet or a poor suffering soul. To convince myself that I am worthy and that what I have to say

> is not a pile of shit. To show that I can and that I will write, never mind their admonitions to the contrary. And I will write about the unmentionables, never mind the outraged gasp of the censor and the audience. Finally I write because I'm scared of writing but I'm more scared of not writing. (*Bridge* 168-169)

ENDNOTES

1 Proposition 209 (also known as the California Civil Rights Initiative) is the 1996 California ballot propositional that amended the state constitution to prohibit state government institutions from considering race, sex or ethnicity, specifically in the areas of public employment, public contracting or public education. The proposition passed with 54.6% of the vote. Its subsequent authorization in December of 1996 at the University of California reflected in low admittance rates of African American and Latino students, where the numbers of students admitted to the UC dropped dramatically in almost every ethnic category except for Asian Pacific Islander and White students.

2 My work with LGBTQ street youth was strictly anonymized and IRB did not allow for any names, places, or information collected that could be linked back to the identities of the youth I talked with. I never asked for names and coded my data by asking youth to give me two letters and two numbers, along with other demographic information. My original fieldnotes are strictly redacted. This may have freed youth to talk openly, yet the politics of the hidden transcript seemed a part of every public observation and every interview.

WORKS CITED

Anzaldúa, Gloria. *Borderlands/La Frontera: The New Mestiza.* San Francisco: Aunt Lute Foundation, 1987.

---. *Making Face, Making Soul/Haciendo Caras: Creative and Critical Perspectives by Feminists of Color.* San Francisco: Aunt Lute Books, 1990.

Butler, Judith. "Contingent Foundations: Feminism and the Question of Postmodernism." *Feminists Theorize the Political.* Eds. Judith Butler & Joan Scott. New York: Routledge, 1992. 3-21.

Freire. P. *Pedagogy of the Oppressed.* New York: Verso Press, 1970.

Gutierrez, Kris D., Morales, P. Zitlali, & Martinez, Danny C. "Remediating Literacy: Culture, Difference, and Learning for Students from Non-dominant Communities." *Review of Research in Education* 33 (2009): 212-245.

Harding, Sandra. *Whose Science? Whose Knowledge?* Ithaca, NY: Cornell, 1991.

Lorde, Audre. *Sister Outsider and Other Essays.* Freedom, CA: Crossing Press, 1984.

Lugones, Maria. "On Borderlands/La Frontera: An Interpretive Essay." *Hypatia,* 7.4 (1992): 31-37.

---. *Pilgrimages/Peregrinajes: Theorizing Coalition Against Multiple Oppressions.* New York: Rowman & Littlefield, 2003.

Martinez, Ernesto. *On Making Sense: Queer Race Narratives of Intelligibility.* Palo Alto, CA: Stanford, 2010.

Mohanty, Satya. *Literary Theory and the Claims of History: Postmodernism, Objectivity, Multicultural Politics.* Ithaca, NY: Cornell, 1997.

Moraga, Cherrie & Anzaldúa, Gloria. *This Bridge Called My Back: Writings by Radical Women of Color.* Boston: Kitchen Press, 1981.

Pérez, Laura E. "Enrique Dussel's Etica de la liberación, US Women of Color Decolonizing Practices, and Coalitionary Politics amidst Difference." *Qui Parle: Critical Humanities and Social Sciences* 18.2 (2010): 121-146.

Quijano, Anibal. "Coloniality of power and Eurocentrism in Latin America." *International Sociology* 15.2 (2000): 215-232.

Saldivar-Hull, Sonia. *Feminism on the Border: Chicana Gender Politics and Literature.* Berkeley: University of California Press, 2000.

Scott, Joan. "The Evidence of Experience." *Critical Inquiry* 17.4 (1991): 773-797.

ANZALDÚA, THE ACADEMY, AND PEDAGOGICAL PRAXIS

"HOW TO TAME A WILD TONGUE": GLORIA ANZALDÚA'S *BORDERLANDS/LA FRONTERA* AND THE 1960S ERA SPEECH TEST AND SPEECH CLASSES AT PAN AMERICAN COLLEGE

ROB JOHNSON AND DEBORAH COLE

Gloria Evangelina Anzaldúa was a student at Pan American College from 1965-1968. She grew up in Hargill, Texas, a small, cross-roads farming community about ten miles from the college. Her family members were farm workers, ranch workers, and migrant laborers (Anzaldúa 227). Anzaldúa matriculated at Texas Women's University in 1962 but returned home after one year of study and eventually transferred to Pan American College. In the early 1960s, few Mexican Americans attended high school, fewer graduated, and even fewer attended college. Pan American was the only four-year college serving the border of south Texas, and its existence offered the promise of higher education and economic opportunity for the local Mexican-American community. Anne Estevis describes the importance of the college to young Mexican-Americans in the late 1950s in her short-story collection *Down Garrapata Road.* "It seemed so unreal, this idea of going to college," says Nilda, a young woman in the collection's final story who is finishing up high school in Edinburg, Texas. "I would be the first in my family to go to college." When her father gives her permission to go to Pan American College, she is speechless: "I was enjoying the feeling of happiness and sense of wonder that had come over me" (118-119).

We would like to be able to write that Pan American College lived up to this "sense of wonder" in the case of Gloria Anzaldúa, and in some respects it probably did: for example, in the Spring semester of 1967, she was able to take a course on "The Frontier in American Literature," a course that could well have started her thinking about the border issues she would later famously write about in *Borderlands*. However, her memories of the school reveal a harsh colonial aspect of her education. In "How to Tame a Wild Tongue," she tells the story of Pan American College's mandatory speech test and its effect on her, beginning with her mother's advice about going to college:

> "I want you to speak in English. *Pa' hallar buen trabajo tienes que saber hablar el inglés bien. Qué vale toda tu educación si todavía hablas inglés con un* 'accent,'" my mother would say, mortfied that I spoke English like a Mexican. At Pan American University, I, and all Chicano students were required to take two speech classes. Their purpose: to get rid of our accents. Attacks on one's form of expression with the intent to censor are a violation of the First Amendment. *El Anglo con cara de inocente nos arrancó la lengua.* Wild tongues can't be tamed, they can only be cut out. (75-76)[1]

This violent colonization of her native south Texas tongue becomes the basis for the chapter's sociolinguistic defense of border languages, and is justly famous as a liberating document for the generations of writers who have felt its influence and were empowered by her words to write in the multilingual language (Spanish, English, Tex-Mex) that was their heritage.[2] The dramatic example she cites above as an attack on this heritage refers to two required speech classes, and our investigations also uncovered a "speech test" (which Anzaldúa does not reference) used to determine whether or not students were required to take the classes. But what was this test and what was the content of these speech classes? Perhaps more importantly, what were the intentions of those who administered the speech test and taught the classes?

TAKING THE SPEECH TEST: INTERVIEWS WITH TWO FORMER PAC STUDENTS

We recently interviewed two former Pan American College students who took the test in 1963 and are now professors in the School of Education at UTPA. Both are harshly critical of the ingrained racism present in the methodology of the test and testify to its longstanding psychological effects on their personal and professional development.

Dr. Alejo Salinas, Jr. began attending Pan American College in 1963. He went on to a successful career in education and was Superintendent of Schools in Hidalgo, Texas for many years. He is currently a professor in UTPA's educational

leadership PhD program. Sitting in his office in the Education School at UTPA, he described his memories of his first day at Pan American College:

> I remember coming out of high school you had this great expectation that you had met the requirements for graduating from high school, which in 1963 was still quite an accomplishment for a Hispanic student—since most of them dropped out in junior high—so you were ready to attend college. I was the first in my class and home to attend college, and when I came to register I realized I had to take a speech test on the spot and without notice. It was given by a lady named Ruth Owens.

The test, he recalls, was designed to trip up the region's bilingual students, focusing on the pronunciation of th, sh, ch, and short i. Only Mexican-Americans had to take the test. If you pronounced these sounds with a Spanish-influenced accent—as almost all Mexican-American students did in the estimation of the test-givers—you were assigned to Speech 113X, a class that met every day. His teacher, Miss Owens, whose "intentions" in correcting their accents were sincere, Dr. Salinas says, was nonetheless unprofessional in the classroom and abusive of students who showed little progress:

> She would sometimes get very upset, and while she didn't throw the book at me, she threw it at other students because they were not making the kind of progress she wanted. So that was embarrassing. It was a humiliating experience and not only for me personally but for a lot of students in the class. We had to take that class to graduate.

Students hated the class and most of the instructors,[3] but there was no mechanism for student evaluation of the class and no possibility in 1963 of protesting against the test and the behavior of the more abusive instructors:

> We put up with it because we didn't know any better. Could we protest? We were not going to do anything like that. The college experience was something brand new to us. We were all wanting to have a positive experience and terrified to even complain about it to anybody because at the freshman and sophomore level you didn't have much say so and you were just lucky to have been accepted, to be in school, and terrified that they might kick you out at any point.

The experience of the speech test and of taking Speech 113X he says was a "traumatic one" that had long-term effects on his personal and professional development:

> It created a situation where I didn't feel I could express myself openly and it kept me from being participatory in class. It wasn't until I started my career and matured that I had confidence—that I realized I could get over all of that. But yes, it had a negative impact on my personality, on

> my career, on what I wanted to do and say, and when you develop this feeling of inferiority it takes a little while to get over it and you have to have a number of successes to offset that feeling of negativity that you develop . . . it definitely was there.

Dr. Miguel de los Santos, whose office is next door to Dr. Salinas's, also matriculated at Pan American College in 1963, and like Dr. Salinas is a former school superintendent (in Edinburg, Texas and San Benito, Texas) now working in UTPA's Educational Leadership PhD program. His memories of the speech test and Speech 113X are bitter ones, too. He emailed the following response to our questions about the test and how students survived the experience in a "spirit of carnalismo":

> Took the oral English test as an entering freshman in 1963 and was found lacking. Don't remember having to take Speech two semesters but was enrolled in a M-F rather than a M-W-F or T-Th course. All of us illiterate Mexicans were to become so proficient in English that semester we would want to lose our Spanish language and culture. I am convinced that that was the psychological objective of the *pendejada*. The only good thing was that my speech instructor, besides being a good teacher, was one of the few at Pan American College who I can objectively say cared about us and believed in our potential. Thank you Mrs. Dahl! Don't remember much except feeling lesser than those who passed. Didn't question because we were not taught to do so. Those of us who failed used to put each other down for not having "passed," yet supported one another in a spirit of *carnalismo*; and, those who passed acted white and also jovially put us down. By the grace of God and a few teachers like Mrs. Dahl we survived PAC's good intentions.

Dr. de los Santos's view that the test and class had as their goal to make the students "lose our language and our culture" is remarkably similar to Gloria Anzaldúa's attack on the speech test in "How to Tame a Wild Tongue." Dr. Salinas, on the other hand, believes that while the intention of the teachers was to better educate the students, their methodology for doing so, for the most part, was a brutal and racist one in its overtones. Were we to interview the literally thousands of Pan American College students who took the speech test from the 1950s to the mid-1970s, we expect that their responses would reflect this range of criticism.

Initially, however, looking at the comments of these two test-takers who went on to become successful educators and who now teach at the university—making them particularly valuable informants—we can re-read Anzaldúa's passage from "Wild Tongue" cited above and understand in more specific terms her anger about the classes and why she saw this not as a simple matter of taking

proscribed courses required in her degree plan. She, along with her peers, as is evident in the interviews above, saw this as a violation of their First Amendment right to freedom of speech. She is thus quite prescient in her conclusion that the only way to "tame" tongues is to cut them out: clearly Anzaldúa and her fellow Pan Am graduates resisted such efforts in both personal and professional ways.

AN OUTSIDER'S PERSPECTIVE ON THE SPEECH TEST IN THE EARLY 1970S

To find out more about the speech test, and from a different angle, we interviewed Dr. Marian Monta, who joined the Communication Department in 1971 at Pan American College. Her job was created following the retirement of Ruth Owens, the strict professor who taught the speech class taken by Dr. Salinas. Dr. Monta, the first woman to graduate with a PhD in Theater from Cornell University (in 1971), has a uniquely valuable insight into the speech test. As an undergraduate student at Fordham University in the late 1940s, she, too, had taken a speech test. It was a common requirement in colleges back east, she says, and even across the United States. At Fordham University, the test was intended to rid the students of their New England accents. Later, in the 1960s, Monta taught at two historically Black colleges, Hampton University and Prairie View A and M. At both schools, a speech test and class were in place to rid the students of southern or southern-black accents. At all of these schools, she says, every student had to take the test, not just a select group. She was surprised, therefore, to find that at Pan Am the test was, by and large, only required of the Mexican-American students and that the Texas Anglo students, whose Texas accent was painfully obvious to Monta's east coast ears, did not have to take the test.

> As an east coast "foreigner," I was amazed to see that the anglos with the thick Texas drawls, who said "git" instead of "get," didn't have to take the test. I would have required [name omitted by editors], one of our faculty members from Texas, to take the class, but he was a test giver, not a class taker.

From her theater background, she says, everyone has accents, but "at Pan Am it meant teaching them to speak east Texan. So it was okay to say 'git' for 'get' . . . but you could not say 'beet' for bit.'" At Freshman orientation, she says, many of the test-givers wouldn't even administer the test—they would just look to see if the student's last name ended in a vowel. Some Mexican-American students with married names or family names that were Anglo, therefore, managed to avoid the test and the class. She recalls the surprise on her colleagues' faces when a Mexican-American student would speak English without the influence of Spanish phonology to a test-giver: "Well, you certainly don't sound like a Rodriguez!" Monta, to this day, supports speech classes that teach "proper" pro-

nunciation and articulation. However, at Pan American College, she says, the experience of giving the test had a distinctly racial tone to it, compared to the many universities where she had studied and taught.

TEACHING SPEECH 113X: OPAL WHITE AND THE SPEECH WORKBOOK

We wanted some insight into how the actual prescribed speech class was taught, so Monta kindly gave us her copy of the workbook that had been used in Speech 113X.[4] This book was authored by Pan American College Communication professor Opal White, who became Monta's mother's best friend shortly after Monta arrived in the Rio Grande Valley. White had been a high school teacher in the Valley and after earning her Master's degree was hired by the Department of Communication at Pan Am. After the death of her husband, White decided to pursue a PhD at the University of Oklahoma, partly to mitigate the grief she felt at her husband's passing. In 1972, at the age of sixty-two, White earned her doctorate, writing a dissertation entitled *The Mexican American Subculture: A Study in Teaching Contrastive Sounds in English and Spanish*. In her dissertation, White provides a socio-historical overview of the uniqueness of this region where the steady influx of new Spanish speakers supports the ongoing use of Spanish if not for all individuals then at least for a significant portion of the population as a whole. She then goes on to provide an overview of the language teaching and learning theories that were current at the time before laying out the general differences between the English and Spanish sound systems.

White was clearly someone who cultivated connections between her pedagogy and her scholarship. Her dissertation explicitly addresses the problem of limited access to education and economic resources that the Spanish-speaking students in the Rio Grande Valley endured in comparison to their English-speaking counterparts.[5] Her research was the first to look explicitly at the phonological aspects of English acquisition by Spanish speaking populations in the area and among the first to look at language issues with respect to Mexican-American populations at all. In her dissertation, White notes the dearth of previous research and says that she must rely for background information on a few studies of Mexican-American populations in other areas of Texas and the Southwest more broadly. The first sentence of the section "Rationale for Study" in her introduction makes her purpose clear: "Granted the significance for educating the Mexican American, the primary rationale for this particular study is that this subject area of concern is the most neglected in the school systems of South Texas" (*The Mexican American Subculture* 9).

Not satisfied with simply describing how language presented a barrier to local students' academic achievement, White sought to provide a tangible, practical way to improve the Mexican-American students' ability to attain upward social

mobility. She believed that helping them to acquire standard American speech would achieve this goal. She went on to author a textbook published in 1979 which was to be used in the speech classes at Pan American University, entitled *General American Speech for the Bilingual Spanish Speaking Student*. The textbook presents the sound system for American English through careful comparison with the sound system for Spanish. The method advocated in the text involves teaching students to use the International Phonetic Alphabet to describe and differentiate the relevant sounds, showing students where to place their articulators in producing the sounds, providing exercises for practicing English sounds in different positions within words, and raising students' awareness about the distinctive differences between the Spanish and English sound systems. Although some particulars with respect to language learning and teaching theory have changed since White's time, the basic facts of the sound differences and the general approach she used are quite similar to those that would appear in language teaching textbooks with a focus on pronunciation published today.

As Alejo Salinas points out, in spite of the sometimes brutal methods employed in the speech classes, the "intentions" of these teachers could be good, and certainly this is true of Opal White's research: she hoped to empower her students through her fine and forward-looking research, not disempower them. Nonetheless—and this is not surprising considering the pre-Chican@ era of her research—White failed to address issues of linguistic colonization later raised by Pan Am College student Gloria Anzaldúa. Unfortunately, these issues remain today, even as the former Pan Am College (now The University of Texas Pan American) is merging with UT-Brownsville and adding a medical school to become The University of Texas Rio Grande Valley (UTRGV), a proposed research-track university that will be one of the largest public universities in Texas, with over 30,000 predominately Hispanic students.

CLASSROOM DISCUSSION OF THE HISTORY OF THE SPEECH TEST AND ANZALDÚA'S *BORDERLANDS*

Forty years after the demise of the speech test, the ongoing contact between Spanish and English in the Rio Grande Valley continues to be a contested ground on the subject of standardization itself, how it is maintained as an ideology, and how it comes into conflict with other views of language that center on variation, like the one championed by Anzaldúa and those currently espoused by sociolinguists and applied linguists.[6] From our perspectives as linguistics and literature professors, the particular grammatical features of codeswitching, the neurological benefits of bilingualism, and the artistic creativity of writing *en dos idiomas* make Anzaldúa's position on translingual wildness a self-evident and easily defendable position. We are sometimes surprised, therefore, to hear current students, many of whom plan to become teachers in local schools,

declare that (a) they believe that they themselves don't speak any language, i.e. they don't speak English or Spanish well, and (b) they believe that codeswitching is wrong and serves as evidence that people are lazy and haven't learned to speak properly. Following in the footsteps of others who have found language courses to be an ideal environment to interrogate linguistic inequalities, we walk into our classrooms with copies of Anzaldúa's "How to Tame a Wild Tongue" thinking that this world-renowned scholar with local roots might just convince our students that having and mixing multiple repertoires is perfectly normal.

What we often find in classroom discussion, however, is that even a half a century later the hegemony of language ideologies seeking to tame wild tongues is still deeply entrenched. As we prepared for our presentation at the Tejas Foco NAACS, Dr. Deborah Cole took this discussion of the speech test at Pan American College into her graduate course, "Problems in dialect, grammar, and language development." Most of these students are in an MA in ESL program and are either already teaching English locally or plan to teach English abroad upon graduation. Having started the semester reading Rosina Lippi-Green's classic sociolinguistic book *English with an Accent: Language Ideology and Discrimination in the United States* and engaging in open discussions about the sociopolitical implications of attempting to change someone's accent, this seemed like the perfect topic to raise in class. The students were assigned the second chapter of Opal White's dissertation, "Retention of Spanish in the Southwest" (White 1972), along with the introduction to White's textbook and the pages that focused on the consonants that Dr. Salinas mentioned being singled out in the speech test. They were told about Johnson's research on the speech test and that we wanted their input for our presentation.

We started class with a general discussion of the readings, and then the students worked in groups to discuss the pedagogical approaches they would use in their own classrooms if they were using Opal's textbook to teach these sound contrasts to English learners. Students were then specifically invited to add anything for sharing during our upcoming presentation. Only two students, both middle aged women from the Rio Grande Valley, took the floor to speak. The first one said that she herself disagreed with Anzaldúa, and that we should know that not everyone around here agreed with her either. She didn't approve of Anzaldúa's use of the word "nosotras," for example, nor with her stance on gender in general. The other student wanted us to know that she felt that speech classes were the right thing for Spanish speakers who learned English and still had a Spanish accent. "Why not acquire a Standard English accent as well?" she asked, sounding remarkably like Gloria Anzaldúa's mother in *Borderlands*. "I don't see anything wrong with having a speech test for doing that," she stated.[7]

These comments resonate with others we've encountered in courses where particularly undergraduates who plan to teach in local schools speak passionately about the need to keep Spanish and English separated and to learn "correct" varieties of each. What this tells us is that though the more overt forms of discrimination (like the speech test) have gone away, forms of covert discrimination held in place by widely shared ideologies have not. If we are to engage in socially responsible teaching, therefore, we may first have to raise student awareness of the historical contexts from which current ideologies and practices emerged. Without this, students may not be prepared to critique the current status quo, much less to resist it. And as the above example reveals, even *with* the historical context and critical discussion of national and local ideologies and practices on the table, changing ideas about language and language speakers that privilege monolingualism remains a challenge – not just in the Rio Grande Valley but also in the wider US and Mexico national contexts. But it is a challenge worth addressing, and the history of the speech test at Pan American College along with Anzaldúa's work on linguistic intolerance provide a rich and timely resource for helping us to do so.[8]

CONCLUSION: WILD TONGUES STILL NOT TAMED

Sometime during the mid-1970s the speech test was phased out at Pan American College; it is now a relic of the past unknown to today's students at The University of Texas–Pan American. Dr. Marian Monta recalls that in 1973 after they had survived their three-year probationary (tenure) period at Pan American College, she and another colleague, Dr. Jim Hawley, took a stand and refused to administer the test anymore. Lecturers were then hired to give the test and teach the classes. The test was on its way out, though: students were becoming vocal about their opposition to the test, and faculty across the college, apparently hearing their students' complaints, began to question the requirement as well. The truth of the demise of the speech test in the mid-70s is probably less dramatic, though: changes in the curricula at Pan American simply couldn't accommodate the six-hour speech requirement any longer. The elimination of the test was long overdue; as early as October 1967, an Anglo reporter for the college's newspaper, Doug Bowe, had ridiculed the speech test in an article on freshman orientation. Describing a revolt by freshmen students against the practice of having to wear beanies, Bowe quotes a freshman on football scholarship saying, "'I ain't gon wear no bee-nee,'" purposefully emphasizing the Anglo-Texan's thick east Texas accent. The next paragraph begins, "The Speech Test . . . If you said 'peach,' you were okeh. If you said 'peash' you took the Speesh. See?" Other anecdotal information shows that students understood the absurdity of allowing Anglos to speak with an accent but not Mexican-Americans. John Simon, a McAllen

businessman who played basketball for Pan Am in the late 1960s, recalls that while most Anglos did not have to take the test, one of their players did—the player was from New Jersey, and "no one could understand what he was saying." Apparently, you could be an Anglo and speak with a Texas accent, but not a New Jersey accent!

While Anzaldúa's protest against linguistic colonization remains a contested point even in her own region, it is also clear that much progress has been made in this area in no small part because of Anzaldúa's writings and, in some ways, because of the speech test itself. It can be no accident that students such as Miguel de los Santos and Alejo Salinas, Jr. went on to highly-successful careers in education, inspired by the negative example of the Speech Test. As Dr. Salinas told us,

> I'm glad things have changed, times have changed, and that the professors themselves have become more acclimated to the type of students we have and more responsive to the needs of the students, and that's a big, big change. The teaching standards at the time and the behavior of the professors were condescending, so that's changed quite a bit. And of course there's so many of us now who came back to participate in the educational program [at UTPA] and we have brought in not only our own ideas and experiences but also the desire to be of true service to the students.

Today at UTPA, students speak Spanish in hallways more often than not and write freely in Spanish and in English. There is an MFA in Creative Writing offering courses in both Spanish and in English or a combination of both, and there is a thriving bilingual, trilingual (including Tex-Mex, as Anzaldúa would have it) regional literary scene. Much of the inspiration for this comes from Anzaldúa's "How to Tame a Wild Tongue," a sacred text that is passed around to aspiring local writers who are struggling to find their voice on the border. Anzaldúa was right: wild tongues cannot be tamed. The speech test failed, everyone passed it, and it's now part of the past.

ENDNOTES

1 "To find a good job you have to know how to speak English well. What is the point of getting an education if you still speak English with an accent?"/ "The Anglo with his innocent face ripped out our tongues."

2 A number of Anzaldúa scholars comment on language suppression and linguistic terrorism in their works, many of them inspired by "How to Tame a Wild Tongue" and by the specific passage on the speech classes we use as our keystone in this essay. See, for example, Lilia I. Bartolomé, "The Struggle for Language Rights: Naming and Interrogating the Colonial Legacy of 'English Only'" and Norma Mendoza-Denton and Bryan Gordon, "Language and Social Meaning in Bilingual Mexico and the United States." However, up to this point, no scholars have investigated the specific historical and social context of Anzaldúa's reference to the speech classes at Pan American College in the mid-1960s.

3 According to Alejo Salinas, Jr., "Of the three people who taught the class, Miss Owens was perhaps the most harsh of them all. Next to her was Mr. Calderon, who was also a Spanish teacher, and he was very harsh. And then Dr. Arthur Hayes was the other professor, and he was a lot more professional in the way that he addressed the students and the way he taught the course; although I never took the class with him, the reputation was out there he was very professional, not like Miss Owens…"

4 An earlier workbook (Self-Improvement Speech Manual) had been authored by an associate professor of education at PAC, Carlos I. Calderon. Its purpose, he told the Pan American newspaper in an interview in November of 1965, was to "correct the most common speech errors made by Spanish-speaking students who are learning to speak correct English" ("Pan" 4). Calderon also wrote articles on this subject for a teacher's journal, Texas Outlook. His MA thesis at UT-Austin in 1950 was entitled "The Education of Spanish-Speaking Children in Edcouch-Elsa, Texas." He also taught Speech 113X, discussed above in footnote i.

5 It is worth noting that she chose Brooks Hill as the chair of her committee. He was the first president of the International Association of Intercultural Communication Studies.

6 See for example recent re-definitions of "Language" as "truncated repertoires" (Blommaert 2010) and critiques of monolithic views of languages as theoretically untenable and empirically unsupportable (Hall 2013).

7 At this point in our research we had not recorded the dramatic interviews with Dr. Salinas and Dr. de los Santos quoted earlier in this article, and it will be interesting to see how future students respond to White's textbook and to the speech test in the context of these testimonios. Video of Dr. Salinas' interview is available on the UTPA Department of English Facebook page and it has recently been screened in a few linguistics and literature classes. Based on those initial classroom discussions, there is good reason to believe that the presentation of a fuller historical record on this subject encourages students to re-evaluate their ideas on "standard" English.

8 See Denham and Lobeck (2010) for collaborations between linguists and public school teachers to raise awareness of and appreciation for linguistic diversity in K-12 contexts globally.

Acknowledgments: The authors would like to thank Dr. Marian Monta, Dr. Alejo Salinas, Jr., Dr. Miguel de los Santos, and John Simon for sharing their experiences with us. We would also like to thank Dr. Frank Guajardo (UTPA School of Education) for his help with our research, and for providing Gloria Anzaldúa's Pan American College transcripts, our thanks to UTPA Registrar Jeff Rhodes. Our additional thanks go out to Dr. Marian Monta, who co-presented with us on our NACCS panel. Thanks also to Erika Garza-Johnson for her translation of a portion of "How to Tame a Wild Tongue."

WORKS CITED

Anzaldúa, Gloria. *Borderlands/La Frontera: The New Mestiza*. 2nd ed. San Francisco: Aunt Lute Books, 1999. Print.

Bartolomé, Lilia I. "The Struggle for Language Rights: Naming and Interrogating the Colonial Legacy of 'English Only.'" *Human Architecture: Journal of the Sociology of Self-Knowledge* 4.3 (2006): 25-32. Print.

Blommaert, Jan. *The Sociolinguistics of Globalization*. Cambridge: Cambridge University Press, 2010. Print.

Bowe, Doug. "Perplexed Fish in Agony." *The Pan American* 5 Oct 1967: 4. Print.

Calderon, Carlos I. *The Education of Spanish-Speaking Children in Edcouch-Elsa, Texas*. MA thesis. UT Austin, 1950. Print.

---. *Self-Improvement Speech Manual*. N.p.: n.p., 1965. Print.

De Los Santos, Miguel. Correspondence with the authors. Feb. 2013. E-mail.

Denham, Kristin, and Anne Lobeck. *Linguistics at School: Language Awareness in Primary and Secondary Education*. Cambridge: Cambridge University Press, 2010. Print.

Estevis, Anne. *Down Garrapata Road*. Houston: Arte Público Press, 2003. Print.

Hall, Christopher J. "Cognitive contributions to plurilithic views of English and other languages." *Applied Linguistics* 34.2 (2013): 211-231. Print.

Lippi-Green, Rosina. *English With an Accent. Language, ideology, and discrimination in the United States*. New York: Routledge, 2012. Print.

Mendoza-Denton, Norma, and Bryan Gordon. "Language and Social Meaning in Bilingual Mexico and the United States." *The Handbook of Hispanic Sociolinguistics*. Ed. Manuel Díaz-Campos. Oxford: Blackwell, 2011: 553-578. Print.

Monta, Marian. Personal interview. Dec. 2012.

"Pan Am Professor Publishes Manual." *The Pan American* 3 Nov 1965: 4. Print.

Salinas, Jr., Alejo. Personal interview. Feb. 2013.

Simon, John. Personal interview. Apr. 2013.

White, Opal Thurow. *General American Speech for the Bilingual Spanish Speaking Student*. Dubuque: Kendall/Hunt Publishing Company, 1979. Print.

---. *The Mexican American Subculture: A Study in Teaching Contrastive Sounds in English and Spanish*. Diss. University of Oklahoma, 1972. Print.

TEACHING PHILOSOPHY AT A HISPANIC SERVING INSTITUTION: PEDAGOGICAL INTERVENTION INSPIRED BY GLORIA ANZALDÚA

CYNTHIA MARÍA PACCACERQUA

"I like very much to see my students use the practical/technical tools that the literary/academic world has appropriated and excluded working class and Third World people from using by mystifying them into boredom and abstraction. Demystifying the use of aesthetic tools in [sic] part of my job as teacher."[1]—Gloria E. Anzaldúa

The academic field of philosophy confronts its practitioners with what at times appears as an insurmountable problem: the failure to achieve inclusiveness. Philosophy's progress towards the inclusion of women and other traditionally underrepresented groups has been slower than the Humanities generally; with respect to women, for instance, philosophy is more comparable to STEM fields (Crouch 224).[2] So, while the above statement by Anzaldúa still applies to higher education as a whole, the current state of philosophy is a particularly poignant reminder of how far one of the most "abstract" fields in the academy is from making a real contribution to the project of undoing the historical intellec-

1 Italics font and underlining emphasis added.

2 In "Implicit Bias and Gender (and Other Sorts of) Diversity in Philosophy and the Academy in the Context of the Corporatized University" Margaret Crouch notes that: "The only disciplines with lower ratios of women to men were engineering, computer science, and physics", 224.

tual, epistemic, cultural violence perpetuated against women, "working class and Third World people" in the United States. Teaching college level courses at The University of Texas–Pan American (UTPA), however, presents my colleagues and me with both a challenge and an incredible opportunity. The challenge resides in the fact that *as is* the academic field alienates women and other traditionally underrepresented groups; the opportunity resides in the fact that at UTPA approximately fifty six percent of undergraduate students are women and ninety percent of all students are Mexican American/Chicano-a/Latino-a or Mexican (Office of Institutional Research & Effectiveness – UTPA 7). So, while on the one hand we are following national trends in losing a significant number of female students for the major, on the other hand we are also in a unique position to foster the inclusion of more philosophical voices and transform the field as a whole. In other words, we have the opportunity to foster the acquisition and use of those "practical/technical tools that the literary/academic world has appropriated" to the exclusion of "working class and people of color."

In what follows I describe some of the pedagogical practices I have developed in an effort to minimize the alienation of students when confronted with philosophy most likely for the very first time, in particular as I use them in my Introduction to Philosophy course. These practices are inspired and informed by Gloria Anzaldúa's work as well as the pedagogical theories and practices of other Chicana and women of color and principles of cooperative learning. The development of these location-specific pedagogical strategies is part of a community effort among Mexican American Studies affiliated faculty to transform learning at UTPA. We seek to teach our students about the life and writings of Anzaldúa and for them to see their concerns, realities, and differential literacy reflected in our courses by simultaneously reshaping and reframing what it means to study and research in our areas of specialization. We do this in efforts toward healing wounds created by historical conditions that have systematically marginalized generations of Mexican Americans from educational opportunities and by contemporary secondary and post-secondary institutions in the Rio Grande Valley that today continue to deny our students the right to learn about themselves, US-Mexico border history, gender and sexuality issues, to name a few. This loss is simultaneous to the ongoing and persistent trend of restructuring public higher education towards the ever more private market demands for specialized workers at the expense, marginalization and continued "mystification" of what in the above quote Anzaldúa identifies as the "practical/technical tools" of the "literary/academic world." Anzaldúa's work is evidence that the promise of these tools lies in their libratory function in excess to any technical specialization made necessary today for economic survival.

As a Latina trained and working in philosophy I am painfully aware of the shortage of women and other traditionally underrepresented groups in general, but I am particularly affected personally and professionally by how few Latinas and other people of color belong to the community. While in 2010 the faculty composition in our program mirrored the gender disparities of philosophy programs across the country, when I was hired I was very excited to join the university due to the unique student population. I knew that philosophy majors and minors in my classrooms at UTPA would be unlike those almost anywhere else in the country and that I would have the opportunity to encourage students to think philosophically from a critical perspective, informed by their lived experience, and in their difference engage in larger philosophical dialogues among its many communities.

THE LANDSCAPE OF PHILOSOPHY'S COMMUNITIES & PRACTICES

The following data on the composition of Philosophy faculty and graduation of doctoral, master's and undergraduate students will help those unfamiliar with the discipline to grasp the dimensions of the problem of underrepresentation of women and other groups.

In 2003, out of all *full time philosophy faculty staff and instructional staff* in degree granting institutions 2.3 percent were Black males, 1 percent Hispanic[3] males, 4 percent male Asian/Pacific Islanders, and 2 percent male American Indian/Alaska Natives. Reporting standards for data were not met in the case of any other categories designating traditionally underrepresented racial and ethnic groups – including women of color (Crouch 224). The 2003 data available on women faculty in philosophy available indicates that women comprise 16.6 percent of the total full time faculty and instructional staff in the field, 26 percent of part-time instructors, and 20.6 percent of the total professionally employed philosophers. Women currently make up nearly 27 percent of the available labor pool in philosophy (Norlock; Mangan; Crouch 224). [4]

The status of women of color faculty in philosophy is very difficult to gauge, as there is little to no intersectional data with regards to gender, race, sexuality, and/or ability. The 2003 data source on women mentions that of the 16.6 percent of full time female instructional faculty, none were women of color. Crouch qualifies these numbers by noting that the 16.6 percent data includes white women alone; the problem is that there is no data currently available for women of color. From the statistics that Crouch does provide, however, one may deduce that in 2003 1.8 percent all full time faculty and instructional staff were

3 Henceforth, the use of the category "Hispanic" reflects its use in the source documents.

4 Also, see Crouch (2012), who notes that these statistics apply to white women only and that for all other categories "reporting standards not met".

women of color. The American Philosophical Association (APA) Committee on the Status of Black Philosophers and the Society of Young Black Philosophers produces the only other intersectional information I could find. According to Haslanger, they report that in 2013 there were 156 Black philosophers in the U.S. This number includes doctoral students and philosophy Ph.D.'s in academic positions. Of these 156 Black philosophers, 55 are Black women; 31 of these Black women hold tenured or tenure-track positions (Haslanger). There is no available data on Hispanic women.

In a document entitled "Minorities in Philosophy" the American Philosophical Association (APA) reports that of *the total completions of philosophy doctorates* in 2009, 4.7 percent were by traditionally underrepresented ethnic and racial minorities. This percentage represents an increase from 2.7 percent in 1995 (the first year recorded), but a significant decrease from 8 percent in 2006, which was the highest percentage ever reported in the field. African Americans comprised 2.48 percent, American Indians or Alaska Natives 0.45 percent, and Hispanics 1.81 percent of the doctoral degrees awarded in 2009 (excluding temporary residents). In "Women in Philosophy" the APA reports that in *2009, 30.47 percent of all doctoral philosophy degree completions were achieved by women.* This is an increase from 19.21 percent in 1987 (the first year recorded) and 24.4 percent in 2007; the highest percent of women graduating with doctoral degrees was in 2004 with 30.89 percent. There is no intersectional data available to determine the percentage of women from traditionally unrepresented racial or ethnic group graduating with doctoral degrees in philosophy.

According to the same "Minorities in Philosophy" APA report, in 2009 the total percentage of traditionally underrepresented ethnic and racial minorities that were *recipients of a Master's* degree in the field was 8.2 percent, an increase from the 6.5 percent of completions in 1995 and a very slight decrease from 8.6 percent in 2004. Of the traditionally underrepresented groups, African Americans comprised 3.1 percent, American Indians or Alaska Natives 0.28 percent, and Hispanics comprised 4.89 percent of the 2009 graduates, making this group the largest among ethnic and racial minority groups. Hispanics are also the fastest growing group among them. In their "Women in Philosophy" the APA reports that the percentage of women completing MA degrees in 2009 was 28.6 percent. The highest percentage of completions reported was in 1991 with 45.8 percent, which culminated a sharp increase begun in the late 1980s.

The APA reports that in 2009, traditionally underrepresented racial and ethnic minorities comprised approximately 12.4 percent of all students graduating with a Bachelor's in the field, a 3 percentage point increase from 1995. Once more, Hispanics make up the largest group among ethnic and racial minorities, contributing the most to this rise. Hispanics were 4.5 percent of the

total Bachelor's degree graduates in 1995 and 6.8 percent in 2009. This compares to 6.7 percent of all 2009 degree completions by African Americans and by 0.8 percent American Indians or Alaska Natives ("Minorities in Philosophy"). In 2009 women who completed Bachelor's degrees in the field comprised 31.2 percent; this gender distribution remained more or less constant since 1987 ("Women in Philosophy").

While these statistics speak for themselves with regards to the historical and contemporary marginal status of women and other traditionally underrepresented communities in the field of philosophy, there are some important observations to draw. First is the fact that the epistemic frameworks currently applied for acquiring this information is inadequate in so far as there is no intersectional data available to identify the percentages of women of color within the U.S. academic philosophy community; nor is there data regarding sexuality or ability. Second is the problem that while the numbers clearly indicate a problem, it is very difficult to ascertain what the contemporary causes for this failure in philosophy are when compared to the relative progress enjoyed in other fields in the Humanities. In fact, in their comparative similarity to STEM fields, these numbers remind us that philosophy is an area that does not quite belong to any one cluster of academic research and thus one may speculate that the distinct nature of the content and its style or method of engagement may play an important role in this historical marginalization. And third is the realization that due to the systematic devaluation of the Humanities in (public) higher education, the rather recent interest in addressing this inclusiveness problem in philosophy suffers from the lack of resources to produce the knowledge necessary to successfully identify the particular root causes and thus create strategies to eliminate them.[5] Statistics produced by government bodies, research funds, and institutional initiatives are geared primarily to solving issues of underrepresentation in other fields that are more readily seen as sites for employment or economic development (e.g., STEM). As a result, in philosophy we often transpose observations, questions, and strategies elaborated in STEM to our discipline with the hope that we gain new insights relevant to our specific problem.[6]

5 This is apparent in the increased discussion of the problem in scholarly journals, conferences, social media and traditional journalistic outlets and the appearance and ever increasing requests for donations from the APA to its individual faculty members for funds that can be directed towards inclusiveness efforts.

6 The clearest example is the APA's Committee on the Status of Women Site Visit Program, which is modeled after a program first developed in Physics to address site specific dynamics that may be negatively affecting women in Physics departments and thus contributing to unequal gender representation. Another such instance is a question posed recently in the Feminist Philosophers' Blog concerning whether or not philosophy too may mirror the sciences in grading practices, where grades are lower than in non-science courses; this is relevant because research has found that higher grades in general pull students towards certain majors and that female students are more responsive to grades than male students. http://feministphilosophers.wordpress.com/2014/03/18/women-grade-sensitivity-and-major-selection/

For the purpose of this essay, it is particularly important to note that recent preliminary studies indicate that the largest percentage drop of women in the discipline takes place between the first exposure to philosophy in introductory courses and the selection of major in the field. Based on a study of fifty-six U.S. institutions of higher education, the average mean percentage of women in introductory classes is approximately 43 percent, while philosophy majors are approximately 35 percent women (Paxton, Figdor and Tiberius 953). A study at Georgia State University based on its own program raises the percentage of women in introductory courses in philosophy to 55 percent, while philosophy majors are 33 percent women (Freeman 9).[7] The first comprehensive study also indicates that a factor appearing to mitigate the attrition rate from women's first exposure to majoring in philosophy is the composition of the department's faculty (Paxton, Figdor and Tiberius 953).

Although still based on a limited amount of studies, these new insights lead me to want to gather a very preliminary quantitative idea of gender representation and attrition rates in the philosophy program at UTPA, so I looked at the percentage of women faculty, majors, and students enrolled in introductory courses in philosophy. Because of the unique student population at UTPA, I also looked at the percentage of women identified as Hispanic/Latina/Mexican American. The sample of this data is very small, so this information is meant only as a first step to what I hope is the gathering of a more comprehensive data set. In contrast to what the data available suggests of the field thus far, of the Philosophy Faculty at UTPA women make up 26 percent of the total full time faculty and instructional staff (compared to 16 percent nationally and 20.6 percent total women philosophers professionally employed nationally, which includes part-time faculty and instructional staff). In addition, of the total full time instructional philosophy faculty, *13 percent are Latinas* (comparative data not available, but in 2003 approximately 1 percent were *male* Hispanic/Latino/Mexican American).

With respect to declared majors,[8] *female students constituted 35 percent of students majoring in Philosophy at UTPA* (compared to 30 percent nationally and approximately 35 percent in the Paxton, et al. study cited above). In addition, of the total enrolled majors in philosophy, *Hispanic women make up 33 percent* (national data unavailable). When it comes to UTPA'a student enrollment in Philosophy introductory courses, *59 percent of all enrolled students are women* (compared to approximately 43 percent in the Paxton, et al. study and 55 percent at Georgia State University study) and *55 percent are Hispanic women*

7 She cites this information from an unpublished presentation by Adleberg, Toni, Morgan Thompson, and Eddy Nahmias entitled "Women and Philosophy: Why Is It 'Goodbye' at 'Hello'?" Paper presented was presented at the Diversity in Philosophy Conference, University of Dayton, May 30 2013.

8 Based on data for the 2013-2014 academic year provided by the Office of the Register's.

(national data unavailable).[9]

Because of the diversity of the studies' source data and methodology, and the very limited information I have available at this time, what can be highlighted regarding gender in philosophy at UTPA is only the following: 1.) Our percentage of women philosophy majors appears to be within the national trends; 2.) As elsewhere, there is also a significant drop in gender proportions between first time exposure to philosophy and enrollment in the BA degree program; and 3.) Since over 90 percent of students at UTPA are Mexican American/Chicano-a/Latino-a or Mexican, we naturally have a large *number* of Mexican American/Chicanas/ Latinas or Mexican women in our courses and majors. The latter point, however, is not an indication of our program being more inclusive due to the extreme difference in the composition of our student population. Thus, at first glance it seems *our program needs to further research what factors may be at play at UTPA in the marginalization of women.* However, because these students registering and majoring in philosophy are predominantly Mexican American/Chicano-a/ Latino-a or Mexican, and knowing that students of color are extremely underrepresented in the field, it also seems incumbent on us to *reflect upon what difference this makes when it comes to learning and practicing philosophy.*

PRACTICING PHILOSOPHY AT A CROSSROADS

The field of philosophy at UTPA stands at the crossroads of not yet having data to better understand the causes of the marginalization of women and other underrepresented groups within the field in general, while simultaneously being the only BA program housed in a U.S. four year university serving a student population that is over 90 percent Mexican American/Chicano-a/Latino-a or Mexican.[10] Until data is generated both locally and nationally, one possible site for untangling whether or not the *difference in our student population at UTPA makes a difference for philosophy educators and whether or not certain pedagogies may be more useful in this context is the theoretical writings of intellectuals who belong to traditionally underrepresented groups in philosophy.* Of particular interest are thinkers who focus on learning and knowledge production as well as the comprehension and critique of sources of marginalization identified from their situated standpoints, specifically, from a South Texas border standpoint. Although she is not alone in fitting this category, one of these thinkers is Gloria Anzaldúa, a Río Grande Valley native and UTPA alumna who majored in

9 Based on data for the 2013-2014 academic year provided by the Office of Institutional Research and Effectiveness at UTPA.

10 The list of Hispanic Serving Institutions surveyed to identify BA degrees offered is based on the 2012-2013 list available through the Hispanic Association of Colleges & Universities. My survey however excludes HIS located in Puerto Rico and other U.S. territories.

English.[11] It is perhaps time for us as practitioners of philosophy to listen to and consider what she has to say that may help us grasp the significance of this local difference independently of our individual specializations.

In the context of our discipline, the area in Anzaldúa's theory and work that most concerns us here is epistemology. From Anzaldúa's perspective epistemology or the *logos* of knowledge is not grounded simply in our ability to justify our beliefs, but also in its embodiment in the subject knower. Both of these grounds have moreover a communal element. The justification of our beliefs relies on the appeal of the forms of thought through which a claim can be accepted as true or false by all who share in such forms of thinking. The embodiment of knowledge in the subject knower relies on the intersubjective space of life experiences that, among other things, constructs our interpretation of the surrounding world and is manifest at the most elemental level in practices elicited from and shared in that social space. In this case, the most radical criterion for the validity of this knowledge is life, by means of what could be identified as a pragmatic judgment of whether or not *it works* in lived experience. In other words, the testament of such validity is what in *Borderlands/La Frontera* Anzaldúa identifies as the survival of *atravesados* (25-6). In adding this pragmatic layer to our more traditional understanding of the *logos* of knowledge, Anzaldúa is claiming that knowing is essentially situated.

Understanding epistemology as comprehending a unity of these two communal elements—thinking and embodiment—invites us to consider whether for Anzaldúa there is necessarily an aspect of knowledge that is *unsaid*. There appears to be an aspect of knowledge that is both operative in how life is led and nonetheless incapable of participating in the proper language of knowledge as recognized publicly. Ironically, this is despite the fact that the embodied element in knowing itself arises out of the social and thus the always already shared space of communal relations. As a result of this gap between what I am calling the unsaid and shared discourse in the production and reproduction of recognized forms of knowledge, one who wills to speak the language of knowledge—the learner, teacher, intellectual—would need to become literate in the unsaid in order to be able to facilitate and acknowledge its function in one's respective work. In becoming literate in the unsaid, we can engage the situated and inter-subjective dimensions of learning, teaching, and intellectual production. In this way we would simultaneously affirm the unsaid's silent embodied existence and function within each of us as well as subject the unsaid to practices of reflection, critique

11 Other examples are Aída Hurtado, who is originally from McAllen and is currently Chair of the Chicano/a Studies Department at UC Santa Barbara; and Norma Cantú, who was born in Nuevo Laredo, raised in Laredo and is currently in the Latina/o Studies Program at the University of Missouri Kansas City.

and transformation of our selves, communities, and ultimately understanding itself. It follows that, since the unsaid of the embodied that grounds Anzaldúa's epistemology arises from the social, to involve ourselves in it is ultimately an engagement with our shared realities, communities and position within them.

This engagement with the unsaid is however a very difficult task because its unspoken nature requires looking for what from the perspective of Anzaldúa's other complementary epistemological ground for knowledge—justification of beliefs—can be described as *in excess* of the explicit propositional language, a language that as we know is the dominant currency in the elaboration of Western theoretical and empirical knowledge. Yet the latter is precisely the language in which educators and intellectuals are most proficient and in which learners have been encouraged and seek proficiency. As a result of the unsaid being in excess of the latter's proficiencies and goals, from an Andalduísta perspective our current epistemic and by default pedagogical skills and practices very likely fall short of enabling the knowledge we desire and imagine or claim to have.

The characteristics of this difficult task of becoming literate in the unsaid will be in part based on the situation or position of the subject knower *vis a vis* others who are also always already differentially positioned. A most important condition differentiating the situated subject knowers and learners is their relationship to privilege. Given the current predicament in fields like philosophy, it seems clear that the demands required for overcoming our illiteracy has been quite trying to our imagination's capacity to envision possible paths for transformation. However, I take Anzaldúa's *Borderlands/La Frontera* as an example of this epistemic work in literacy of the unsaid. In this text, an important key to access the excess of what is affirmed in discursive knowledge is the understudied and unrecognized history of Mexican Americans in the United States.

In *Borderlands/La Frontera*, Mexican American history necessarily permeates the distinct embodiments of *what works* within contemporary conditions. For Anzaldúa this is an intimate past that most immediately concerns her and allows her to begin the process of figuring her subject position. Her recounting of the multiple cycles of colonization that have kept the Border/wound from healing functions as a key that opens up the multiple dimensions of her communal existence: race, gender, sexuality, language, knowledge and subjectivity (25-6). This historical horizon moreover allows her to identify, interpret and critique the particular cultural norms dominant within her family, Mexican American and U.S. culture at large. To do this is to begin to grapple with the *unsaid* that works in sustaining life in the Río Grande Valley. The process, however, is not simply a naïve celebration of an embodied pragmatic knowledge; it includes a critical eye towards normative aspects of the communities' practices that have not and do not work equally in fully sustaining and nurturing life, her life. This is to say,

they do not always work in the specificity of her lived experience as a Mexican American woman, queer, and prieta, for instance.

Borderlands/La Frontera does the work of identifying unique historical conditions, of interpreting them relative to Anzaldúa's experiences, and of engaging in a transformative critique through means other than the dominant and institutionalized language that serves to communicate knowledge. Instead we find her appealing to a multitude of approaches and literary tools for the transfiguration of the *unsaid* into coherent discourse; these are approaches and tools that are not traditionally deemed conducive to clear thinking, communication, and understanding. She uses poetry, letter writing, *testimonios*, idioms (e.g., *hablar pa'tras*), pre-Colombian concepts and mythologies among others to bring the embodied aspect of knowing that orients her life and the life of those in her diverse communities into public space. As a result of the historical and systematic exclusion of "working class people and people of color" from the sphere of learning and legitimized knowing, an exclusion that directly affected her subject position as knower, to bridge the epistemic gap between the unsaid and the possibility of discourse for the purpose of knowledge requires a simultaneous process of authorizing her agency as knower. By entering into the historical horizon that determined her social conditions and through the use of these apparently disparate approaches and tools that are conducive to her authorization, she transfigures the unsaid into a form of linguistic, coherent, and communicative element of knowing. In other words, in her will to speak knowledge we witness her become literate in the unsaid.

The work of transfiguration is necessary because what is otherwise claimed to be the known within existing discourse is constructed on the basis of the embodied knowing of predominantly Western and privileged intellectuals whose subject positions, inter-subjective relations and social space caused their own segregation from the knowledge of others. By denying the embodied knowing present in the communities of traditionally marginalized peoples, the existing institutionalized discourses of truth are the result of what Mills coins "an epistemology of ignorance" (18). This means that practices *validated* by what has been shown to work in the survival of those excluded from the academic world never formed part of the institutionalized *unsaid* implicitly informing the concerns, elaboration and construction of what is discursively recognized. Only the embodied knowing of those individuals situated so as to have exclusive authority to legitimize what is true is immanent to otherwise justified knowledge. From an Anzalduísta epistemological perspective that affirms the necessary role of embodiment for knowledge, it also means that so-called legitimized knowers remain blind to their own institutionalized *unsaid* extant in excess of their discourses of truth. As a result, Western knowledge is

deficient in both satisfying the epistemic conditions for its claim to truth and its ability to account for Anzaldúa's embodied knowing as a queer dark-skinned Chicana from the borderland

Therefore, from an Anzalduísta perspective, unless the excess in the propositional language of knowledge is recognized and we become literate in the unsaid, our epistemic and by default pedagogical practices remain inadequate. This is particularly the case in contexts of encounters between those who have been historically-generationally excluded from access to the learning and use of *tools that work* in the institutionalized social spheres of knowledge production and have become naturalized to those who have long inhabited these privileged spheres. What we find in this encounter are: a body of knowledge that does not contain the embodied knowing of those historically marginalized; a set of tools and skills in the production of legitimized knowledge that have been developed in exclusive social spaces; an element of knowing that is *unsaid* and likely very different due to the differential positions of the subjects and groups involved in the encounter; and a shared desire for teaching, learning and benefiting in some way from these varying subject positions. If this reading of Anzaldúa's epistemological and pedagogical insights is true to her work, then given the character of its faculty and student population together with its borderland location, *what makes a difference in philosophy at UTPA is the degree to which this encounter is almost continuously sustained between faculty and students, and the challenge that it presents in finding the unsaid that works to sustain life both within the institution and community to which it and we all ultimately belong.*

One attempt to respond to the trying task of becoming literate in the unsaid at UTPA has been to reorient my teaching approach in my Introduction to Philosophy course. The course is organized around the philosophical concern with the nature of a person's membership in civil society, the political state, and the human-natural world. This is a concern that strategically raises numerous dimensions of our experiences as ethical, political, cultural, and biological subjects. The aim of the design is to learn how our basic understanding of what it means to be human affects our justifications for building particular types of relationships with people and nature together with the consequences that follow from these, including whether or not those consequences lead to fulfilling lives. Unlike other more traditional approaches to introducing philosophy to students, organized around different subfields of philosophy (e.g., epistemology, God's existence, metaphysics, personhood, moral philosophy, etc.) or historically surveying the most recognized thinkers of Western philosophy, my course introduces some of the main concerns of philosophy by focusing on one theme throughout the semester. The preference for this layout is to enable students to go in depth into one philosophical problem by approaching it from multiple

critical perspectives, realizing thus the diverse dimensions involved in satisfactorily addressing a concern essential to our human condition.

STRATEGIC PEDAGOGICAL INTERVENTION

Based on Anzaldúa's insights, the main strategy I use for this course is twofold: content selection and assignment design. As to content, I insert the works of two traditionally underrepresented thinkers in a historical philosophical conversation with more canonical figures; to put them in conversation means that they are not mere tokens of representation but rather clear interlocutors that address very specific ideas in that history with their own unique concepts and frameworks. At the same time, these authors also bring into their theoretical positions critical issues of gender, sexuality, race, language, citizenship and wealth grounded in historical and contemporary processes and experience. At the end of the course I introduce a historical event that critically brings all of the interlocutors' ideas into play. The authors and the sequence of their introduction are as follows: Plato (*Republic*), Gloria Anzaldúa (*Borderlands/La Frontera*), John Locke (*Second Treatise on Government*) and Charles Mills (*The Racial Contract*). The historical event is the 1994 Revolution in Chiapas of the *Ejercito Zaptista Liberación Nacional (EZLN)*. For the purpose of this essay, I will briefly describe the particular position and grounding function of Anzaldúa's work within the course's philosophical concern. I do this by identifying some of the points of intersection with the other thinkers. Since she is the second author, most of these points will speak to Plato's work.

Having introduced philosophy through sections of Plato's *Republic*, Anzaldúa is first and foremost studied as a paradigmatic philosopher or lover of wisdom. In *Borderlands/La Frontera* we see that the problems, questions and ideas she engages with and develops explicitly intersect with principal parts of Plato's philosophical inquiry:

1. For both thinkers the successful journey towards leading a life concerned with bringing about a world that is just and good is enabled by strengthening one's soul or self, which entails a certain type of harmonious relationship among its parts. For Plato these parts are *logos*, spirit, and appetite; for Anzaldúa the particular parts are relative to the subject position of the person (i.e., Chicana, queer, feminist, and prieta parts, among others). They also conceive the soul as active with the capacity or *facultad* that if nurtured leads to and sustains unity.

2. Ignorance plays a role in initiating this journey and is impossible to fully overcome due either to the bodily entrapment of the soul or the situated character of knowledge. To be cognizant of one's ignorance entails the recognition that one's reactions to the world are embedded in one's cultural

understanding and the identification of unjustified beliefs that otherwise inform one's cultural understanding and habitually direct our responses to the world.

3. Plato's account of the primary vehicle for getting closer to the truth of justice and the good is essentially an inner intellectual activity of the soul—its highest form of learning is by thinking itself. Anzaldúa, on the other hand, adds historical orientation, cultural practices and symbolic forms as critical sites with resources for philosophical engagement. In *Borderlands/La Frontera* she effectively extends our understanding of the philosophical life by partly grounding the practice in the concrete conditions of the South Texas U.S./Mexican border. Thus in the context of UTPA, her work introduces philosophy as practiced *locally*.

4. Since the philosophical life is the outcome of the healthy soul's desire for the wisdom to positively transform the political and ethical conditions in our communities and in our ignorance this desire can never be fully satisfied, the philosophical differences between Plato and Anzaldúa simply highlight the open-ended character of their positions. The relentless questioning in the pursuit of justice and the good frees us to be critically accountable for our claims, agency and relationships—nothing other than an invitation to dialogue and reevaluation. Whether the philosopher or *la new mestiza-nepantlera*, both thinkers envision a persona committed and with the strength to confront and transform their community.

I designed the course so that Anzaldúa's theory provides a natural transition into the second part, bridging the political philosophies of Plato, Locke, and Mills. This is because despite the many intersections with Plato's thought, Anzaldúa's concrete and contemporary concerns are tied to ideas and conditions that are alien to the Ancient Greek philosopher, but born out of the legacy of Western Modernity. For instance, while Plato's political thought addresses different forms of constitutions that differ according to the source of power (wisdom, honor, wealth, the people, or fear), Anzaldúa's political thought addresses problems that arise from Western assumptions embedded in the modern concepts such as political power and the nation-state (i.e., the nature and rights of human beings, the social contract or the correspondence between the body politic and its national identity). And, as we move from Locke's theory of the social contract to Mills theory of the racial contract, Anzaldúa's work speaks, for intstance, to the lived experience of the system of racial marginalization that Mills theorizes. Her unique borderland perspective brings to life the consequences of what Mills identifies as a concrete and conceptual racial contract that founds white supremacy as a political system in the United States and permeates a global

political order born out of European colonization. As seen above, Anzaldúa's critical approach to knowledge and philosophical position also speaks to what Mills identifies as an "epistemology of ignorance" that sustains white supremacy (18). For Mills, the reason political philosophers have been blind to the founding "racial contract" results partly from the systematic exclusion of peoples of color from the field—both as members of the community or independent sources of knowledge. Anzaldúa joins in this epistemic critique of the academy and notably her philosophical voice is one of the traditionally excluded voices.

Finally, by introducing the case of the EZLN's revolution in Chiapas, Mexico at the end of the course we are able to witness a late 20th Century embodiment of all of the ideas we have learned up until then. To mention a few: a differential indigenous position that grounds a philosophical framework and worldview that conflicts with and denaturalizes the Western ideas informing the current global world order; the Mexican government's failure to perform the function that legitimizes its political power, which is to protect the natural rights of its citizens; the right to revolution in light of this failure; different conceptions of property or relations to the natural world; the reformulation and embodiment of what a democratic society can look like; the critique of the power embedded in the media, which limits political discourse and perpetuates dogma; and the possibility for change and vision of a new global community that includes human beings and the environment.

The assignments that I believe create an intervention in what I describe above as the ***almost continuously sustained difficult encounter between learners and teachers at UTPA*** are the inclusion of personal stories and a final digital testimonio project. The personal stories are students' written responses to weekly or biweekly assigned "prompts" that ask them to recount a first-person experience of undergoing or witnessing an event that reveals something very specific and that is tied to the subject matter we are discussing via the readings. Every "prompt" I assign focuses on moments of experiencing or witnessing such events as learning, community, justice, cultural alienation, contractual relations, competing ethical demands, racism, sexism, among others. The exchange of these stories enables a process of bridging the epistemological gap in the encounter between students and me. Whether we are working on Plato, Anzaldúa, Locke or Mills, there is always a connection to be drawn between the ideas of the authors and the stories that are put in writing and then shared in the classroom. By moving back and forth between the lived experiences and the philosophical concepts and frameworks, we develop the tools and skills necessary in the transfiguration between the unsaid embodied knowledge they own and the articulation of that knowledge into different forms of philosophical discourse. Their stories show that they know in their bodies what racism is like and pragmatically ***know how*** to live under a culture of racism. Of

course, part of the learning process is not only to fully articulate this knowledge philosophically, but also reflect upon whether or not there can be more strategic practices of what works in pursuit of a life they conclude is a "good life." The back and forth between lived experiences and "abstract" ideas in the course thus transforms our inter-subjective, social space of learning; the experience of this process creates the possibility of resituating ourselves with respect to one another and expanding or ideally transforming our embodied knowing.

The final digital *testimonio* project does two things: creates an oral embodiment of their stories that exists independent of its author and requires a very specific and concrete application of the concepts learned in light of their individual stories. I call it a *testimonio* because in digital form, the author has an opportunity to hear him or herself as an interlocutor in a shared space inhabited by his fellow students and me. This creates an extra layer of witnessing or bearing testimony that the recounting of their story in written responses to prompts and their telling the story in person in the classroom do not allow. I believe this extra layer creates the opportunity for them to witness their ability to participate in and contribute to public discourse, to enact their public personas.

A VISION OF THE DIFFERENCE

In order to evaluate whether or not these strategies accomplish my intended introductory philosophy within the institutional difference present at UTPA, I have asked students to respond to questions regarding the course. I would like to share with you some of the student responses I received, specifically on: 1) whether or not they appreciated studying Anzaldúa's work; 2) which of her ideas or concepts were most salient to them; and 3) what their experiences were like in completing the Final *Testimonio* Project. These are some student responses to the first question:

> *As someone who rarely identifies themselves as "Hispanic" or "Latino," Borderlands does give me insight on the historical and cultural facets of living in the Valley. It is both interesting and illuminating in terms of race and culture, and I enjoy her arguments and wish to learn more about the region's history.*
>
> *Plato and Locke deal more with concepts and theories, which Anzaldúa draws more actively from personal experience. I much prefer her style and rhetoric as opposed to Plato's asking simple questions, and extracting abstract concepts from his form of dialogue.*
>
> *Yes, she motivates me to keep studying and working hard.*
>
> *I actually like her reading; I thought it was interesting. I think that this kind of readings give the confidence and acceptance to the people that have the same problem as Gloria. Being different.*

Eye opening to see what other people actually go through.

Yes, knowing something from someone born/raised here actually made it, is astonishing.

Very glad, because it strengthens the way I think and how to sort of explain my thought, can use her as motor, a source and help to pursue my ways.

Here are student responses to the second question regarding the ideas that stood out for them in Anzaldúa's work:

Equality, her being a 'gay' 'Latina'. I know what it's like growing up with the problem in a 'Hispanic family and environment.'

I am glad. It helps me connect to the other work [covered].

It's good to let everyone know about our culture and how people react because of our sexuality and I think that her readings teach the people equality; that none can judge us no matter of your sexuality preference.

Addresses the intersection of queerness, border living, and womanhood. It's exactly what a person like me wants to read because it applies to me as a queer brown woman from the RGV.

I would say it makes me glad someone explains a certain culture that in fact many can't or won't understand unless they come here.

As to the Final *Testimonio* Project, some student reflections include:

Despite the universal awkwardness I think everyone felt, I did enjoy the final testimonio project. It was an experience to hear our thoughts out loud to an audience of your peers and receive feedback. Listening to everybody's testimonial, you can't help but feel a sense of connection with other students. I think this is critically important to helping understand who we are, and how we relate to the people around us.

Listening to my voice in front of everybody made me a bit self-conscious of my experience. But it's helpful in helping me to identify my experiences and how they relate to philosophy. It gave me a hands-on opportunity to relate what I've learned with what I've experienced. As a whole the experience was positive and helped give me a better understanding of philosophy.

... hearing yourself on a recording is also very different from just reading it in my mind. It gave me another perspective and allowed me to make critiques as if I was listening to somebody else's work.

> *The experience of having to hear my digital testimonio in class with the rest of my classmates was a good experience. We all got to hear feedback from our classmates and professor as well... Overall the final digital testimonio and analysis was a good experience, where I got to see what I got out from this whole course.*

Finally, I share a reflection written by an upper division student who registered in a few of my courses, including a Feminist Philosophy course where for the first time I included some written *testimonio* assignments and a digital one.

> *First of all, I would like to thank you for making this course as enjoyable as it was. I cannot even begin to tell you how this course has changed the way I think and treat other people as well. My favorite assignment, without doubt, was the Digital testimonio as it allowed me to express true feelings. I am very grateful for the opportunity to have learned so much from my classmates through that exercise as well. I would also like to say that it has been a pleasure to have taken all of my upper level courses with you as I note that you do not test one's abilities but strengthen them. Continue with this strategy as your feedback was of great help and guidance. Again, thank you for this philosophical journey, I assure you that I will continue to read and learn of these fascinating topics.*

This reflection is particularly significant to me and to the question of whether or not Anzalduísta pedagogies may contribute to nurturing the public voices of students belonging to communities that have been historically de-authorized from participating in the public sphere. After taking my course, this student registered in Creative Non-fiction where she transformed the *testimonio* that she had digitalized into a new poetic piece that she then performed at the local International Museum of Arts and Sciences in McAllen as part of the communities celebration of *el Día de los Muertos*. There she shared the story of a family member victim of domestic violence. She did so creatively while speaking critically to her community, which she sees as honoring the dead who no longer suffer without asking about the fate of those in the community who are "with lively flesh pretending to be alive." She speaks of recognized and valorized cultural beliefs, appeals to their significance to the community's conceptions of life and death, and transfigures women's knowing how to survive into a critical perspective on how life and death are culturally gendered. She reconceives these in light of domestic abuse. In her eyes the latter is outcome of cultural conditions that appear to conduce and not intervene in situations of domestic violence, thus obstructing the safety and life possibilities of female members of the community. She transfigured the embodied knowledge of *what works unequally*—the unsaid —into an idea expressed in public language.

The inner and outer transformative events communicated by my students' responses signal the possibilities for growth inherent to an alternative philosophi-

cal pedagogy that not only teaches philosophical positions, but lends approaches and skills to articulate the *unsaid* grounded in embodied knowing. Given the epistemic ignorance that inhabits the discursive practices in institutions of higher learning, the creation of concepts and frameworks that adequately reflect the realities we all inhabit is imperative to the survival and flourishing of life. From the Anzalduísta perspective developed here, this requires first the recognition of a new epistemology that forces those of us for whom legitimate knowledge assumes a naturalized *unsaid* that is immanent to what we deem worthy of learning, teaching, and using and then the self-reflective work to denaturalize the latter. It also requires us to recognize the *unsaid* brought into our classrooms by increasingly diverse student populations and into the academy through alternative forms of philosophical literature. This recognition means learning the necessary skills to transfigure the *unsaid* into forms to be publically engaged for the purpose of creating more adequate concepts and frameworks. Since the *unsaid* is the embodied knowing of *what works* and as such arises from social relations and conditions, learning these skills will entail subjecting ourselves to new forms of academic spaces that because of our position of authority will require our leadership to construct.

A pedagogical intervention informed by perspectives of intellectuals who have experienced first-hand learning as members of traditionally underrepresented communities may be one promising piece in a larger project to address the problems of inclusivity in the field of philosophy and to engage critically the difference made in settings such as UTPA where our students are predominantly Mexican American/Chicano-a/Latino-a or Mexican. However, my vision in seeking and practicing pedagogical interventions is not the recruitment of students into the major or into professional careers in philosophy. I wholeheartedly believe in the liberatory potential of philosophical engagement. As Anzaldúa and Plato foreground, philosophical lives are not about thinking for the sake of thinking. The philosophical life seeks to materialize justice in our communities and the good in ourselves; it is essentially a transformative practice lead by intellect, courage, and ultimately, love. To translate the essay's opening epigraph: As a teacher, part of my job is to demystify the practical/technical tools that the academic world of philosophy has appropriated and excluded working class and Third World people from using by way of dogmatically associating them with boredom and de-authorizing their engagement with the illusion of the impracticality of abstraction.

WORKS CITED

American Philosophical Association (APA). "Minorities in Philosophy." The APA Online. 2013. Web. 28 Sept. 2013. http://c.ymcdn.com/sites/www.apaonline.org/resource/resmgr/Data_on_Profession/Minorities _in_Philosophy.pdf

---. "Women in Philosophy." The APA Online. 2013. Web. 28 Sept. 2013. http://c.ymcdn.com /sites/www.apaonline.org/resource/resmgr/Data_on_Profession/ Women in_Philosophy.pdf

Anzaldúa, Gloria. Gloria Evangelina Anzaldúa Papers, Benson Latin American Collection, University of Texas Libraries, the University of Texas at Austin.

---. Borderlands/La Frontera: The New Mestiza. 3rd Edition. San Francisco: Aunt Lute, 2007. Print.

Crouch, Margaret. "Implicit Bias and Gender (and Other Sorts of) Diversity in Philosophy and the Academy in the Context of the Corporatized University." JOURNAL of SOCIAL

PHILOSOPHY, Vol. 43 No. 3, Fall 2012, 212–26. Web. 19 April 2014.

Freeman, Lauren "Creating Safe Spaces: Strategies for Confronting Implicit and Explicit Bias and Stereotype Threat in the Classroom." APA Newsletter on Feminism and Philosophy. Ed. Margaret Crouch. APA Spring 2014 2-12. Web. 26 April 2014

Haslanger, Sally. "Women in Philosophy? Do the Math." The New York Times. 22 Sept. 2013. Web. 22 Sept. 2013. http://opinionator.blogs.nytimes.com/2013/09/02/women-in-philosophy-do-the-math/?_php=true& type=blogs&_r=0

Hispanic Association of Colleges & Universities. "List of Hispanic Serving Institutions 2012-2013." Web. 15 April 2014.

Mills, Charles. The Racial Contract. Ithaca: Cornell University Press, 1987. Print.

Mangan, Katherine. "In the Humanities, Men Dominate the Fields of Philosophy and History." The Chronicle of Higher Education. October 29, 2012. Web. 17 Sept. 2013. https://chronicle.com/article/Men-Dominate-Philosophy-and/135306/

Norlock, Kathryn J. "Letter to the APA Committee on the Status of Women" February 2011. Web. Sept. 9 2013. https://docs.google.com/viewer?a=v&pid=sites&srcid=ZGVmYXVsdGRvbWFpbnxhc%20GFjb21taXR0ZWVvbnRoZXN0YXR1c29md29tZ-W58Z3g6NGQxNWNhYWIzNmExOWNhZg

Paxton, Molly, Carrie Figdor and Valerie Tiberius. "Quantifying the Gender Gap: An Empirical Study of the Underrepresentation of Women in Philosophy." Hypatia, Vol 27 Issue 4 (Fall 2012), 949-57. Print.

Office of Institutional Research and Effectiveness. "Stats at a Glance." University of Texas – Pan American, Fall 2013. Web. 25 Sept. 2013.

Anonymous. "Women, Grade Sensitivity, And Major Selection. Feminist Philosophers Blog. March 18 2014. Web. Sept. 17 2013. http://feministphilosophers.wordpress.com/2014/03/18/women-grade-sensitivity-and-major-selection/

LA LLORONA AND THE ACADEMY: WAILING/ WRITING AS ACTIVISM AND EMPOWERMENT

JODY A. BRIONES

I am a Chicana academic, and my voice, my "wailing" for activism and empowerment, is heard through written form. Sociocultural and sociopolitical activism, however, is often not valued within the academy (Baez; Cancian; Flores Niemann). The "publish or perish" doctrine of the academy has commodified student and faculty writing by placing more value on research-based, canonically-inspired works rather than on works written to empower and inspire activism, which are often written by people of color and marginalized scholars. The devaluing of the epistemological, personal, cultural, and social contributions of these types of scholarship is a tactic used by the hegemonic academy to silence Chicanas and marginalized faculty. In this chapter, I use Gloria Anzaldúa's unfinished doctoral dissertation "Llorona, the Woman Who Wails: Chicana/Mestiza Transgressive Identities" to explore how the Chicana body can be used as text to empower and promote activism in written form to resist the hegemonic and oppressive forces of the academy. I will use Anzaldúa's concept of ***autohistoria-teoría*** as she explains it through the embodiment of the mythological/folkloric figure of La Llorona. Anzaldúa uses La Llorona as the embodiment of Chicana identity because, as she explains, "[f]or the Chicana feminist exploring her female ancestors, time is collapsed, present, past, future,

are like rooms in one house. *La llorona* for me is such a house" ("Llorona, the Woman Who Wails" 2).

La Llorona, also referred to as the "Weeping/Wailing Woman," is a central mythological/folkloric figure in the Mexican and Mexican American culture that has significantly influenced Chicana identity politics. Although La Llorona has many narratives, her central mythos is that she killed her children for her lover and now roams the earth, guilt stricken, searching for them as penance. La Llorona's hegemonic master narrative has historically served as a cautionary tale to control unruly children and serves as a "bad mother" archetype for Chicanas, pitted against the "good mother" archetype of La Virgen de Guadalupe, another significant figure in Chicana identity politics. La Llorona's wailings were meant to scare women and children into submission. But Anzaldúa was not afraid of La Llorona; she found strength in her:

> *La llorona* is a scream that punctures a hole in space, a bloodcurling wail that keeps alive the trauma of the past, a trauma frozen in time, eternal, a trauma of separation and death. The scream is followed by a slow prolonged moaning. She is thus the symbol for exile and isolation, for journey/*viaje*/quest/wandering...we who diveate [sic] from culturally imposed roles are *lloronas*...*La Llorona* is a symbol of victimization, vengeance, and a longing for historically denied social justice for women, Chicano and Mexican people and the dominated who have been stifled and silenced ("Llorona, the Woman Who Wails" 9, 16-17).

Thus, Anzaldúa was empowered by La Llorona: "To me she was the central figure in Mexican mythology which empowered me to yell out, to scream out, to speak out, to break out of silence" (*Interviews/Entrevistas* 229). This empowerment led Anzaldúa, as well as other Chicana feminists, to reclaim the mythology and symbolism of La Llorona to create counter narratives that call on all Chicanas to use their "wailings" as voice for social activism and empowerment.[1]

In her revised but unfinished dissertation "Llorona, the Woman Who Wails," Anzaldúa argues that the physical body of the Chicana serves as a site of *nepantla*, where the psychic, temporal, and symbolic identities of the *mestiza* superimpose themselves onto the physical body of the Chicana. Thus, as *naguals*, shapeshifters of transgressive identities, Chicanas' physical bodies are texts of *autohistorias* ("Llorona, the Woman Who Wails" 4), using personal experiences to reflect on

1 Chicana feminist texts that create an empowered, counter narrative of La Llorona include Sandra Cisneros' *Woman Hollering Creek and Other Stories*, Helena María Viramontes' *The Moths and Other Stories*, Domino Renee Perez' *There Was a Woman: La Llorona from Folklore to Popular Culture*, and Sonia Saldívar-Hull's *Feminism on the Border: Chicana Gender Politics and Literature*.

and rewrite hegemonic historical and cultural master narratives to "create new stories of healing, self-growth, cultural critique, and individual/collective transformation" (*The Gloria Anzaldúa Reader* 319). Interpreting La Llorona's wails as voice of the Chicana *autohistoria*, Anzaldúa identifies La Llorona as a representation of the Chicana body, as shown in Figure 1, to illustrate how the inner consciousness, in the form of the psychic, temporal, and symbolic identities of the *mestiza*, superimpose themselves onto the outer consciousness that is the physical body of the Chicana.

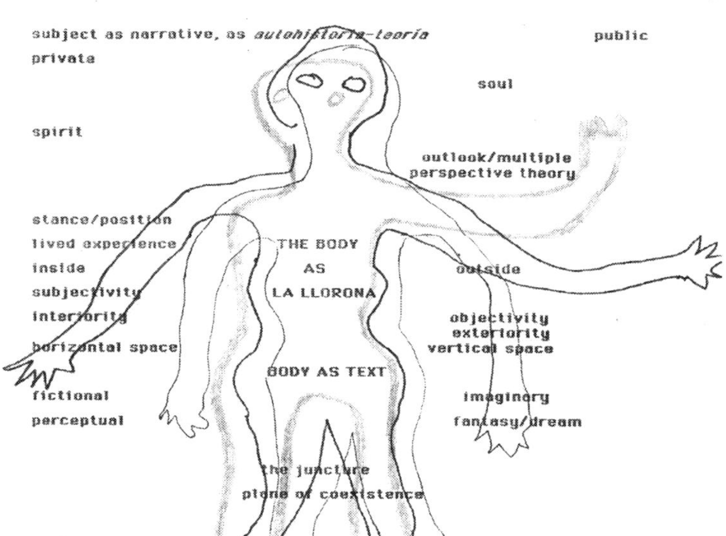

Figure 1. "The Body as La Llorona" ("Llorona, the Woman Who Wails" 4) © Gloria E. Anzaldúa Literary Trust

It is through these transgressive planes of being that Chicanas can "denot[e] the presence of an absence" ("Llorona, the Woman Who Wails" 4) and use the concept of *autohistoria-teoría* to create narratives that promote intracultural collective identity and Chicana empowerment.

Anzaldúa urges us to (re)create our cultural history by reclaiming La Llorona, by creating a counter narrative that rewrites La Llorona and other Chicanas as *gritonas* for activism and empowerment. For Chicana academics, these "wailings" of activism and empowerment are enacted in written form through conference proceedings, journal articles, and monographs. However, the hegemonic forces of the academy resist and often punish Chicanas for these "wailings." These oppressive academic conditions are well documented, the most recent of which are in *Presumed Incompetent: The Intersections of Race and Class for Women in Academia.*

In *Presumed Incompetent*, contributing authors, all women of color within the academy, share their *testimonios*, or "wailings," regarding their experiences as racialized and sexed subjects within the hegemonic patriarchy of the academy. For example, contributing author Yolanda Flores Niemann, Full Professor of Psychology and current Senior Vice Provost at the University of North Texas, shares how she endured and overcame racism, sexism, and tokenism at one of her first institutions as a tenure-track junior faculty member. Flores Niemann explains that when her scholarship would focus on issues affecting the Mexican American population, "I was considered the ethnic researcher. This label also meant that my research was undervalued and not considered scholarly" (343), stating one seasoned professor in her department asked her, "'What are you, a scholar or a Mexican American?'" (340), confirming that the hegemony within her institution did not consider ethnic research scholarly. I, too, have encountered this at my institution.

I am a tenure-track Assistant Professor of English at a Hispanic-Serving Institution in South Texas where I serve as Coordinator of Freshman and Sophomore English. Upon my mid-career review (which was one year late), I was told that only scholarship which focused on Composition Studies would count towards my tenure and promotion—scholarship that focused on Chican@ Studies would not count. This surprised me because this stipulation was not in my contract, and neither my department chair nor dean had ever mentioned this. It also worried me because most of my scholarship is rooted in Chican@ Studies. When I asked why scholarship in Chican@ Studies would not count towards my tenure and promotion, I was told that it was because I was hired for my specialization in composition, hence my position as Coordinator of Freshman and Sophomore English. This decision by my all-White fourth year committee showed that they do not value Chican@ scholarship—they think it unworthy of academic status.

Experiencing this type of racial/ethnic discrimination felt personal because most of my scholarship is rooted in the personal, so it felt as if the committee was saying *I* wasn't good enough, not worthy enough for tenure and promotion, and that the *gritos* that are my scholarship are "wailings" of a hysterical and vengeful woman, like La Llorona—and I would say that they are half right. I am not hysterical, but I am vengeful. Hysteria will "depotenize *el grito de la llorona*" ("Llorona, the Woman Who Wails" 10). As a Chicana academic, I want to use my writings/wailings, my scholarship, as passive vengeance in the form of Chicana activism and empowerment to create and enact social justice. Flores Niemann explains:

> people of color who pursue an academic career and conduct ethical, culturally-sensitive research...are role models and mentors for other

> students, faculty, and community members. Through their research, they can facilitate understanding of and improvements in their communities and [create] more trust in academic institutions. (353)

It is by "wailing" that these social justices can occur.

La Llorona, the woman who wails, is a source of empowerment for Chicanas. A proto-*mestiza*, La Llorona represents the transgressive and symbolic identities Chicanas embody and the *autohistorias* Chicanas create. These *autohistorias* are the counter narratives that resist the oppressive forces of the academy. Writing/wailing empowers Chicanas to psychologically, spiritually, and physically resist discriminatory academic hegemony and other psychological, spiritual, and physical oppressions. Thus, I say to all *mujeres*, especially those within the academy, *¡adelante gritonas!*

WORKS CITED

Anzaldúa, Gloria. *The Gloria Anzaldúa Reader*. Ed. AnaLouise Keating. Durham: Duke UP, 2009. Print.

---. *Interviews/Entrevistas / Gloria Anzaldúa*. Ed. AnaLouise Keating. New York: Routledge, 2000. Print.

---. "Llorona, the Woman Who Wails: Chicana/Mestiza Transgressive Identities." Box 93, Folder 14. "Llorona, the Woman Who Wails: Chicana/Mestiza Transgressive Identities" 8 June 2002. Gloria Evangelina Anzaldúa Papers, 1942-2004. Benson Latin American Collection, University of Texas at Austin, Austin, TX. 1 Nov. 2013.

Baez, Benjamin. "Race-Related Service and Faculty of Color: Conceptualizing Critical Agency in Academe." *Higher Education* 39.3 (2000): 363-391. *JSTOR*. Web. 1 Sep. 2014.

Cancian, Francesca M. "Conflicts between Activist Research and Academic Success: Participatory Research and Alternative Strategies." *The American Sociologist* 24.1 (1993): 92-106. *JSTOR*. Web. 1 Sep. 2014.

Cisneros, Sandra. *Woman Hollering Creek and Other Stories*. New York: Vintage Contemporaries, 1991. Print.

Flores Niemann, Yolanda. "The Making of a Token: A Case Study of Stereotype Threat, Stigma, Racism, and Tokenism in Academe." *Presumed Incompetent: The Intersections of Race and Class for Women in Academia*. Ed. Gabriella Gutiérrez y Muhs, Yolanda Flores Niemann, Camen G. González, and Angela P. Harris. Boulder: UP of Colorado, 2012. 336-355. Print.

Pérez, Domino Renee. *There Was a Woman: La Llorona from Folklore to Popular Culture*. Austin: University of Texas P, 2008.

Saldívar-Hull, Sonia. *Feminism on the Border: Chicana Gender Politics and Literature*. Berkeley: University of California P, 2000. Print.

Viramontes, Helena María. *The Moths and Other Stores*. Houston: Arte Público, 1995. Print.

CAR[T]AS: ROOTING OUR PURPOSE AS ACADEMICS IN A TIME OF TRANSFORMATION

NATALIA DEEB-SOSSA, GLORIA M. RODRIGUEZ, INÉS HERNÁNDEZ-AVILA, AND YVETTE G. FLORES

"Because who would believe/ the fantastic and terrible story of all our survival/ those who were never meant/ to survive?"—Joy Harjo

In our workshop at El Mundo Zurdo 2013: An International Conference on the Life and Work of Gloria E. Anzaldúa, we presented our book project, *CAR[T]AS: Letters to the Next Generation.* These letters to the next generation of Chicana/Latina and Indigenous scholars address how to go beyond survival in the academy. They include our own stories of survival and struggle, our issues with work-life balance, our heartfelt research, and the methodologies that we have found useful to our survival and development as scholars. Our letters also include *advertencias*, or forewarnings, about some surprises that we encountered on our path, and for which we want to prepare our students.

This collection is a follow-up to the book *Telling to Live: Latina Feminist Testimonios,* written more than a decade ago. In that volume, the contributors explored their personal experiences of *latinidad,* offering *testimonio* of their own lives. Seven years before that, a group of Chicana scholars contributed to *Building with Our Hands, New Directions in Chicana Studies*, edited by Adela de la Torre and Beatríz M. Pesquera, which explored cutting-edge research on

Chicanas from a variety of disciplinary perspectives. This anthology is another forum that emphasizes the personal *testimonio* while exploring the intersection between our lives as Latina and indigenous women and the scholarship/research/creative work we pursue. *Testimonios* as a method is gaining currency because of its value in generating stories. Storytelling is basic to *testimonio*, but the key to writing *testimonios* is finding our voices, our "I" voices, which have been buried under the rubble of academic language.

In her piece path to *conocimiento* in *This Bridge We Call Home*, Gloria Anzaldúa gives us a template for self-awareness that organizes our collection of letters. *Conocimiento es otro modo de conectar* across colors and other differences to allies also trying to negotiate racial contradictions, survive the stresses and traumas of daily life, and develop a spiritual-imaginal-political vision together. *Conocimiento* shares a sense of affinity with all things and advocates mobilizing, organizing, sharing information, knowledge, insights, and resources with other groups. (Anzaldúa, "now let us shift" 571). There are seven stages to the process, and each stage is a section in our proposed book of letters. Anzaldúa describes a synergistic seven-stage process, in which the etapas or "spaces" might be recursive and nonlinear:

(1) The Rupture: "el arrebato...rupture, fragmentation...an ending, a beginning" (546); crisis, betrayal, illness. (2) Nepantla: "neplanta...torn between ways" (545); opposing forces, the site of transformation, questioning. (3) The Coatlicue State...desconocimiento and the cost of knowing; withdrawal; "desire for love & connection" (550); trauma; new landscapes. (4) The Call to Action: "the call...el compromise...the crossing and conversion" (554); "longing for your potential self" (556). (5) Re-membering Coyolxauqui: "putting Coyolxauhqui together...new personal and collective 'stories'"; "passing the turning point", shedding, releasing, repairing, healing, rewriting (558). (6) The Clash of Realities: "the blow-up...a clash of realities"; reframing, shifting, accepting ambiguity, spiritual techniques, connections (563). And (7) Spiritual Activism: "shifting realities...acting out the vision or spiritual activism"; acting with compassion, neutrality, a "'nos/otras' position—an alliance between 'us' and 'others'" (558).

OUR WORKSHOP

The Workshop consisted of three parts: We first shared our prayers, followed by some of our cartas and *testimonios*. Second, we discussed the importance of sharing our stories of survival and struggle in academia. The discussion focused on the meaning of mentorship, our best and worst mentors, how each of us have been mentors, and the consequences of being mentors to so many students. Third, we welcomed participants to engage in the writing process that we

ourselves have undertaken so they could discuss what they want in their mentors and their top two questions they wished they could ask their mentors but have been afraid to ask.

Only four CAR[T]ISTAS were able to participate at the conference: Inés Hernández-Avila, Yvette Flores, Gloria Rodriguez, and Natalia Deeb-Sossa. Our workshop was moderated by Irene Lara and took place on Friday, November 15, 2013.

OUR PRAYERS

We began our session with each of us reading our prayers. Gloria began: I am calling out to all of our mothers who have borne us, who have nurtured us, who watch over us—not just the ones whom we know but the ones who have adopted us, good, bad, and ugly—bringing us into their arms and sheltering us, but also teaching us how to be *chingonas* when we need to be. Please be with us to reclaim and embody our deepest sense of humanity as we share ourselves with people who are likely also in pain, struggling, and also striving to (re)member themselves...Allow us to stay grounded in our compassion for all forms of life—to appreciate and love all the beauty, strength, and flaws that make us human. Help us to be connected to our history. Help us to be connected to our future generations. Help us to be connected to ourselves and each other. Help me to find my voice and the courage to speak, even when I'm setting out on a path that has yet to be defined.

Her prayer was followed by Ines' prayer: We want this to be a session full of light, a session that lifts up the spirits of everyone present, a session that lights up the spirit of Gloria Anzaldúa. We want to speak from the heart, to hear with our hearts/spirits, to listen carefully and lovingly to everyone's *palabra*. We want the writing space to be blessed, to be a space of trust, a safe space. We will be speaking about the path to *conocimiento*, as written by our ancestor spirit, Gloria. It is good to focus on what she has written; we do not always have to agree, she would have and will understand this. We want to honor her as a philosopher, as a major thinker in the world, as someone who emerged from South Texas and became who she was and is. We want to demonstrate the compassion she speaks of in the section "spiritual activism," we want to demonstrate collectivity, individual *energías* coming together to co-labor, to work together. We want the audience to leave with something they have written that will speak to what they heard through all their senses, what they heard from Spirit.

Then, Natalia followed by reading: *Hoy, mañana y siempre*, let me and those around me be open-minded, and sensitive to other people's pain and alienation. Let our *espiritus* be *rebeldes* and *revoltosas*. Let us never give up our political selves and faith in the goodness and wisdom of others around us. And if those around

us have already rejected us, discriminated against us, and made us feel invisible, let us *nunca*, never, give up on the belief that they can change and that we all can make the world, *nuestra comunidad*, a just one. Let us all help each other heal by sharing our own stories of struggle and survival, and encourage each other to create radical visions for personal and communal transformation. In these times of corporatization of the US academic industrial complex, the expansion of the prison industrial complex and the military industrial complex, as well as the relentless US imperialist foreign policy I encourage all of us to accept and extend Gloria E. Anzaldúa's invitation to transformation.

Lastly, Yvette shared: In remembrance of all the women who came before us, who lived remarkable lives, and those whose name and stories were not recorded, for all of those *quienes pasaron desapercibidas*, seemingly without being known or noticed, let us all mindfully, lovingly record our stories. May we be guided to give voice to our sorrows, our joys, our fears and our victories. May we be guided to continue our *transformacion*.

SHARING OF OUR WORK AND OURSELVES

After the prayers and a moment of silence, **Inés** explained how the book project—letters to the next generation of Chicana/Latina scholars about how to survive in the academy—emphasizes the personal *testimonios*, the intersection between work and our lives as Latina and indigenous women and *advertencias* about some challenges that we encountered and for which we want to prepare our students.

Inés then explained how we use Gloria Anzaldúa's seven stages to the process of *conocimiento* as a template to organize our collection of letters. Conocimiento is, according to Gloria Anzaldúa, "*otro modo de conectar*...to negotiate racial contradictions, survive the stresses and traumas of daily life, and develop a spiritual-imaginal-political vision together" ("now let us shift" 571). Each of us, Inés explained, would read a short essay we wrote which represents one of these stages.

Gloria began by defining the *etapa* of rupture. This is the first stage: "*el arrebato*... rupture, fragmentation...an ending, a beginning" (546). It is characterized by crisis, betrayal, illness. She elaborated drawing directly from Anzaldúa's essay, "now let us shift":

> Every *arrebato*—a violent attack, rift with a loved one, illness, death in the family, betrayal, systematic racism, and marginalization—rips you from your familiar "home," casting you out of your personal Eden, showing that something is lacking in your queendom...Cada *arrebatamiento* is an awakening that causes you to question who you are, what the world is about. The urgency to know what you're experiencing awakens

> *la facultad,* the ability to shift attention and see through the surface of things and situations...You honor what has ended, say good-bye to the old way of being, commit yourself to look for the 'something new,' and picture yourself embracing this new life. But before that can happen you plunge into the ambiguity of the transition phase, undergo another rite of passage, and negotiate another identity crisis. (546-47)

This is Gloria's testimonio:

I have come to realize that I have "nested ruptures" that interrelate but are rooted in the manner in which I was shaken from the person I thought I was—or, perhaps the performance of success that came easy for me until I went to graduate school. I always hated school, but not because I hated learning and knowledge—in fact, I was blessed always to have many people around me in my family who taught me things that I still think of as the most important things of my life. I hated school because it was the first and enduring rupture in my life, that moment of separation from the sense of well-being that I drew from all the people who cared for me unconditionally but who kept me from being too self-centered by reminding me that I had to learn to share and give back in some way to others. I always had a strong sense of myself as a Chicana, even though I called myself Mexican at school. I learned Spanish first, but I spoke mostly English both at home and, of course, at school. I would spend hours on my own listening to music or sitting on my tricycle outside and singing at the top of my voice when I was at home.

At school, I had to take naps on the floor lying on a towel, and the teacher would put on records to soothe us to sleep, but I would lie awake, trying to learn the words. Then we got up from nap time and resumed the noisy activities that I found meaningless and alienating; however, I quickly learned what I needed to do to succeed—because when I was succeeding in the teacher's eyes, she (all but a few were "she's" through high school) would leave me alone, give me a good mark, and let me move on.

When I would come home from school, I would typically hear my dad playing his guitar each evening but not in a movie-like scene where we all stood around and sang. No, I learned from my dad that his music was his escape—even from those who loved him so dearly. My mom and I would even try to penetrate that wall by acting silly, singing, and dancing around or near him, and he would half-smile, shake his head a bit, and just keep right on playing, in his own world, re-connecting with his spirit, after each day of having to put up with no doubt boundless ignorance and perhaps exploitation by his bosses and co-workers, even though these same folks generally seemed to like my dad.

The layers of ruptures thus begin with this sense of self being constantly interrupted by a schooling process that only really taught me one thing: do what you must to get these people off your back so you can do what you really want to do. That is when I began to hone my skills of embracing my inner nerd, and most of what my teachers wanted from me was not that difficult to achieve, so I often exceeded their expectations.

Then, fast-forward to college. My friend's comment helped to create another rupture for me. We were in a class called "History of Economic Thought" and we'd gotten our mid-terms back, and I got a good grade on it, as did my friend, after which she said to me, "I peeked at the other students' papers, and some of them got lower grades than we did, and they're White. I wonder if the professor is just so racist that his expectations of us were low and that's why we got such good grades." The rupture here is not one that actually had to result in changes in what I was doing to keep moving forward with schooling; rather, it was an internal rupture to the things I thought I knew about myself—that I may not get by on being pretty, but I could definitely move ahead in life with my brains. It interrupted my thought that I knew how this game was played and was succeeding, so I could do whatever I wanted, into realizing that I had an obligation not to accept just other people's expectations of me as the sole arbiter of my development and success. My friend's comment kept nagging at me, so that from that point forward, I couldn't—still can't—quite trust positive feedback about my intellectual work.

Natalia followed by reading a poem that discussed the dislocation suffered by Chicana/o students at UC Davis. This poem reflects the third-stage of conocimiento, or the Coatlicue state, which is characterized by *desconocimiento* and the cost of knowing, withdrawal, "desire for love and connection," and trauma. Many students have confided to Natalia how they experienced micro-aggressions at the hands of other students, faculty, staff, and administration. At UC Davis Chicana/o and Latina/o students feel disregarded, alone, frustrated, and with a diminished sense of confidence:

> There is a lot of racism and discrimination on this campus / I am always seen as someone who does not belong here / I feel like I'm in a world that does not accept me / wants me to fail / My skin color and accent make me look as a stranger.
>
> We are tokenized... / and then left floundering without resources or support / White students and professors / discount my experiences/ I'm left feeling invisible / I've experienced culture shock / Most of my neighbors in student housing were white / I didn't feel comfortable speaking in class/

I carry battle wounds / I remember being tracked in high school and not knowing it / taking woodshop over computer science, choir over math / people assume I'm a heavy drinker / I like posole over coke / and I can only clean because that is what Mexican women do.

I don't feel safe / as I continuously hear when I walk through campus / "don't be ghetto"/ "she's a bitch" / "I raped that test…" / I'm exhausted 96% of the time / Large part of the exhaustion is trying to navigate / the sexist, racist, abilist, queerphobic university system/ and I doubt myself always it seems...

I was in complete shock / not many people on this campus looked like me / many did not even understand what I said / I felt left out / isolated / intimidated / I am constantly asked where I am from / I am from San Fernando Valley / I am not even aware I had an accent / Many days I keep my mouth shut / because I have been put down before / I do not feel smart enough / I don't fit in.

I come from East Oakland / I have been asked several times if I speak English / my accent has been pointed out several times / I have felt guilt for being here / working on my "success" / leaving my family behind with problems /an alcoholic brother / who would come home beating up on everyone that crossed his path / a dad that would get in really bad fights with my brother / a little brother who would cry / a mother who would faint every time and /a sister who would get "ataque de nervios."

When I first moved to Davis / two students yelled / "Go back to Mexico" / A classmate said to me / I was not like the Mexicans from his hometown: / they steal car parts /
are in gangs / drop out from high school / do nothing but insult people.

I am an economics major / professors think I cheat simply because I am brown / they assume I am not good in math / Even in high school / my calculus teacher / after hearing me playing the guitar / told me / "you should stick to music" / Is that a compliment to my skills / or a statement that I'm not that good in math? / what do *you* think?

The high school I went to / did not prepare me to get into college / let alone succeed in college / I feel that I am having to learn everything / others already know / and that I am being judged / based on the color of my skin.

It is so easy to fall behind / It is so stressful in college / There are so many other things to worry about / I work to pay for rent / clothes / food / gas / books /school / I work 35 hours a week / and still find myself broke / I am constantly busy with school / work / and struggle to balance / school / work / health / fitness / friends / family /life. / Is it any surprise I feel like I'm barely surviving?

This campus is very hostile / especially for Latinos in engineering / I was the only Latino in my lab class / students bragged about how their families worked for Apple, IBM and Chevron. / How can I relate to that? / My dad is a construction worker / my mother works in a *maquila* / I struggle due to lack of resources / I don't own a computer/ I have to check out the books out of the library.

My biology advisor / did not motivate me to keep going / he advised me to look into another major / saying "things will not get easier for *you*." / In addition / a teaching assistant told me / this school was not a place for a "girl like me!" / What do you think they meant by: "not for *me*?"

When I got here / I heard the following comments: / "Oh, your English is so good," / "You're Mexican? But you're so light!" / I feel confused / angry / I wrestle with either challenging their ignorance and racism / (becoming the angry Latina) / or letting it go / (and somehow being complicit in their racism and ignorance).

It is a very lonely place / I hardly see people who look like me / people who come from a similar background / I get glares / because of the way I dress / I don't have a lot of money / to buy fancy things.

I am Chicano / and went to the Silo for food / I paid for it / but later on, I was accused of stealing the food / Even though I cleared up what happened / Everyone around me /
still thought I was a thief / The cashier would never have accused me of stealing / This would never have happened / if I was white.

In my first year / I was riding my bike back to my dorm / I had a hoodie on and it seemed to invite / the UCD patrol unit / to follow behind me / they followed closely / until I went into my dorm / it was racial profiling / I felt harassed / I felt stereotyped / The message was clear: / I should not be out at night / I do not belong at UCD.

Some weeks I don't have money to buy food / even though I work on campus / I go hungry some days / I often times don't make it to the food bank / I work or I am in class when they are open / My family cannot help / I can't ask my friend to pitch in / I wonder if I can do my homework/ while I go hungry another day.

Bathrooms / Who would think of bathrooms / but there are not enough gender neutral restrooms / It is a matter of safety / should I risk my safety when I need to pee?

The environment in my pre-med classes / is extremely intimidating / I am silenced in these classes / I am shut down/ what I have to say is undervalued / what I have to say is not respected / It is exhausting being me / I feel tired of being Mexican / I doubt myself / specially when people say / it was easier for me

to get into college / "because I'm Mexican."

Such hostile campus climate / renders invisible / alienates/ discriminates/ and marginalizes / our students of color / transgendered students / mothers / low-income students / undocumented / women / queer students / Many students this quarter / have struggled with depression / some have become suicidal / yet the campus administration / hardly talks about campus climate / its hostility / its effect./ I am left to wonder / what will administration's response be / to the real effects of the hostile campus climate / and to my students' words?

I will end by asking / Whose voices and perspectives on campus are you listening to? Also consider what other Chicanas/os and Latinas/os on campus are invisible? / The institution makes invisible—literally, ethnically and culturally—custodians, landscapers, cooks, staff members, and faculty./ What is our responsibility towards them?

Yvette followed with her *testimonio* titled "A Call to Action." This personal essay brings to life what Anzaldúa is having us explore in "the call" stage. The fourth-stage of *conocimiento* is defined as: "the call…*el compromiso*…the crossing and conversion" (554); "longing for your potential self" (556).

> I lie in a fetal position, clutching my stomach, the core of my being. Silent screams erupt from my belly; tears flow endlessly. I do not sleep. I am no longer wanted as a wife, lover, partner, friend. He needs space, he says. He appreciates everything I have done for him. But he does not want to be a burden to me, he insists. This is better for me, he pronounces. I am paralyzed by rage/pain/loss. How dare he tell me what I need or want, or what I can or cannot handle? How dare he hide his desire for freedom under a cloak of presumed caring for me? How dare he refuse to acknowledge that he is simply exercising his patriarchal right to discard that which is no longer of use to him? How can he leave me? How dare he destroy our love and my trust in him at a time when I am most in need of his support? I am preparing my packet for promotion to full professor. I need to organize my writings and write a narrative about my accomplishments and seek reviewers who understand my work and my contributions to the academy (will they have any idea of what the journey to this moment in my academic life has been, since it is an unspoken story for so many women of color?). My home life always has been my base, my source of strength. When I felt loved, I believed I could do anything. How can I go on when I am no longer loved?
>
> I cannot breathe. My lungs fill with unshed tears despite weeks of crying. My western physician tells me I have pneumonia. She asks me what is wrong. I tell her my marriage may be ending (I am still in denial that it

is over and has been for months); she corrects her diagnosis. It is emotional pneumonia she says and shows compassion.

My Serbo-Croatian healer tells me my grief and his betrayal has blocked my qi, my life force. My life energy is blocked by pain, by sorrow, by unspoken fears and psychic wounding. She massages my body and prays for healing for my broken heart. She burns sage and gives me tea. You must learn to find love within yourself, she says. I hear her words but I feel nothing. I have already built up the walls that my love for him had torn down. How is your heart, she asks. I respond "encased in cement; protected by barbed wired." She seems concerned, unaccustomed to hearing Latina melodramatic descriptions of romantic pain.

How can I put myself together enough to prepare my promotion packet, teach my classes, do the service work? Do I seek solace in books, as I did when as a child life made no sense? Do I throw myself into my academic work? Do I continue to teach/to profess about *familia y salud mental* when for the first time in my life I feel the need for antidepressants to get through the day. Valeriana, acupuncture, and all my other therapies do not seem to work. I do not want to lie on anyone's couch and talk about the pain. I JUST WANT NOT TO FEEL IT.

Why am I letting a man and a failed romantic relationship tear me apart?? How could I not? I was socialized to love men; to nurture them as a mother should, to love them as a *puta* and as a docile wife? How could I not put all my eggs into this heterosexual basket when that is what every woman in my family has done before me?

I acknowledged that when one's heart has been broken, one has to find the inner strength and resilience that has survived the attacks of patriarchal violence, whether from a man or an academic institution. I had suffered that pain before; however, I managed not to internalize the attacks that occurred within the academy. This violence was more personal because it came from someone who mattered, not an institution inhabited by other wounded souls like mine. I could contextualize the assaults from the academy as political and I could try not to take them personally. However, to be cast aside "for my own good" was too big a lie to swallow. I felt abandoned. I could not see a way out of this darkness.

Somewhere along my educational trajectory I had become westernized, acculturated, disembodied, partly cut off from the healing knowledge imparted by my *tias*—the family *curanderas*—and my clairvoyant maternal grandmother and mother. The trauma created by institutionalized oppression while a student and young professor, the daily doses of marginalization and erasure, had torn me asunder and created amnesia. To survive

in the midst of violence, the victimized often dissociate—separate mind from heart and spirit. I relied on my brain and devalued my intuition as I was dismembered by the daily indignities I faced as a woman of color in the academy. I silenced my own suffering out of guilt about my privilege, always comparing myself to those who had it worse than I—a lesson in self-erasure I had internalized long ago. The loss of my marriage led to an *arrebato*—a crisis of meaning—from which I feared I would not recover.

After months of going through the motions of living—dissociated from heart and mind—so that I could continue to perform my academic duties, after weeks of grief and denial, physical illness and moments of extreme self-loathing, I fell asleep and had a dream.

I am riding in an old yellow school bus. My friend of nearly 30 years, mentor and spiritual guide (when I let him) sits next to me. The bus is proceeding slowly down a long narrow country road. Suddenly the bus stops and my friend tells me it is time to get off. I protest: "I am not ready." He smiles and with his eyes bids me farewell. I step off the bus onto a warm, sunny day. The bus disappears and I walk into a field of maize. I am overwhelmed by the brightness of the yellow that envelops me. Suddenly I feel a presence, Her presence. She appears before me, tall and beckoning. Her long braids of grey-black hair lay against a sky blue rebozo. Her deep brown eyes look through me to my core. I do not feel afraid. I know she has been waiting for me. I know it is now my time to accept her invitation. She opens her arms and I walk into her sweet soothing embrace. I feel her warmth and the warmth of all the women in my lineage who came before me—the dreamers, the seers, the healers, the mothers and grandmothers, the daughters and granddaughters who share our history of pain and sorrow and survival. No words are spoken. She holds me and I know I will be alright.

I awoke with tears falling down my face—not the tears of despair/rage/pain that have been my companion for the past few months. They are cleansing tears. I get out of bed, shower, open the windows that have been shut for weeks, and begin to clean my house. I let the light in. I have been blessed. My path has been shown to me.

I must find my way back to myself and rebirth the woman I am meant to be. Over the next few months I slowly and mindfully rebuild my life as a woman without a man.

I begin to transform my teaching; I begin to relearn the old ways of knowing and healing. I seek ways to find and reconnect my body/mind/spirit. I did not share my dream with any of my friends for a long time. I did not need to look for outside sources of validation. I had the answers within myself; I needed to trust my knowledge. I knew that She came to me

in the dream to soothe my pain and help me birth the new me. The search for wholeness began. To rebuild myself, I had to go back and I had to go inside—to reclaim ancient ways of knowing and recover the teachings of the elders in order to find healing and transform my life.

I now walk in the knowingness that I am guided, I am blessed, I am taken care of and I deserve to be who I am in this moment, in this time, and in this place.

Finally, **Inés** ends by reading her essay on the seventh stage of *conocimiento* or Spiritual Activism, which is characterized by "shifting realities...acting out the vision or spiritual activism"; acting with compassion, neutrality, a "'nos/otras' position—an alliance between 'us' and 'others'"(570). Inés' *testimonio* begins with a poem she wrote in the 1970s:

> Guerrillera soy/ En cada suspiro, pensamiento, lágrima, y beso / En cada momento que / me encuentres / Guerrillera soy
>
> I am a spiritual warrior, eso es lo que soy, desde hace mucho. Entiendo que la Guerra es interna tanto como externa, que la luz de iluminación, la luz de la conciencia es mi meta, que soy la serpiente, y estoy dispuesta a que la flecha de la luz de la conciencia me penetre, para que mi ser pueda lograr una transformación espiritual. I used to relate to the Corazón sacrificado, I was attracted to it, I wanted it as my emblem, in my trajes de danza, I would use it as my imagen sagrado, but then after many years, I began to understand that I was bringing pain upon myself—that pain, yes, is part of love, amoridolor, como deciamos aquí en Tejas en los setenta, creating our own difrasismo, BUT, el dolor de esta vida es tan profunda que no tenía porque buscar más dolor, solo basta con saber lo que pasa en el mundo, and this is more than enough. The heart surrounded by the crown of thorns, the heart with the sword piercing through it, that has been me for so long, my childhood, my adolescence, my first marriage, my divorce, my life filled with sexual experiences of violation and rape, degrading hurtful, sombras de traiciones, mi vida en Tejas en el movimiento, mi vida como mujer/madre soltera, my moving to California, being in the Indian community, yearning for a partner, picking the wrong undeserving men, being hurt again and again, finally meeting the one who was meant for me, who was born for me.
>
> My precious Spirit, I didn't understand or remember, o más bien, no me dí cuenta que tan cerca estabas, protegiéndome, showing me how to be well, loving to dance, all my life, loving to dance, probably was conceived after my parents had a night of dancing, probably went to dances while I was forming in my mother's womb, knowing from the womb that dance

is life and life is dance, learning later about the sacred nature of dance, learning later about the cosmic dance of life, becoming a danzante, keeping the beat of my feet with the beat of the drum heart, the EarthMother drum, being with the rhythm as Grandpa Tom used to say, know that the rhythm is you, that it is yours, that it belongs to you, that you came into this world in this life on this earth with the rhythm, that the rhythm will guide you, the rhythm will heal you, the rhythm will help you when you are lost, the rhythm will help you when you are down, the rhythm will console you when you are sad, the rhythm is what you will leave this world with, Huehuecoyotl, Ancient One, I know your sacred dance, it is the dance of the Giver of Life, Mother and Father, it is the dance of my people, it is the dance that has saved my life.

Spiritual Warrior, remember that we have moved into the Sexto Sol, it is time to act with consciousness of the new time that has arrived, it is time to manifest the change(ing). Se tienen que acabar los juegos. Hay que percibir y recibir este sol con amor, entusiasmo, respeto, bondad, porque es un bebito y hay que tratarlo con much ternura. Pero llegó con toda su sabiduría, don't forget, because it is recently here from the spirit world where it was gestating in the cosmic womb. We must fine-tune the ears of our heart to learn from this Sol. We must work together for this. We must. The heart is the center. Cuerpo, Conciencia, Voluntad, Espíritu, Corazón. Magic, Sacred, Number 5. Nez Perce way.

Gloria Anzaldúa says, capturing beautifully a concept that resonates with so many indigenous peoples, "The heart es un corazón con razón, with intelligence, passion, and purpose, a 'mindful' heart with ears for listening, eyes for seeing, a mouth with tongue narrowing to a pen tip for speaking/ writing" (571). My first book of poems was titled *Con Razón, Corazón* (1976). I knew back then, I learned/knew from childhood, from my mother and father, how to see with the heart, hear with the heart, speak with the heart, be with my heart. I didn't realize at first that early on I was already engaging in spiritual activism, because when I spoke I spoke from the heart, I understood spirit and did my best to move with spirit. At marches, rallies, demonstrations, when I would be called upon to speak, and I would look out into the faces of the people listening to us as we delivered our messages of Movimiento, I felt I was connecting with each person. I looked intently at them. I heard my own voice speaking. I didn't think about what to say. I opened my mouth and my heart took over. I have made grievous mistakes along the way. Reflection is the key. To see myself with my heart, to hear myself with my heart, to be myself with my heart. To admit my mistakes, to own them, to be honest with myself, and then to forgive myself with

compassion. This is the secret of spiritual activism, at least for me. To learn to be with yourself, deeply, honestly, compassionately, lovingly. Then the Spiritual Warrior cannot be defeated, ever, no matter what. It is an ongoing process, sí? We are never done, because from moment to moment we are shifting, moving, shedding, transforming. This is how I see my work, my life, as a Spiritual Warrior.

ENGAGING WITH OUR WORKSHOP PARTICIPANTS

After each of us read our testimonios, we encouraged the audience to write their own cartas or personal *testimonios*. We started by using the following prompt, and gave them only five minutes to free-write: "Gloria writes often about the space of doubt, of questioning. Write about a moment or moments in your life when doubt has been your friend, making you reflect in new and different ways about something you were working on." After the five minutes had passed, we asked them to do a second writing exercise, also for five minutes, following this prompt: "Write a letter to your younger self in which you might offer *advertencias* or forewarnings, suggestions, praises, or words of healing." After the five minutes had passed, we asked for people to share, if they wanted, their free-writes. The *testimonios* read out loud were powerful, insightful, heart-breaking and at the same time hopeful. They all reminded us how the personal inspires and challenges us to theorize experience—the moving, the funny, the disturbing, the angering—and further *concientización* and direct action.

A letter to myself by Irene Lara

Bella Irene del espíritu brillante. Sí, eres tu. No te escondas. No mires hacia abajo. Mira a tu alrededor. Eres esta belleza, este milagro. Déjate brillar. No tengas miedo. Transformalo. Has lo que tengas que hacer. Vamonos.

La duda by Maria Figueroa

Lo dudo...dudar is a dicho I've often heard from my mother, mi mamá. The place of doubt has and did recently become an intimate comadre. She came in the form of my grandmothers, abuelitas, in my dreams and in my running, sweaty prayers. La duda, the doubt I could feel in my core, en el vientre desde el cenote de conocimiento. When I knew, I just know because La duda as my intuition would tell me, warned me that something was wrong, that mi compañero was not being fiel. His disloyalty came con La duda. So like a wise messenger, I did not shoot the messenger, mi comadre La duda. Instead, I embraced her, thanked her for bringing me all of those messages that would eventually lead to my path of recovery.

A letter to myself by Maria Figueroa

Mija, mija chiquita linda,
quierete, amate, abrazate
come bien y se feliz
love your lonjita because many times you will be told to hate it
quierete, amate, abrazate
mija, roller-skate through pebbled streets
be an osicona y no te dejes de nadien
si te pegan, hit them back where it really hurts
so they'll never do it again
si quieres comer pan dulce, los cochinitos son los mejores
con un basito de leche or un chocolatito

We thank all those who shared the *testimonios* for this essay and at the workshop. They were profoundly moving, and do what the best *testimonios* have always done: allow us to know and care about other academic-activistas-chingo-nas/os in struggle, and motivate us to create and support positive action. Thanks for your coraje—in both senses of the word—por el valor y la rabia.

WORKS CITED

Anzaldúa, Gloria E. "now let us shift…the path of conocimineto…inner work, public acts," *this bridge we call home: radical visions for transformation*. Eds. Gloria E. Anzaldúa and AnaLouise Keating. New York: Routledge, 2002. 540-78.

Harjo, Joy. "Anchorage." *She Had Some Horses*. New York: Thunder's Mouth Press. 1983. 15. Print.

HOW TO DE-ACADEMIZE THEORY: ACCOUNTABILITY AND REPRESENTATION

RUFINA CORTEZ

Gloria Anzaldúa's work urges for the de-academization of theory and for the fluidity of connectivity between the community and academy. To accomplish this, our research must serve to historicize the relationship between the university and community. It must also depict both the physical and cultural marginalized spaces in which people in the community negotiate their lives. For many of us who are insiders within—who come from the same communities we research—we inscribe our histories and interweave our narratives against the hegemonic discourse. In doing so, we challenge the inscribed tenets of invisibility and muteness as this relates to marginalized peoples. While objectivity is encouraged in scholarly work, the reality is that as marginalized subjects ourselves, we have the responsibility to expose our own vulnerabilities, our own positionalities—if we are to expect the same from those we research. This work primarily addresses two main questions: (1) What accountability do Chicana/ Latina scholars have in the production of new knowledge, and (2) How should scholars of color represent their own research when directly associated with those same communities which they come from?

Mujeres scholars of color are at the forefront of intellectual discussions of how disrupting homogeneous discourses constructs counter-narratives and new ways of knowing and imparting research. Our research often utilizes our untold stories because of the marginalization we have experienced and are documenting. My position as a scholar-activist is a contradictory one: As a first-generation Latina with a terminal degree, I am granted certain privileges but also find myself negotiating my insider-outsider role within academia. Women of color conducting research in communities they belong to while at the same time centralizing their *testimonios* puts them in vulnerable positions in which they share often intimate experiences for the sake of exposing the marginalization we often research.

When I first started graduate school I recall asking my advisors to introduce me to the texts that amassed all the theory I needed to master within the field of education. *"Where is the dictionary of all the theories?"* I thought. I envisioned there being one text that decoded everything I needed to know. I did not realize that these theories were just the foundation from which more theory would be created. As I became more immersed in graduate work I came to the realization that we are always creating theory from lived experience, especially as marginalized groups that traditionally are not recognized in canonical writings. Our own lived experiences and those day-to-day experiences of participants in our work are constructions of theory. Counter to the expectation of "objective research," it is vital that we pull from our own *conocimiento* to de-academize theory.

My "theoretical home" is pulled from my own *conocimiento* in seeing and theorizing the world (Preuss and Saavedra 2). Institutions of higher education teach us to distance ourselves from our research—to remain "objective"—but from my experience as part of different collaboratives throughout my years in academia, it is precisely in these spaces of community that we can dismantle traditional discourses of power. Writing and reading groups, a radio collective, and a critical research collaborative influenced my graduate school training. These collaborations allowed me to interpret my work through different lenses and influences while centering and privileging my own lived experience. We worked side-by-side, not always in agreement but always in solidarity. This constituted a way of disrupting the traditional approach to research. As part of the critical research collaborative and radio show collective, we listened to one another—we allowed for dialogue exchanges to fuel and grapple with our ideas about projects focused on social justice, and equipped us to take action. These spaces provided the opportunity to work with graduate students across disciplines, ideologies, and backgrounds. Such spaces provide a platform where we are able to practice defending our positions, provide a different perspective with which to think about research, and provide a safe space in which to think

out loud and develop theories from lived intimate experiences without feeling penalized for challenging the status quo.

Our research comes from an intimate space that has not always been encouraged. It is difficult to delve into painful memories; we endure much suffering in our work, such as the indifference that often times the dominant society displays to learning our language, the language which, according to Anzaldúa, "reflects us, our culture, our spirit" ("Speaking in Tongues" 183). We continue to be told that we need to separate ourselves from our research in order to uphold an objective analysis; we continue to be bordered by the limitations inscribed in the canon. Nevertheless, for many of us, our research and writing represents a liberatory practice where we can unleash all of those emotions, contradictions, and tensions that are ever present in our own lived experiences—and which are not often mentioned in canonical texts.

We must always remain aware of the role we play as "border crosser" researchers (Villenas). Research is traditionally implicated in the exclusion of alternative knowledges. As women of color researchers, we must also remain cognizant and vigilant about our own complicity as scholars conducting research in communities with which we closely identify. Borders are always present in research and prominent in the everyday lives of those who are constantly fighting for, reconciling, or negotiating those spaces that keep them in the margins of societal progress, advancement, and mobility. Thus, as women of color in the academy we have the responsibility to rewrite our histories. Through the deployment of this framework, we can further disrupt the violent notions of homogenization attributed to the communities that continue to be vastly under valorized. For example, in my work on the experiences of Chicanas/Latinas in doctoral programs, the narratives collected served to document the agency, activism, and survival of marginalized graduate students at predominantly White doctorate-granting research universities—and further elucidated potential areas of action for university leadership.

I utilized *testimonio* as a tool to characterize oppression, marginalization, agency, and empowerment. *Testimonio* has the effect of privileging and centering the subaltern experience and voice in ways that traditional research tools fail to do so. The Latina Feminist Group conceptualizes *testimonio* "as a crucial means of bearing witness and inscribing into history those lived realities that would otherwise succumb to the alchemy of erasure" (2). In this sense, *testimonios* serve to challenge the status quo and power structures found in academia and other spaces. In using *testimonio* as a method and political tool, we are able to "expose the complexities within Latina lived experience[s] and engage[s] individual stories to facilitate an understanding of the larger collective" (Espino, Vega, Rendón, Ranero, and Muñiz 446).

Rising women of color scholars are indebted to the intellectual contributions made by Anzaldúa and other critical pedagogues. It rests on those of us who have been greatly influenced by their work to now build on the knowledge and construction of critique and analysis introduced and utilized by these scholars. It is our responsibility to build the next *Bridge*. But how is this to be done, and for what purpose? It requires that we become nakedly open with our own oppressions, with our own prejudices, and with our own wounds. We have to give ourselves with no reservations to our research from a space of complete surrender and trust in our lived pedagogies and collective memory, which ultimately constitute our own theoretical contributions to our respective fields. There is so much one has to negotiate and give of oneself; all must be communicated in our writing. In bringing my whole person into the research process, for example, I am able to critically interrogate and challenge power structures that continue to suppress disfranchised communities of color. In grounding my work in my lived history and those of the communities that inform my scholarship, I am privileging the participants' narratives to contribute to new forms of knowledge. We must continue collaborating, building on each other's work, and participating in writing groups where we can privilege our own production of knowledge.

This work proposes that by employing a framework that privileges critical narratives we can engage various degrees of the embedded complexities in research such that those conducting the fieldwork also are members of the marginalized communities being studied. Employed in this manner, the work of women of color scholars speaks to both their social agency and commitment in disrupting the boundaries that have historically silenced dialogue. We must always ask what our indebtness and *obligación* is to the communities we study. By constantly interrogating our own ethics, positionality, responsibility, and representation within our areas of research, we can solidify the perspectives with which we approach our work. It is important to always locate our research historically and geographically, and additionally reflect on who is producing the research. What is the responsibility of the researcher towards the participant? We also need to come to peace with what it is that we can contribute to and give back to our respective communities—those historically marginalized. Our research should be about our commitment to produce the best scholarship we can to further the understanding about our communities and, with agency and purpose, replace deficit models. Although the academy tends to be an isolating place, it does not have to be one. This transformation requires digging deeply into those innermost intimate places within ourselves, which often unleash vast pain and emotions that we would rather hide, but which we need to confront in order to fully produce transformative research—research that matters.

WORKS CITED

Anzaldúa, Gloria, ed. *Making Face, Making Soul/Haciendo Caras: Creative and Critical Perspectives by Feminists of Color*. San Francisco, CA: Aunt Lute Books, 1990. Print.

---."Speaking in Tongues: A Letter to Third World Women Writers." In *This bridge called my back: Writings by radical women of color*, edited by Cherríe Moraga & Gloria Anzaldúa, 183-193. 3rd ed. Berkeley, CA: Third Woman Press, 2002. Print.

Espino, Michelle M., Vega, Irene, I., Rendón, Laura, I., Ranero, Jessica J., and Muñiz, Marcela, M. "The Process of *Reflexión* in Bridging *Testimonios* Across Lived Experience." Equity & Excellence in Education 45.3 (2012): 444-459. Web. 25 March 2013.

Preuss, Cara Lynne and Saavedra, Cinthya M. "Revealing, Reinterpreting, Rewriting Mujeres." *International Journal of Qualitative Studies in Education* (2013): 1-21. Web. 24 April 2014.

The Latina Feminist Group. *Telling to live: Latina feminist testimonios*. Durham: Duke University Press, 2001. Print.

Villenas, Sofia A. "The Colonizer/Colonized Chicana Ethnographer: Identity, Marginalization, and Co-optation in the Field." *Harvard Educational Review* 66.4 (1996): 711-732. Web. 20 May 2012.

SPIRITUALITY AND STORYTELLING

LEARNING FROM ANZALDÚA: TOWARD A THEORY-PRAXIS OF WOMANIST SPIRITUAL ACTIVISM

ANALOUISE KEATING

Conocimiento urges us to respond not just with the traditional practice of spirituality (contemplation, meditation, and private rituals) or with the technologies of political activism (protests, demonstrations, and speakouts), but with the amalgam of the two—spiritual activism, which we've also inherited along with la sombra. Conocimiento pushes us into engaging the spirit in confronting our social sickness with new tools and practices whose goal is to effect a shift. Spirit-in-the-world becomes conscious, and we become conscious of spirit in the world. The healing of our wounds results in transformation and transformation results in the healing of our wounds. —Gloria Anzaldúa, "Let us be the healing of the wound"

Throughout her career, from "The coming of el mundo surdo" (in the late 1970s) to "Let us be the healing of the wound" (2003), Gloria Anzaldúa worked to develop a theory and practice of what, in her later writings, she named "spiritual activism"—a post-secular approach to metaphysics, ontology, and ethics driven by a desire for healing, progressive social change, and inclusionary communities. I describe Anzaldúa's approach as "post-secular" to underscore her movement through secularity and her intentional description of reality (visible, invisible, and semi-visible) as sacred.[1] Anzaldúa drew from both secular and religious traditions, creating an innovative animist-inflected ontology and ethics.

Unlike secularism, which separates the sacred from the non-sacred, Anzaldúa's spiritual activism posits the sacredness of all existence. And unlike organized religions, which are outwardly imposed and directed; rely on external rules, doctrines, and authorities; and reinforce a collective, hegemonic, often-monologic "Truth," Anzaldúa's spiritual activism thrives on multiplicity and has its source at least partially within each individual. Influenced by indigenous philosophies and esoteric thought, as well as her own experiences with curanderas and folk Catholicism, Anzaldúa's spiritual activism represents a metaphysics and ethics of interconnectedness that insists on our inter-relatedness with all existence.

I have been drawn to the term "spiritual activism" since the first time Anzaldúa mentioned it to me, in a 1989 conversation, where she described it as an "aspect" of her theory of conocimiento:

> You could say that conocimiento is basically an awareness, the awareness of facultad that sees through all human acts whether of the individual mind and spirit or of the collective, social body. The work of conocimiento—consciousness work—connects the inner life of the mind and spirit to the outer worlds of action. In the struggle for social change I call this particular aspect of conocimiento spiritual activism. (Interviews/Entrevistas 178)

I was completely captured by this phrase, and I have been using it ever since. Unlike the word "spirituality" which can be misinterpreted as disembodied escapism, passivity, or religiosity, "spiritual activism" clearly foregrounds the political implications and the necessity of action because "spirituality" functions as an adjective modifying the noun, "activism." As I use the term, "spiritual activism" represents a politics of spirit and a holistic worldview which can transform—simultaneously and reciprocally—one's self and one's worlds. Whether she discusses it as "conocimiento," "la facultad," "El Mundo Zurdo," "las nepantleras," "nos/otras," "mestiza consciousness," or "the New Tribalism," spiritual activism was central to Anzaldúa's life and work.[2]

Until fairly recently, however, Anzaldúa's theory-praxis of spiritual activism was generally ignored or in other ways under-valued in the scholarship on her writing.[3] This avoidance is not surprising, given the "academic spirit-phobia"[4] we so often encounter. Those of us working in conventional academic settings have been trained to rely almost exclusively on rational thought, anti- or non-spiritual forms of logical reasoning, and scientistic-empirical demonstrations.

References to spirit, souls, the sacred, and other such apparently nonmaterial topics are often condemned as essentialist, escapist, naive, superficial, "New-Age," and so on; and scholars who insist on bringing spirit into academic conversations can be dismissed as apolitical and/or backward-thinking. As Irene Lara

notes, "Within a western framework, writing about spirit and spirituality, as well as writing from a spiritual epistemology that is embodied and ensouled in a woman of color consciousness, is cause for silencing and marginalization" (30). This silencing is particularly intense when we bring spirit (or metaphysics and ontology, more generally) into highly theoretical discussions. As M. Jacqui Alexander explains, despite recent scholarship linking spirituality with socio-political change, "there is a tacit understanding that no self-respecting postmodernist would want to align herself (at least in public) with a category such as the spiritual, which appears so fixed, so unchanging, so redolent of tradition."[5] Moreover, words like "spirituality," "holistic," and "metaphysics" have become so commodified as to be robbed of their potentially progressive meanings.

Even feminist-identified scholars—who can be more skeptical about Cartesian-based thought and thus more open-minded than their colleagues—are often deeply suspicious of anything related to the spiritual. There are many valid reasons for this suspicion, including inaccurate conflations of spirituality with organized religions, destructive encounters with patriarchal religious practices, and negative reactions towards cultural feminists and other "pro-goddess" feminists who, in their eagerness to escape patriarchal thinking, have sometimes essentialized, oversimplified, and in other ways misrepresented concepts of womanhood which exclude far more people than they include. Fortunately, this automatic rejection or denial is slowly changing, thanks especially to the work of Anzaldúa and other women-of-color authors including Alexander, Delgadillo, Leela Fernandes, Layli (Phillips) Maparyan, Irene Lara, Laura Pérez and Michelle Rowley.

In this essay, I draw from Anzaldúa's explorations of spiritual activism, focusing especially on some of the most provocative yet foundational elements, to develop a preliminary theory-praxis of womanist spiritual activism. I describe this theory-praxis as "womanist" both to distinguish it from the many other versions of spiritual activism circulating in contemporary culture and to underscore the radically inclusive, deeply multicultural nature of this enterprise.[6] And, I use the term "womanist" rather than "feminist" because I believe womanism to be more radical in its transformational promises, more able to embrace contradictions and ambivalence, and more inclusive in its vision. Whereas feminism seems almost always to foreground gender (in practice, if not in theory), womanism does not. As Layli (Phillips) Maparyan explains,

> Unlike feminism, and despite its name, womanism does not emphasize or privilege gender or sexism; rather, it elevates all sites and forms of oppression, whether they are based on social-address categories like gender, race, or class, to a level of equal concern and action. ("Womanism: On Its Own" xvi-xviii)[7]

"Womanism," as I use the term, signals a multicultural approach to social-justice issues and underscores the formative role played by women-of-color thinkers. I locate womanism's radical potential in its insistence on the reality of spirit—defined broadly and in post-secular terms.[8] As I suggest in the following pages, this emphasis on spirit has important implications for individual and collective identity (among other things). My point here is not to prove that this spirit (force, divine, God, call-it-what-you-will) "really" exists (although I believe that it does). Rather, I am interested in the work it can do in the world.

To be sure, Anzaldúa did not define herself as a womanist and would probably claim that her feminism is as broad as the womanism Maparayan describes, thus making womanism redundant. I do not disagree. However, Anzaldúa's feminism is not the norm; the feminisms I encounter (in feminist theory, at academic conferences, and on listservs) are generally more narrow than Anzaldúa's feminism, and so I prefer the term womanism.[9] But labels can only take us so far, and I hope that my decision to use the word "womanist" rather than "feminist" will not prevent you from considering the dynamic process I describe. Womanist spiritual activism is complex and multidimensional, with metaphysical, ontological, epistemological, and ethical components. In the following pages, I offer several preliminary observations.

Womanist spiritual activism posits a metaphysical, vibrational component--an ontology that defines "material" in spirit-inflected terms. (I think here of Ralph Waldo Emerson's description of Spirit as matter stretched "o so thin!" [234].) This material-spiritual vibrational component is foundational and serves as the ground of being—the framework and creative force underlying everything that exists. As Layli Maparyan explains,

> Womanism assumes an immanent spiritual reality. What this means is that "spiritual stuff" is the substrate of all reality and that it pervades everything. Everything is a manifestation of spirit; nothing is without spirit—a perspective I call "Innate Divinity." Spirit, a/k/a divinity, is present and active in all things. Because Spirit is alive, everything is alive. Stated differently, spirit is what is "real"; it is at the bottom of things or what is behind everything. In addition to being the basis of life, i.e., alive, spirit is full of power, beauty, splendor, etc., and its qualities transcend or exceed what is typically visible or manifest at the mundane level of life. (35)

As Maparyan's use of various terms to describe this "spiritual stuff" indicates, for womanist spiritual activists the specific names we call this ontological "stuff" are much less important than the work it does in the worl—ensuring both the sacredness of and our interconnectedness with all existence. As Anzaldúa explains in an early interview, "Spirit exists in everything; therefore God, the

divine, is in everything—in blacks as well as whites, rapists as well as victims; it's in the tree, the swamp, the sea...Some people call it 'God;' some call it the 'creative force,' whatever. It's in everything" (*Interviews/Entrevistas*100).

In womanist spiritual activism, this cosmic force is radically democratic, embodying itself in, and as, every thing—all physical, nonphysical, and semi-physical forms. As Anzaldúa asserts in *Borderlands/La Frontera: The New Mestiza*: "every cell in our bodies, every bone and bird and worm has spirit in it" (36). Unlike organized religions, which generally establish hierarchical ontologies that locate "God" or some other type of divinity at the top, elevate human beings (generally "made in God's image") over other life forms, and locate "dead" matter at the bottom of this hierarchy, womanist spiritual activism insists on a nonhierarchical ontology that neither centers the human nor elevates the human above other aspects of life. Anzaldúa illustrates this nonanthropocentric worldview throughout "now let us shift...the path of conocimiento...inner work, public acts." After describing nature as "alive and conscious," and the world as "ensouled," she "become[s] reacquainted with a reality called spirit, a presence, force, power, and energy within and without." This "reality called spirit" transforms her perceptions:

> With awe and wonder you look around, recognizing the preciousness of the earth, the sanctity of every human being on the planet, the ultimate unity and interdependence of all beings--somos todos un paíz. Love swells in your chest and shoots out of your heart chakra, linking you to everyone/everything—the aboriginal in Australia, the crow in the forest, the vast Pacific ocean. You share a category of identity wider than any social position or racial label. (558)

The implications of this shared identity category "wider than any social position or racial label" are immense, transforming our individual and collective self-definitions, and thus our epistemologies and ethics.

To begin with, positing a shared spirit-inflected identity can trigger a profound shift in self-understanding, analogous to what Leela Fernandes terms "disidentification." As Fernandes explains, disidentification is a "twofold process":

> At one level, it rests on a letting go of all attachments to externalized forms of identity as well as to deeper ego-based attachments to power, privilege, and control. At another level, disidentification is not simply a negative process of detachment but *a positive movement of creating a different form of self.* This disidentified form of self draws on a spiritualized perspective that does not need to resort to traps, limitations, and temporary security of identity. (27, my emphasis)

By positing a shared cosmic identity infusing all existence, womanist spiritual activism facilitates this "positive movement" and creates "a different form of

self." Disidentification does not negate personal identity but instead re-situates it within a much larger context, inviting us to expand our emphasis from an exclusive focus on a narrow self-enclosed personal identity to a cosmic Selfhood, or what psychologist Linda Myers and her colleagues describe as an "optimal conceptual system." As they explain, within this framework,

> Self...is seen as multidimensional encompassing the ancestors, those yet unborn, nature, and community...From the perspective of an optimal conceptual system, self-worth is assumed intrinsic in being. People are worthy because they are unique expressions of spiritual energy. Spiritedness or the condition of being spirit is acknowledged and lived. As reality is defined in terms of a spiritual-material unity, individuals are empowered to confront old ideas of alienation and separation. The purpose of life and its meaning come into clearer focus as human beings recognize how self is connected with all of life. (56)

Letting go of narrow self-definitions, womanist spiritual activists open ourselves to alternative possibilities, perceptions, and realities. Our world shifts and expands, enabling us to create new knowledge. Thus for example in her 1999 writing notas, Anzaldúa commands herself to release her personal and socially-inscribed value system: "Surrender your personal point of view of right and wrong. Surrender the walls between you and the others. . . . See through all your identifications, your labels of classification, the barrier that our ethnic origins set up, our cultural traditions and religious beliefs." Similarly, in "now let us shift" she suggests that detachment facilitates perceptual change: "You shed your former bodymind and its outworn story like a snake its skin. Releasing traumas of the past frees up energy, allowing you to be receptive to the soul's voice and guidance" (559). Through this process of letting-go, Anzaldúa aspired to attain a broader (dare I say more universal?) vision; she sought to activate her connection to all existence, to what she describes in her writing notas as the "oneness with life, with the Creative Intelligence." Importantly, this "oneness" is not synonymous with "sameness" but instead indicates complex commonalities defined as relational differences. When we claim commonalities we're not ignoring or even downplaying the specificity of each person's experiences, beliefs, and desires. Instead, we're adopting an inclusive, both-and perspective. Take, for example, Anzaldúa's theory of El Mundo Zurdo ("The Left-Handed World"), a theory she first articulated in *This Bridge Called My Back* and was still developing at the time of her death. El Mundo Zurdo represents a visionary collective identity mobilization in which people from a variety of different backgrounds, with a variety of needs and concerns, co-exist and work together to effect progressive social transformation. El Mundo Zurdo represents relational difference, inclusive communities based on commonalities (not sameness). As

Anzaldúa explains in her 1981 autohistoria, "La Prieta," the inhabitants of El Mundo Zurdo are not all alike; our specific oppressions, solutions, and beliefs are different. Significantly, however, these differences can co-exist within the spaciousness of El Mundo Zurdo: "these different affinities are not opposed to each other" but instead function as catalysts, facilitating the development of new, potentially transformative alliances.[10] Like womanist spiritual activists, Anzaldúa replaces oppositional difference with a dialogic, relational approach.

Anzaldúa's interrogation of conventional identity categories in her later work illustrates this dialogic approach. While she does not reject social identities like "Chicana," "lesbian," and "woman," she moves through them, enacting a version of what Maparyan has described as a womanist maneuver called the "fly-over."[11] Look, for example, at this passage from "now let us shift":

> Being Chicana (indigenous, Mexican, Basque, Spanish, Berber-Arab, Gypsy) is no longer enough, being female, woman of color, patlache (queer) no longer suffices. Your resistance to identity boxes leads you to a different tribe, a different story (of mestizaje) enabling you to rethink yourself in more global-spiritual terms instead of conventional categories of color, class, career. It calls you to retribalize your identity to a more inclusive one, redefining what it means to be una mexicana de este lado, an American in the U.S., a citizen of the world, classifications reflecting an emerging planetary culture. (561)

This call for an emerging planetary culture is so profound, so risky, so huge. Not only does Anzaldúa move through and beyond the various identity categories she occupies by virtue of her particular status as a human being, but she invites us to shift beyond the human. In so doing, she illustrates womanist spiritual activism's radical potential.

ENDNOTES

1 My definition of "post-secular" differs from those contemporary theorists (like Rosi Braidotti) who define the term as a return to fundamentalist forms of organized religion which deny the separation between religious views and the state by imposing religious views on the state.

2 For an analysis of Anzaldúa's spiritual activism, see my article, "'I'm a citizen of the universe': Gloria Anzaldúa's Spiritual Activism as Catalyst for Social Change."

3 As Theresa Delgadillo asserts, "The aspect of *Borderlands* that remains still in the shadows . . . is its spirituality, which is not unconnected to its queerness or its forward-looking perspective." I agree with Delgadillo's assessment of the text: "In *Borderlands* spirituality informs the theorization . . . and imagination . . . of the psychic, intellectual, emotional, discursive, and material components of a process that can shift the borderlands from a world of 'isms' to a more just order. Anzaldúa emphasizes the development of a spiritually informed critical awareness and its employment rather than the achievement of a prescriptive consciousness. This unique and radical contribution to feminist thought . . . insists not on epistemic privilege but on unceasing epistemic inquiry." Anzaldúa's spirit-inflected theory and praxis includes a holistic-critical consciousness which employs nonbinary, potentially transformational critique.

4 I coined the term "academic spirit-phobia" in "I am a citizen of the universe," in order to describe many academics' knee-jerk negative reactions to any reference to spirituality, spirits, and so on.

5 See also Theresa Delgadillo: "In the course of my research and teaching I have also encountered those who urged, for ideological reasons, particular scholarly approaches: some attach greater value to theologically informed analyses, and others respect only work grounded in European philosophies. I have been cautioned about the negative consequences of critiquing well-established religions, accused of thinking myself above religion, advised to be a 'good Catholic,' taken to task for a pro-choice essay, mistaken for a conservative religious scholar, accused of proselytizing, sneered at for wearing my Guadalupe/Goddess necklaces, and condescended to for considering the study of representations of religion to be worthy of scholarly attention." Laura E. Pérez makes a similar point, noting the ways discussions of spirit "are largely marginalized from serious intellectual discourse as superstition, folk belief, or New Age delusion, when they are not relegated to the socially controlled spaces of the orientalist study of 'primitive animism' or of 'respectable' religion within dominant culture" (37-38).

6 Although Anzaldúa did not originate the term "spiritual activism," she didn't borrow it from elsewhere but came up with it on her own. It seems that the term was used by various people almost simultaneously. In recent years, "spiritual activism" has become increasingly popular. A recent Google search turned up over 53,000 hits, and there are at least five books that use "spiritual activism" in the title (Claudia Horwitz's *The Spiritual Activist: Practices to Transform Your Life, Your Work, Your World*; Wanda Krause's *Spiritual Activism: Keys for Personal and Political Success*; Michael McColly's *The After-Death Room: Journey Into Spiritual Activism*; and Avraham Weiss's two books: *Principles*

of Spiritual Activism and *Spiritual Activism: A Jewish Guide to Leadership and Repairing the World*), as well as a "Spiritual Activism Movement" (www.spiritualactivism.org).

7 For further discussion of womanism and its connections with feminist thought, see Layli Maparyan's *The Womanist Idea*. As Maparyan notes, not all versions of womanism are so broadly multicultural; some focus primarily on racialized gender.

8 While I define spirit in post-secular and post-religious terms, many womanists probably would not. See, for instance, Sanders et. al., "Roundtable Discussion: Christian Ethics and Theology in Womanist Perspective."

9 For a lengthier discussion of these distinctions between womanism and feminism, see my book, *Transformation Now! Toward a Post-Oppositional Politics of Change*. In terms of my decision to put Anzaldúa in dialogue with womanist thought, it's important to emphasize that Anzaldúa's work—particularly her theory of spiritual activism and her discussions in the interviews collected in *Interviews/Entrevistas*—influenced Maparyan's definition of womanist praxis. Anzaldúa and I had many "kitchen table" discussions about feminism and womanism, and Anzaldúa never ran screaming from the room (so to speak) when I dis-identified with feminism and called myself a womanist. She did, however, insist that she saw me as a feminist. Ultimately, the names we call ourselves are far less important than the work we do in the world.

10 See also Anzaldúa's discussion of El Mundo Zurdo in "now let us shift," where she explains that "[t]he left hand is not a fist pero una mano abierta raised with others in struggle, celebration, and song." She associates her onto-epistemological theory, conocimiento, with El Mundo Zurdo, and here, too, we see her relational approach to differences: "Conocimiento es otro mode de conectar across colors and other differences to allies also trying to negotiate racial contradictions, survive the stresses and traumas of daily life, and develop a spiritual-imaginal-political vision together. Conocimiento shares a sense of affinity with all things and advocates mobilizing, organizing, sharing information, knowledge, insights, and resources with other groups" (570).

11 The fly-over is a context-specific, self-reflective act driven by urgency and visionary pragmatism. As Maparyan explains in *The Womanist Idea*, the fly-over entails "jumping over certain discursive steps or layers of an ongoing social conversation in order to arrive more quickly at a needed endpoint, idea, or practice . . . . So, let's say you are talking about intersectionality and you need to get to cosmic humanness or whatever, you just 'fly over' the intervening steps of tediously unpacking everything intersectionality *could* mean and you just jump into using the humanness frame right away."

WORKS CITED

Alexander, M. Jacqui. "Remembering This Bridge, Remembering Ourselves: Yearning, Memory, and Desire." *this bridge we call home: radical visions for transformation*. Ed. Gloria E. Anzaldúa and AnaLouise Keating. New York: Routledge, 2002. 81-103.

Anzaldúa, Gloria. *Borderlands/La Frontera: The New Mestiza*. San Francisco, CA: Aunt Lute, 1987.

---. "The coming of el mundo surdo." 1977. *The Gloria Anzaldúa Reader*. Ed. AnaLouise Keating. Durham, NC: Duke University Press, 2009. 36-37.

---. "El paisano is a bird of good omen." 1983? *The Gloria Anzaldúa Reader*. Ed. AnaLouise Keating. Durham, NC: Duke University Press, 2009.

---. *Interviews/Entrevistas*. Ed. AnaLouise Keating. New York: Routledge, 2000.

---. "La Prieta." 1981. *The Gloria Anzaldúa Reader*. Ed. AnaLouise Keating Durham, NC: Duke University Press, 2009. *This Bridge Called My Back: Writings by Radical Women of Color*. 38-50.

---. "Let us be the healing of the wound: the Coyolxauhqui imperative—la sombra y el sueño." *One Wound for Another/Una herida por otra. Testimonios de Latin@s in the U.S. through Cyberspace* (11 de septiembre de 2001-11 de marzo 2002). Eds. Clara Lomas and Claire Joysmith. Mexico City: Centro de Investigaciones Sobre América del Norte (CISAN), at the Universidad Nacional Autónoma de México (UNAM), 2005.

---. "now let us shift...the path of conocimiento...inner work, public acts." *this bridge we call home: radical visions for transformation*. Ed. Gloria E. Anzaldúa and AnaLouise Keating. New York: Routledge, 2002. 540-78.

Braidotti, Rosi. *The Posthuman*. Cambridge: Polity, 2013

Delgadillo, Theresa. *Spiritual Mestizaje: Religion, Gender, Race, and Nation in Contemporary Chicana Narratives*. Durham, NC: Duke UP, 2011. Kindle file.

Emerson, Ralph Waldo. "Experience." 1944. *Selected Essays, Lectures, Poems*. Ed. Robert D. Richardson, Jr. New York: Bantam Classic, 2006. 229-52. Kindle file.

Fernandes, Leela. *Transforming Feminist Practice: Non-Violence, Social Justice and the Possibilities of a Spiritualized Feminism*. San Francisco: Aunt Lute Books, 2003.

Horwitz, Claudia. *The Spiritual Activist: Practices to Transform Your Life, Your Work, Your World*. New York: Penguin, 2002.

Keating, AnaLouise. "'I'm a citizen of the universe': Gloria Anzaldúa's Spiritual Activism as Catalyst for Social Change." 34 *Feminist Studies* (2008): 53-69.

---. *Transformation Now! Toward a Post-Oppositional Politics of Change*. Urbana: University of Illinois Press, 2013.

Krause, Wanda. *Spiritual Activism: Keys for Personal and Political Success*. San Francisco, CA: Turning Stone Press, 2013.

Lara, Irene. "Goddess of the Américas in the Decolonial Imaginary: Beyond the Virtuous Virgen/Pagan Puta Dichotomy." *Feminist Studies* 34.1-2 (Spring 2008): 99-130.

Maparyan, Layli. *The Womanist Idea.* New York: Routledge, 2011.

McColly, Michael. *The After-Death Room: Journey Into Spiritual Activism.* Brooklyn, NY: Soft Skull Press, 2006.

Myers, Linda J. et al. "Identity Development and Worldview: Toward an Optimal Conceptualization." *Journal of Counseling & Development* 70 (1991): 54-63.

Pérez, Laura E. "Spirit Glyphs: Reimagining Art and Artist in the Work of Chicana Tlamatinime." *Modern Fiction Studies* 44.1 (1998) 36-76.

Phillips, Layli. "Womanism: On Its Own." *The Womanist Reader.* Ed. Layli Phillips. New York: Routledge, 2007.

Rowley, Michelle. "Rethinking Interdisciplinarity: Meditations on the Sacred Possibilities of an Erotic Feminist Pedagogy." *Small Axe* 12.2 (2007): 139-53.

Sanders, Cheryl J., Cheryl Townsend Gilkes, Katie G. Cannon, Emilie M. Townes, M. Shawn Copeland, and bell hooks. "Roundtable Discussion: Christian Ethics and Theology in Womanist Perspective." *Journal of Feminist Studies in Religion* 5.2 (1989): 83-112. JSTOR.

Weiss, Avraham. *Principles of Spiritual Activism.* Kvat Publishers, 2001

---. *Spiritual Activism: A Jewish Guide to Leadership and Repairing the World.* Woodstock, VT.: Jewish Lights, 2013.

RECOGNIZING THE SPIRITUAL AS A VEHICLE FOR SOCIETAL TRANSFORMATION: ANZALDÚA'S SPIRITUALIZED POLITICS AND THE SECULARITY OF WOMEN'S AND GENDER STUDIES

APRIL L. MICHELS

As revealed throughout her groundbreaking works, Gloria E. Anzaldúa dedicated her life to healing the wounds inflicted upon all beings by dualistic-oppositional frameworks that serve to keep us detached from and divided against each other, thereby making us complicit in our own disempowerment and the subjugation of all planetary beings. Knowing that a drastic shift in human perception must occur to bring forth the dawning of a socially just world, Anzaldúa beckons her readers to relinquish their adherence to status-quo stories and embrace a consciousness of radical interrelatedness:[1]

> What we do has a ripple effect on all people and the natural environment. ...Let's acknowledge the harm we've done...let's put our dismembered psyches and patrias (homelands) in new construction...May we allow the interweaving of all minds and hearts and life forces to create the collective dream of the world and teach us how to live out ese sueño. May we allow spirit to sustain and guide us from the path of dissolution. ("Let us begin the healing of the wound" 313-14)

This passage illuminates Anzaldúa's long-standing belief that interacting and communicating with the omnipresent realm of spirit inspires individuals to

enact radical self, societal, and worldwide transformation. As Anzaldúa explains in a conversation with AnaLouise Keating,(re)connecting to the sacred life force that permeates all of creation spurs the realization that self is not an enclosed entity but is inextricably linked to all beings, human, animal, mineral, and vegetable, all of which have a consciousness, a pulse, and a soul (*Interviews/ Entrevistas* 160). Thus, I intend to illustrate that the spiritualized consciousness of interconnectivity that Anzaldúa seeks to awaken in her readers has the potential to inspire a profound sense of cosmic accountability and ignite an inclusive, spiritual activist movement that is devoted to ensuring the peaceful survival of all planetary beings.

While Anzaldúa's spiritualized vision for enacting multi-level transformation exemplifies Women's and Gender Studies' commitment to dismantling systems of inequality, the spiritual dimensions of her work remain largely under-examined in WGS scholarship.[2] As Keating notes, "All too often . . . scholars avoid Anzaldúa's politics of spirit. Although they celebrate her groundbreaking contributions to feminist theory and her innovative formulations of the Borderlands and the new mestiza, they rarely examine the important roles Anzaldúa's spiritual activism plays in developing these theories and many others" ("citizen of the Universe" 54). This omission seems to be informed by the secular/spiritual binary that prevails in western academic and even WGS epistemologies. While I do acknowledge that this bifurcation is influenced by the academy's overemphasis on rational logic and the fact that spiritual authority is frequently used as a weapon of oppression, I am inclined to assert that if WGS does not critically examine the possible ramifications of this normalized dichotomy, the field may inadvertently facilitate the dismissal of Anzaldúa's transformative theories.

To be clear, my intention is not to imply that WGS, feminism, or activists must be spiritual to truly do work that matters. Rather, I am concerned that the spirit-phobic nature of WGS and the academy may unintentionally cause Anzaldúa's spiritualized-intellectual legacy to disappear into the forgotten shadows of academia.[3] In short, my overall goal is to promote academic appreciation and validation of Anzaldúa's spiritually infused philosophies. In doing so, I discuss some of the possible reasons the secular/spiritual binary is maintained in WGS, the impact it has on what is regarded to be appropriate WGS scholarship, and the influence it tends to have on scholarly examinations of Anzaldúa's visionary works. Next, I illustrate that Anzaldúa's (re)configuration of spirituality, which subverts conventional religious, intellectual, and some mainstream, academic feminist (mis)conceptions, aims to initiate and achieve the global transformation that WGS has long envisioned: a world in which all forms of injustice are non-existent.

PRIVILEGING SECULARITY, DISMISSING SPIRITUALITY

In some ways, the tendency to privilege secularity and deemphasize spiritual/ religious rhetoric within WGS scholarship and disciplinary practices is understandable and justifiable. First, the academy's overemphasis on westernized rational thought trains scholars to rely almost exclusively on tangible, discernible, and quantifiable evidence to assess and justify knowledge claims. Furthermore, as Keating explains, academics who engage with spiritual ways of knowing/ being in their scholarship risk marginalization and invalidation: "When we talk about spirit worlds, soul, transformation, interconnectedness, the sacred, and so forth, we risk accusations of essentialism, escapism, or other forms of apolitical, naive thinking" ("Shifting Perspectives" 242). Laura E. Pérez provides a strikingly similar observation:

> Beliefs and practices consciously making reference to the s/Spirit as the common life force within and between all beings are largely marginalized from serious intellectual discourse as superstition, folk belief, or New Age delusion...Even in invoking the spiritual as a field articulated through cultural differences, and in so doing attempting to displace dominant Christian notions of the spiritual while addressing the fear of politically regressive essentialisms, to speak about the s/Spirit and the spiritual in US [academic] culture is risky business that raises anxieties of different sorts. (37-38)

As Keating and Pérez reveal, the academy's strict adherence to and valorization of rationalistic standards promotes the trivialization of spiritually oriented scholarship. In fact, even when scholars clearly emphasize that spiritualized epistemic frameworks have the power to enact radical societal transformation, their scholarly endeavors are often dismissed as being regressive, anti-intellectual, and atavistic (Keating, "Citizen of the Universe" 55). Since such accusations may jeopardize one's academic reputation and career, the scholarly omission of the spiritual is certainly justified, for the mantra of the westernized academy appears to be "secularity or perish."

FEMINISM'S SUSPICION OF RELIGION

While the secular climate of WGS is influenced by academia's claim that rigorous research must be uninfluenced by spiritual sensibilities, the field's resistance to incorporating spirituality into its theoretical and analytical discourses also seems to stem from feminism's long-held and reasonable skepticism towards institutionalized religion. As early as the suffrage movement, activists such as Elizabeth Cady Stanton and Matilda Joslyn Gage regarded religion, with its androcentric interpretation of scripture that blamed women for bringing sin and death into the world, to be one of the major impediments to achieving female

liberation.[4] Similar to their foremothers, radical feminists like Mary Daly, as Linda Woodhead notes, asserted that since patriarchal exegeses deemed women's subordinate status to be divinely mandated, all forms of religion were "inimical to the feminist project" (54). Thus, second wave feminist activist movements, which played a vital role in establishing WGS as credible academic field, equated female emancipation with the complete rejection of overtly and covertly patriarchal religious traditions. While the tendency of some mainstream and academic feminists to label all religions and, by extension, spiritual traditions as inherently oppressive to women has been critiqued by several WGS scholars, such as Layli Maparyan, Leela Fernanades, and Audre Lorde, the antagonism towards religion/spirituality seems to remain entrenched in WGS.[5]

To be fair, WGS' lingering suspicion towards institutionalized religion and even spirituality is understandable. As Sheila Ruth explains in *Woman's Spirit and Man's Religion*, terms, such as "sprit" and "sacred" which tend to be associated with organized, patriarchal religion, can summon forth extremely painful memories of ostracization, subordination, and condemnation:

> For those of us who fled, religion had functioned as the worst kind of binding, as an unfriendly master we had been expected to serve and revere... The authority of religion over our conceptual lives and behavior was final and absolute. In its rigid exclusivity, its nice demarcations of social groups, it proposed to determine who was friend and who was enemy...As source of all Truth, religion was primary arbiter in matters of consciousness and morality. (Thou shall not disobey...thou shall not enjoy the body—regardless of how sane it seems to do so; thou shall not doubt God or priests or book—for this you will suffer death or hell or both or worse.) (494-95)

Considering Ruth's reflection, I am inclined to suggest that WGS hesitates to incorporate spiritualized or religious rhetoric into the field's discourses because doing so may unintentionally re-wound scholars, teachers, and students who have been scarred by institutionalized religion. Providing further insight into WGS's compulsory secularity, Fernandes notes that the "rise of religious fundamentalist movements across the world has seemed more than ever to underlie the immense importance of defining clear secular boundaries for contemporary visions of justice" (8). Given the fact that religion has often been utilized to justify acts of violence, some feminist academics might reasonably argue that incorporating spirituality and religion into WGS discourses runs the risk of inadvertently reifying extremist views that have served to normalize systemic injustice.

THE STAKES OF SECULARITY

While arguably well-founded, the secular impulse of WGS, albeit inadvertently, casts all manifestations of spirituality as being diametrically opposed to

feminist epistemologies, politics, and activism, thereby implying that serious WGS scholarship and academics should be uninfluenced by and unconcerned with spiritualized world-worldviews. As Karlyn Crowley asserts, "In WGS, the 'progressive-secular imaginary' has been inextricably linked to female emancipation...That is, secularism is assumed to be what reasonable, modern people aspire to," while spirituality is "seen as atavistic and uninformed" (244-45). Making a similar observation, Michelle M. Lelwica notes that the anti-spiritual current in mainstream and academic feminist discourse maintains that "a truly feminist consciousness is a secular consciousness" (114). Consequently, spiritually based perspectives are labeled as an archaic and apolitical "false consciousness" that must be remedied by an academic feminist ethos (114). In other words, WGS practitioners who seek to be validated as political and transformative feminist scholars are conditioned to believe that they must check their spiritual sensibilities at the proverbial door of the academy. As Keating reveals, the overtly secular climate of academia and WGS has affected Anzaldúan scholarship in a number of interrelated ways: "We might admire Anzaldúa's bold spirit vision yet fear that if we explore it in our work, we will harm our careers. . . . Or, we might appreciate Anzaldúa's spiritual activism yet worry if we try to discuss in print, our colleagues will re-evaluate her writings in negative ways and reject her theoretical contributions as . . . escapist ramblings" ("Citizen of the Universe" 55). While I do not wish to diminish the negative consequences that may result from risking the spiritual, neglecting the transformative implications of Anzaldúa's spiritually infused theories and politics inadvertently implies that Anzaldúa's spiritualized tongue must be "tamed" by the decrees of westernized, academic secularism in order to validate the significance of her intellectual legacy. In this way, the censorship Anzaldúa's spiritualized rhetoric runs the risk of perpetuating the Eurocentric acts of "linguistic terrorism" that Anzaldúa speaks out against in *Borderlands*. As Anzaldúa proclaims, "Until I am free to write . . . without having to always . . . accommodate the English speakers rather than having them accommodate me, my tongue will be illegitimate" (81). While it might appear that I am making a leap by drawing a parallel between "linguistic terrorism" and academic spirit-phobia, both, albeit in different ways, facilitate the delegitimization of Anzaldúa's lived experiences and theoretical contributions.

To clarify, my point is not to suggest that WGS, motivated by racist, imperialist, and elitist incentives, purposely aims to muffle Anzaldúa's spiritualized narratives. However, I feel that it is vital in our attempt to create an all-inclusive and polyvocal discipline, for us, as WGS scholars and activists, to challenge our preconceived and perhaps misconceived notions of spirituality. For starters, we must acknowledge that heteropatriarchy is not the sole possessor or disseminator of spiritualized knowledge and politics. When we uncritically

dismiss spirituality as being nothing more than the oppressor's tool, we unintentionally and misguidedly surrender the powers of spirituality to the unjust social forces that will continue to use spirituality as a weapon against marginalized individuals and communities. To borrow the words of Fernandes, "What is needed . . . is simply a racial form of liberation of the divine—within ourselves, our communities, our world. . . . It is precisely this kind of liberation which is needed if the tremendous transformative power of spirituality is not to be continually colonized by [the] structures of inequality and the social groups that mistakenly believe they benefit from them" (116). Like Fernandes, Anzaldúa believes that true societal transformation cannot occur as long as spirituality is held captive by heteropatriarchal-colonial narratives. As such, Anzaldúa mission is to liberate the sacred from the shackles of oppressive religious institutions and reconnect humanity to the divine presence that animates all of creation.

INSTITUTIONALIZED RELIGION AND THE USURPATION OF THE SPIRITUAL

Spirituality has nothing to do with Religion, which recognizes . . . spirit, and then puts dogma around it. . . . Religion eliminates all kinds of growth, development, and change, and that's why I think any kind of formulized religion is really bad. —Gloria Anzaldúa, Interviews/Entrevistas

Often, institutionalized religious doctrine depicts the sacred as existing on a disembodied and transcendental realm that is diametrically opposed to the physical. To gain access into this ethereal realm and experience a communion with the divine, one must rebuke the ways of the world, renounce the desires of the flesh, and focus on preparing the soul for its celestial ascension. In addition to casting the material as a hindrance to the spiritual, the rhetoric of divine chosenness that is expressed in some organized religious discourses implies that only followers of the so-called true faith will be granted eternal bliss while the rest of humanity languishes in perpetual condemnation. These entrenched dualistic assumptions can present a number of barriers to enacting social change. First, the over-emphasis on divine transcendence and personal salvation can cause people to direct their consciousnesses inward to the self, outward to the celestial, and away from earthy concerns, thereby allowing one to escape from and dismiss issues of social injustice (Keating, "citizen of the universe" 53-54). Moreover, the dichotomous and exclusionist notion of "chosenness" fosters epidemic spiritual narcissism that divides religions into opposing camps that fight amongst and against each other in order to assert and validate their spiritual superiority.

In extreme cases, religiously induced "us vs. them" mentalities serve to justify the victimization of those who do not conform to a specific religion's sanctioned codes of righteousness. Consequently, Anzaldúa rejects organized religion as a fraudulent institution that monopolizes the spiritual and normalizes

rigid demarcations to promote hatred of the body, fear of the "other," vicious intolerance:

> All religions impoverish life because they renounce it. They especially divorce the flesh from the spirit. . . . To me, it always seemed that this division is where the oppression of myself as a woman, as a lesbian, as a brown woman, as a working class woman comes in. To me religion has always upheld the status-quo, it makes institutions rigid and dogmatic. Anything threatening—people like me (dykes, creative people, heretics of some sort)—must be eliminated. (*Interviews/Entrevistas* 95)

The internalization of the view that the body, sexuality, and human nature are fundamentally debased, according to Anzaldúa, conditions individuals to believe that they must reject and eradicate the so-called impure aspects of the self in order to obtain divinity (*Borderlands* 59). This assumption can foster a profound sense of self-loathing that eventually emanates outwards, detrimentally affecting the ways we interact with others. As Anzaldúa writes, "There are many defense strategies that the self uses to escape the agony of inadequacy and I have used all of them. I have used rage to drive others away and to insulate myself against exposure. I have reciprocated with contempt for those who have aroused shame in me" (67). In this passage, Anzaldúa offers a plausible explanation for religiously motivated violence. At its worst, the belief that divinity is transcendent of materiality gives rise to the misconception that physical realm and humanity are manifestations of depravity that threaten to further solidify the soul's estrangement from the divine. In a misguided attempt to alleviate the pangs of one's own sense of spiritual inadequacy, lay claim to absolute righteousness, and ensure salvation, some resort to utilizing rage and cruelty against those who evoke, within the embattled self, feelings of shame, fear, and spiritual insecurity . Thus, by concealing the inherent and infallible sacredness of the corporeal and human nature, institutionalized religion, as Anzaldúa suggests in the above passages, utilizes spirituality to induce hatred of the self, promote disdain for others, and barricade individuals within impenetrable, adversarial encampments. These divisive tactics serve to keep us in a perpetual state of internal/external fragmentation to ensure that we remain indoctrinated and weakened by status-quo narratives.

MATERIALIZING THE SPIRITUAL, HEALING WOUNDEDNESS, AND RECLAIMING THE DIVINE WITHIN

Aware that enduring social change cannot be achieved and sustained in the absence of spiritually transformed beings, Anzaldúa beckons her readers to take the path of conocimiento. As I define the term, the path of Conocimiento is an internal journey of self-excavation and spiritual rejuvenation that individuals

must undergo to see past the illusion of impenetrable borders, reclaim the divine within, and achieve a holistic awareness that perceives the sacredness of all that exists. As Anzaldúa reveals in *Borderlands* and "now let us shift," this voyage, while therapeutic and necessary, is often tumultuous, unpredictable, and, extremely painful. During the Coatlicue state, for instance, we are ripped away from our uncomfortable surroundings and plunged into the terrifying depths of the underworld. Left without the possibility of transcendence, we are forced to confront our woundedness, the pain we have inflicted upon others, and the aspects of the self we have forsaken: "You're infuriated with yourself for not living up to your expectations...Tormented by self-contempt, you reproach yourself constantly...Self-pity swamps you...you're unable to climb out of the pit that is yourself" ("shift" 551). This agonizing experience, however, is not one of total despair. While in the midst of this dark abyss, we become reacquainted with the "divine within" (*Borderlands* 72). This illuminating inner force urges us to surrender to Coatlicue's transformative power: "Come, little green snake. Let the wound caused by the serpent be cured by the serpent...*Coatlicue states*...are exactly what propel the soul to its work: make soul, increase consciousness of itself. Our greatest disappointments and painful experiences—if we make meaning out of them—can lead us to becoming more of who we are" (68, Anzaldúa's emphasis). Thus, the Coatlicue state, if we allow it, can be a realm of self-healing, spiritual-growth, and re-birth. Reflecting on her personal descension into Coatlicue's regenerative womb, Anzaldúa proclaims that being devoured by the serpent leads to a metamorphic, ecstatic moment of divine oneness and wholeness: "I feel everything rushing to a center. . . . All the lost pieces of myself come flying from the deserts . . . valleys, magnetized toward that center. *Completa.* Something pulsates in my body, a luminous thin thing that grows thicker every day. Its presence never leaves me. . . . And I am not afraid (73, Anzaldúa's emphasis). Ultimately, by granting us the opportunity to let go of past traumas, Coatlicue empowers us recognize our inherent sacredness, intertwine the spiritual with the material, and enact radical self-transformation.

Awakened to the realization that the spirit is enfleshed, we rebuke dichotomous paradigms that divorce divinity from materiality and devote ourselves to fully inhabiting the body and attending to soul's desires. This newfound commitment expands our perception, allowing us to "link inner reflection and vision—the mental, emotional, instinctive, imaginal, spiritual, and subtle bodily awareness—with social, political action and lived experiences to generate subversion knowledges" ("now let us shift" 542). This interconnected and holistic way of knowing shatters the arbitrary divisions that have been naturalized by those in power to ensure that we remain imprisoned in our isolated cells, utterly detached from ourselves, others, and the world around us.

No longer seduced by status-quo narratives, we are able to perceive the inherent sacredness, interconnectedness, and interdependence of all that exists:

> With awe and wonder you look around, recognizing the preciousness of the earth, the sanctity of every human being on the planet. . . . Love swells in your body and shoots out of your heart chakra, linking you to everyone/everything—the aboriginals in Australia, the crows in the forest, the vast Pacific Ocean. You share a category of identity that is wider than any social position or racial label. This conocimiento motivates you to work actively to see that no harm comes to people, animals, oceans—to take up spiritual activism and the work of healing. ("Shift" 558)

As the passage reveals, Anzaldúa's (re)conceptualization of the spiritual as an embodied and embedded presence that intertwines all that exists, replaces rigid, exclusionary identity-based categories with a radically all-inclusive concept of identity that extends far beyond the limitations of racial, ethnic, gender, religious, and even organismic classifications.[6] In doing so, Anzaldúa, invites all individuals to participate in the materialization of an anti-oppressionist planetary culture, in which differences are neither ignored nor regarded to be insurmountable barriers. Joining hearts, hands, and life forces, the citizens of this emergent community utilize their profound sense of spiritual interconnectedness to enact revolutionary transformation. [7]

USING SPIRITUALITY TO TRANSFORM THE WORLD

While recognizing the divine interrelatedness of all beings and engaging in personal spiritual practices, such as meditation and daily affirmations, are vital components of spiritualized activism, Anzaldúa does not believe that achieving a higher state of awareness automatically brings about far-reaching and enduring social change. For instance, in "El Mundo Zurdo," Anzaldúa asserts, "The vision of our spirituality provides us with trap door solution no, no escape hatch tempting us to 'transcend' our struggle. . . . We must perform visible and public acts that may make us more vulnerable to the oppressions we are fighting. But our vulnerability *can* be our source of power—**if we use it**" (195, Anzaldúa's emphasis). Far from promoting escapism, Anzaldúa's conceptualization of spirituality requires activists to daily confront the reality of oppression, accept accountability for the suffering of all beings, and to fully commit themselves to the advancement of social justice, even when doing so requires venturing out into unfamiliar territories without the guarantee of a safe passage. Thus, while Anzaldúa's spiritualized theory and activism begins with an inward looking view that inspires individuals to begin the process of spiritual growth and healing, transformation does not stop at the self. Rather, it emanates

outward to dissolve all dichotomous paradigms, revealing that there is no "other," as everyone and everything are inextricably linked within the spiritual-cosmic-whole. Accordingly, every being must be equally respected, valued, and nurtured to ensure the optimal health of the planetary community.

To achieve and sustain global transformation, we must accept Anzaldúa's invitation to embrace our interconnectedness. This radical act of compassion will prompt the dissolution of dualistic categorizations that serve to trap within it a constant battle over what truly constitutes transformational and significant feminist/WGS scholarship. As Maparyan reminds us, "More than serving the function of unifying and connecting feminists [and WGS academics] the project of definition has tended to separate feminists, create conflict, and divert energy into semantic and ideological debates and away from concreted social change action" (21).While I do believe that academic disputes can often lead to innovative theoretical insights and strategies, spending a significant amount of time and energy locked within a besiegement mentality ultimately squanders the strength needed to advance global justice.[8] Undoubtedly, WGS has significantly contributed social and academic change through its commitment to valuing the experiences, realties, and knowledges that have been subjugated by heteropatriarchal and colonial discourses. As WGS continues to grow, however, we, as academics and activists, must critically (re)examine the ways the field's normalized presumptions may inadvertently privilege certain narratives and identities while simultaneously effacing others. As we work to create an all-inclusive discipline, we must remember that despite our various and seemingly divergent affiliations, we share the common desire to live in a world in which social injustice is nothing but a distant memory of past world we left behind.

ENDNOTES

1 I borrow the term "status-quo narratives" from AnaLouise Keating. As Keating states, "Status-quo stories limit our imaginations and prevent us from envisioning alternative possibilities—different ways of living and arranging our lives. Status-quo stories train us to believe that the way things are is the way they always have been and the way they must be" (23). For a more detailed discussion, refer to the first chapter of Keating's *Teaching Transformation.*

2 For the purposes of this paper, I use the acronym "WGS" to refer to Women's and Gender Studies and similar fields/programs, such as Women's Studies, Gender and Sexuality Studies, Feminist Studies, Gender Studies, and so forth.

3 "Spirit-phobia" is a term coined by Keating to refer to academia's aversion towards spirituality. For a more in-depth discussion on academic spirit-phobia, see Keating's "'I'm a Citizen of the Universe': Gloria Anzaldúa's Spiritual Activism as Catalyst for Social Change."

4 Stanton's most extensive critique of Christianity is offered in *The Woman's Bible,* in which Stanton proclaims, "The Bible teaches that woman brought sin and death into the world, that she precipitated the fall of the race, that she was arraigned before the judgment seat of Heaven, tried, condemned, and sentenced" (7). As a result, Stanton asserts that women's true emancipation rests on revising and challenging Biblical Scripture that is used to perpetuate the notion that female subjugation is the infallible Word of God (11). While Stanton does not argue for the total rejection of the Bible, Matilda Joslyn Gage, in *Woman, Church and State,* advocates for no less than a complete "overthrow" of "every existing form" and doctrine of institutionalized religion (544-45).

5 For details, see Maparyan's *The Womanist Idea,* Fernandes' *Transforming Feminist Practices,* and Lorde's "Letter to Mary Daily" in *Sister Outsider.*

6 As Keating eloquently states, Anzaldúa shifts "beyond the culturally specific, beyond the human, beyond the entire material world [to posit] a new commonality: Each human being's radical interconnectedness with all existence" (181). Moreover, Keating utilizes Anzaldúa's visionary reconfiguration of identity to discuss the transformative implications of planetary citizenship, a term Keating has coined to "generate new forms of empathy and action" that encourages individuals to "make connections with differently situated, differently located, differently embodied others" (180). In short, planetary citizenship replaces immutable divisions with "porous boundaries" and inspires individuals to find commonalties in their differences so that they can build alliances to enact far-reaching material, social change (181). For a more in depth discussion on Keating's theory of "planetary citizenship," see chapter six of *TRANSFORMATION NOW!.*

7 For examples of how the inhabitants of this emergent planetary culture utilize fluid notions of identity to build coalitions across differences, see Anzaldúa's discussion of El Mundo Zurdo in "La Prieta" and Maparyan's *The Womanist Idea,* especially page 12.

8 Allison Piepmeier asserts that "within a besiegement mentality, an insistence on ideological purity makes sense: every compromise seems a concession, one step closer

to letting the walls crumble and the enemy in" (133). For a comprehensive examination of the besiegement narrative in WGS, see her article, "Besiegement," included in *Rethinking Women's and Gender Studies.*

WORKS CITED

Anzaldúa, Gloria. *Borderlands/La Frontera: The New Mestiza.* 1987. San Francisco: Spinsters/Aunt Lute, 1999. Print.

---. "El Mundo Zurdo." *This Bridge Called My Back: Writings by Radical Women of Color.* 2nd ed. Ed. CherrìeMoraga and Gloria Anzaldúa New York: Kitchen Table, 1983. 195. Print.

---. *Interviews/Entrevistas.* Ed. AnaLouise Keating. New York: Routledge, 2000. Print.

---. "La Prieta." *This Bridge Called My Back: Writings by Radical Women of Color.* 2nd ed. Ed. CherrìeMoraga and Gloria Anzaldúa New York: Kitchen Table, 1983. 198-209. Print.

---. "Let us Begin the Healing of the Wound: The Coyolxauhgui imperative—la sombra y el sueño." *The Gloria Anzaldúa Reader.* Ed. AnaLouise Keating. Duke UP: Durham, 2009. 303-14. Print.

---. "now let us shift....the path of conocimiento...inner work, public acts." *this bridge we call home: radical visions for transformation.* Ed. Gloria Anzaldúa and AnaLouise Keating. New York: Routledge, 2002. 540-78. Print.

Crowley, Karlyn. "Secularity." *Rethinking Wome's and Gender Studies.* Ed. Catherine M. Orr, Ann Braithwaite, and Diane Lichtenstein. New York: Routledge, 2012. 240-57. Print.

Fernandes, Leela. *Transforming Feminist Practice: Non-Violence, Social Justice, and the Possibilities of a Spiritualized Feminism.* San Francisco: Aunt Lute, 2003. Print.

Gage, Matilda Joslyn. *Woman Church and State: A Historical Account of the Status of Woman Through the Christian Ages: With Reminiscences of the Matriarchate.* 2nd ed. 1893. New York; Arno, 1972. Print.

Keating, AnaLouise. "'I'm a citizen of the Universe': Gloria Anzaldúa's Spiritual Activism as Catalyst for Social Change." *Feminist Studies* 34.1/2 (2008): 53-69. Web. *Academic Search Complete.* 20 May 2013.

---. "Shifting Perspectives: Spiritual Activism, and the Politics of the Sprit." *Entremundos/ Among Worlds: New Perspectives on Gloria Anzaldúa.* Ed. AnaLouise Keating. New York: Palgrave-Macmillan, 2005, 241-245. Print.

---. *Teaching Transformation: Transcultural Classroom Dialogues.* New York: Palgrave-Macmillan, 2007. Print.

---. *TRANSFORMATION NOW!: Towards a Post-Oppositional Politics of Change*. Urbana, UP of Illinois, 2013.

Lelwica, Michelle M. "From Superstition to Enlightenment to the Race for Pure Consciousness: Antireligious Currents in Popular and Academic Discourse." *Journal of Feminist Studies in Religion* 14.2 (1998): 108-23. Web. *JSTOR*. 15 June 2013.

Lorde, Audre. "An Open Letter to Mary Daily." *Sister Outsider: Essays and Speeches by Audre Lorde*. Berkley: Crossing, 2007, 66-71.Print.

Maparyan, Layli. "Feminism." *Rethinking Women's and Gender Studies*. Ed. Catherine M. Orr, Ann Braithwaite, and Diane Lichtenstein. New York: Routledge, 2012. 17-33. Print

---. *The Womanist Idea*. New York: Routledge, 2012. Print.

Pèrez, Laura E. "Spirit Glyphs: Reimagining Art and Artist in the Work of Chicana Tlamatinime." *Modern Fiction Studies* 44.1 (1998): 36-76. Web. *Project Muse*. 21 July 2013.

Piepmeier, Allison. "Besiegement." *Rethinking Women's and Gender Studies*. Ed. Catherine M. Orr, Ann Braithwaite, and Diane Lichtenstein. New York: Routledge, 2012. 119-34.

Ruth, Sheila. "Women's Spirit and Men's Religion." *Issues in Feminism: An Introduction to Women's Studies*. 5th ed. Ed. Sheila Ruth. Mountain View: Mayfield, 2001. 488-96. Print.

Stanton, Elizabeth Cady. *The Woman's Bible*. 1895. Introduction Barbra Welter. New York: Arno, 1974. Print.

Woodhead, Linda. "Secular privilege, religious disadvantage." *The British Journal of Sociology* 59.1 (2008): 53-58. Web. *SocINDEX*. 22 July 2013.

HEALING OUR WOUNDS THROUGH OUR WORDS: ANZALDÚA, VIOLENCE, AND STORYTELLING

ADRIANNA MICHELLE SANTOS

Chicana and Mexicana writers have documented violence in a variety of texts including *Las Hijas de Juan: Daughters Betrayed* by Josie Mendez-Negrete, *Amá, Your Story is Mine: Walking Out of the Shadows of Abuse* by Ercenia Cedeño, *So Far From God* by Ana Castillo, *Mother Tongue* by Demetria Martinez, *Forgetting the Alamo, Or, Blood Memory* by Emma Pérez, *Black Widow's Wardrobe* by Lucha Corpi, and *Desert Blood: The Juarez Murders* by Alicia Gaspar de Alba, among others. Survival as a central theme, and the term survivor as applied to women of Mexican American descent, is an important paradigm for considering the ways in which Chicanas represent experiences of violence. Chicana writers demonstrate a commitment to breaking the silence concerning sexual assault by incorporating themes of healing and resistance through experiences of trauma. Gloria Anzaldúa, especially, was a forerunner in examining the power of transformation in recovering from the devastation of violence. In *Borderlands*, she proposes the "New Mestiza Way" of a shifting border consciousness, or "third space" state of being, as a method of combating a fragmented and violated self. She acknowledges the physical and metaphorical border as an open wound, a trauma from which Chicanas are constantly attempting to heal. She argues, however, that "A massive uprooting of dualistic thinking in the individual and collective con-

sciousness is the beginning of a long struggle, but one that could, in our best hopes, bring us to the end of rape, of violence, of war" (102). Anzaldúa goes on to describe the link between the creative self and the total self, the *facultad* and *nahual* that the artist possesses to give birth to new ways of understanding Chicana subjectivities. I argue that an adoption of a Chicana survivor identity is an important move in promoting solidarity between people who have been victimized by violence, both interpersonal and institutional. Representations of these survivor identities and survival stories can be found within the pages of social protest literature written by Chicanas. Through methods of radical storytelling, these narratives are shared, witnessed, and become part of an active process of transforming communities that have been scarred by violence. My essay springboards from these ideas and considers the writing and publishing of contemporary Chicana rape narratives as part of an empowered struggle to fight violence, and discusses the manner in which these texts focus on storytelling, healing, and survival as key components of the ongoing Chicano movement for social justice.

Violence is an important paradigm for understanding social problems in Chicana/o communities, especially because of a history of colonization, the effects of which still permeate imbalanced relationships of power in the United States. Further, gender violence as a focal point unearths an insidious problem that plagues women in particular. This research examines contemporary Chicana texts that address gender violence, which I refer to as *survival narratives*. I contend that certain texts articulate subjectivities beyond "victim" for survivors of violence. Each describes a process of politicization that occurs for survivors when they understand the social conditions under which they have been victimized and choose to resist. By bringing grave issues of sexual violence to light, "survival narratives" build bridges between victims and survivors, individuals and communities, and artists and activists. Understanding survival narratives further as border narratives also helps us to recognize the potential spark for political action through creativity, by articulating the multiple worlds that border crossers straddle. I argue that the authors of specific texts, like those mentioned above, engage in radical storytelling as a theoretical and practical framework for ending violence against women. The texts shape public and academic discourse by creating subversive, unconventional methods of reading and understanding rape. Survival narratives re-inscribe experiences of violence through representation as sites of transformation. These writings can potentially lead to political action through an empathetic readership that promotes what human rights activist Yuri Kochiyama calls principled activism. In solidarity with survivors of sexual violence, I explore Anzaldúa's work through the lens of women of color feminisms and discuss the links between the historical legacy of

colonization to both the limitations and transformative potentials of the modern anti-violence movement.

To clarify, I make use of the term "survivor" to describe those who have been victimized by violence for very specific reasons. First, I employ this term in order to call attention to the stakes. In a MELUS Interview with Elsa Saeta, Ana Castillo remarked, "Survival means you exist and we're not just survivors. We are women who go way beyond survival. We don't just exist. We have great faith and optimism in the future" (148). While I agree with this sentiment, I would argue that focusing on "survival" as a theoretical concept is an important means to fighting oppression based on gender violence. It is significant that the characters in many of the texts I study ultimately expire before the end of the novel. First of all, death is the most common reported fear that survivors remember having during a rape. Second, according to the US Department of Justice's "Full Report of the Prevalence, Incidence, and Consequences of Violence Against Women," Hispanic women are significantly less likely than white women to report the attacks to seek help when they are abused or to report the assault to the authorities.[1] They are more likely to internalize this abuse, develop eating disorders, and abuse alcohol and drugs due to rape trauma syndrome. This can often lead to feelings of depression, fragmentation, and hopelessness (Tjaden and Theonnes 35). Furthermore, in the "State of Hispanic Girls" the National Coalition of Hispanic Health and Human Services Organizations has found that young Hispanic women are much more likely than non-Hispanic girls to attempt suicide, develop severe depression, abuse drugs and alcohol and become pregnant as teen-agers. According to this report, "The incidence of sexual abuse by family members and friends is clearly connected to subsequent depression among Hispanic girls" (26-27). Shockingly, one in three Hispanic girls consider suicide. More than any other racial group, Hispanic girls and women lead the United States in attempted and completed suicides, which is inexorably linked to the culture of silence that encourages the internalization of sexism, assault and harassment. These findings are significant for understanding Chicanas' experiences of gender violence in the United States. Therefore, the irony with which I label these texts "survival narratives" serves to highlight the potential impact to further anti-violence discourse and challenge both interpersonal and state-sanctioned violence. To use the label survivor as a rallying cry is to point to the injustice by delineating the victimization, because the alternative is death. Not just social, metaphorical or imagined death, but the real eradication of cultural traditions, bodies, and entire populations.

Another reason I chose the term "survivor" as a theoretical marker is particularly to avoid the label of victim, which is the commonly accepted legal term for a person who has suffered violence. A victim is a person who has been

injured or killed as the result of a crime or accident, or someone who has been tricked or duped. The term "victim" implies passivity, a lack of choice, and calls attention not only to the injured but the injurer. On the other hand, "survivor" implies one who has come through a trauma to the other side, and even points to empowerment through its use. Despite a growing awareness of violence against women as a pressing social problem, the system still works to benefit the accused, not to protect and support the victim (INCITE!). Furthermore, even if they decide to come forward, women of color and immigrant women face additional obstacles to social services including language barriers, economic and cultural differences, and tenuous citizenship status (Crenshaw). What's more, the anti-violence movement has been co-opted by state funded organizations whose ultimate goal is to place blame on a pathological predator complex, which absolves the state of any accountability for the effects of institutional violence to facilitate interpersonal violence. Because of this disconnect between victims' needs, social services, and the influence of institutional oppressions, survivors find other pathways to healing irrespective of whether or not they choose to report to the police. There are a great variety of ways that survivors begin to heal from violence. Many of these also involve coming to an understanding of themselves as survivors of violence and members of larger communities that have been victimized. According to Nancy Naples:

> The term *survivor* is typically reserved for those who have self-consciously redefined their relationship to the experience from one of "victim." This redefinition can be accomplished through a combination of influences, including personal reformulation of earlier experience, therapeutic interventions, identification with cultural products such as "incest poetry" or survivor narratives, and discussion with others who self-define as survivors. Often incorporated as evidence for survivor status are presentations of public testimony or public claims that take the form of speaking out in the media or in other public forums. (1151)

Many people who have been victimized by sexual violence rally behind the term "survivor" because of this potential for transformation and healing through alternative methods. The label is useful for galvanizing Mexican American women around a cause not only because of the aforementioned implications. In a human consciousness-raising project, Chicanas model "survival" by bringing personal stories of abuse and violence into the public realm of understanding, outside the oppressive institutions of government, the prison industrial complex, criminalization of people of color and the targeting of immigrants, the medical industrial complex, the sexual and reproductive attack on women of color, the federally funded and de-politicized non-profit industrial complex, the silencing of queer voices, and the collusion of formerly radical organizations with the

state, which reinforces structural violence in its myriad forms. Therefore, I use the terms "survivor" and "survival narratives" in my research to emphasize the links between victimization, speaking out, and political action. Women who call themselves survivors know that by invoking this term, they are connecting themselves to a broader group of women who share similar experiences of victimization and who are fighting to change the social conditions that put them at risk of such violence.

It is also important to consider that when Chicana writers attempt to represent rape they must face the challenge of speaking the unspeakable, articulating that which a patriarchal society has a limited discourse to articulate—the survivor's perspective. The language of sexual violence is one that survivors are compelled not to speak. Social norms position survivors in the role of "victim" or passive object and encourage those who have been violated to keep their peace, hold their tongue and not speak out against oppression. In "now let us shift...the path of conocimiento...inner work, public acts," Anzaldúa suggests, however, that:

> By redeeming your most painful experiences you transform them into something valuable, algo para compartir or share with others so that they too may be empowered. You stop in the middle of the field and, under your breath, ask the spirits – animals, plants, y tus muertos – to help you string together a bridge of words. What follows is your attempt to give back to nature, los espíritus, and others a gift wrested from the events in your life, a bridge home to the self. (80)

According to Anzaldúa, even the most violent and seemingly irredeemable experiences are potential offerings to the world, and effective pathways to spiritual growth. These nods to what she elsewhere deems "spiritual activism" make evident both the embodiment and effervescence of transformation. Through making meaningful connections with others, it becomes possible to give the gift of life, through the language of survival.

Moreover, because of the failure of state-funded anti-violence models to address the needs of women of color, it is more crucial than ever to study radical art forms as pathways to education and awareness. Chicana cultural forms in particular shed light on issues of abuse and address violence from the survivor's perspective. When survivors connect with texts that tell their stories in new and innovative ways, that allow them the choice to understand themselves and their situations, they take steps forward in healing. They become intimately connected with a web of other survivors. Their victimization becomes something both within and outside themselves. It is transformative. When words are brought forth into the world that do not victimize, but empower, they are given potential access to new ways of thinking about themselves and their experiences. They

are free to choose their methods of understanding. They can move forward and help others, share their stories in ways that are healing for them. They become liberated from a system that so often ends up favoring the perpetrator. Profoundly, communication, art and aesthetics become transformative methods of healing. For example, Josie Mendez-Negrete, author of the incest memoir *Las Hijas de Juan*, in the epilogue describes her own process of healing as she wrote the book. She becomes the archetypal "wounded healer" as she guides the reader through instances of violence and survival. In an interview with Mendez-Negrete, she briefly mentioned public readings, where "the community has embraced it. When I've had readings there's been a lot of coming outs, and testimonios" (Interview with Mendez-Negrete April 22, 2012). According to Mendez-Negrete, survivors are often compelled to share their own stories when they hear the authors' words. Another important emphasis in her memoir is the power of the love relationships between her mother and her sisters. They are able to endure abuse and incest, to survive, through their love for one another. Similarly, a character named Caridad, a rape survivor in Ana Castillo's *So Far From God*, ultimately becomes a curandera after a brutal sexual assault. She survives a vicious attack only to spend the remainder of her days healing others. She also develops an intimate relationship with a woman from the local rape crisis center and, through love, is liberated from the patriarchy. In this way, Chicana writers who document violence point to methods of healing that involve not only breaking the silence, but also emphasizing love for oneself and others, healing through community action and "giving back."

Furthermore, for Chicana/o communities, speaking collective truths is also a matter of cultural survival. For instance, Emma Pérez argues that Chicanas share a cultural memory as well as a legacy of violence. The scars of colonization are inherited through the survivors of torture, murder and enslavement. Moreover, Antonia Castañeda writes specifically about rape and other forms of violence against women of color as "a logical extension of sexism and the politics of male domination...the legacy of the Americas is violence and exploitation based on sex, gender, race, sexuality, class, culture, and physical condition – based on the power and privilege to exploit and oppress others that each of those elements confer on us. We all share the historical legacy – it is our common heritage" (319). These Chicana writers, as well as many others, highlight the connections between memory and trauma, as well as the systemic forces that affect the individual survivor as part of a marginalized and disempowered group – in this case, brown women. Lazaro Lima also specifically addresses the representation of violence in Chicano literature. He writes, "The value of the text lies in its ability to narrativize the collective Chicano experiences of national subjection, dispossession, and disenfranchisement through its symbolic positing

of the suffering Chicano body as evidence of the national crime wrought against Chicanos" (135). Each of these scholars insists that our cultural wounds are shared and that understanding violence in a historical context of oppression and subjugation, drives us to consider new pathways to healing and new ways of building movements against violence.

Additionally, multiple Chicana fiction writers represent sexual assault or rape in the form of a metaphor that is symbolic of the ideological and physical subordination of women within patriarchal society. For example, in "The Politics of Rape: Sexual Transgression in Chicana Fiction," Dr. Maria Herrera-Sobek notes that rape has often been represented as metaphor in Chicana literature to critique white, mainstream, heterosexist norms as well as heteropatriarchy within Chicana/o communities (246). Metaphors allow us the opportunity as readers to imbue meaning in signs and symbols in significant ways. They also present the opportunity to redirect power through re-signification and innovation. In a culture that often blames the victim, metaphors open spaces for conversation about the causes, effects, and nuances of intersecting forms of violence. Anzaldúa expounds in "Border Arte," "through the centuries a culture touches and influences another, passing on its metaphors and its gods before it dies. (Metaphors *are* gods.) The new culture adopts, modifies, and enriches these images, and it, in turn, passes them on" (180). Anzaldúa's observations about the expansive power of metaphors to adapt and morph depending on context is useful to interrogating the dynamic significance of storytelling. I would argue that the use of certain metaphors is a productive way to understand our culturally specific experiences of trauma. For example, in Lucha Corpi's *Black Widow's Wardrobe*, the cultural icon of La Llorona is invoked as a metaphor for the ways in which women's behaviors are regulated and controlled by the state, the proliferation of constrictive gender norms, and the historical restriction of women's movement through acts of violence. In *So Far From God*, as well, Caridad is assaulted, not by an individual, but by an ominous dark cloud she calls "la malogra," a potent symbol of patriarchal control. Through this shifting of expectations, interpersonal assault becomes a focal point for examining the larger problem of violence against women. In this way, metaphors are an important tool of radical storytelling.

It is also significant that these kinds of metaphors are not only employed in writing, but also in everyday interactions of Chicana survivors. For instance, in "Talkin' Sex," Pat Zavella describes a research study in which most of the women she interviews use metaphor as a way to talk about sex, something that was just "not talked about" in their homes. Zavella notes that in her interviews, "the pervading themes of silence and violence were clear…and…processes of silence can be devastating for those who have been sexually abused – every

woman who disclosed abuse to me felt that she had been at fault or had done something wrong. This has a damaging effect on women's self-esteem and makes standing up for themselves when confronted with other systems of power very difficult, though not impossible" (247). Chicana communities create their own networks of understanding that complicate traditional white, mainstream, heterosexist means of understanding identity, memory and survival. A culture of victim-blaming suffuses women's self-images and means of identity construction. By recognizing themselves as part of a patriarchal system, however, it may be possible to re-imagine alternative ways of thinking about one's body and the violent acts committed upon it, as well as the psychological trauma that comes from this kind of suffering in silence. It is important that Chicana feminisms address the stifling of sexuality through an empowered process of questioning, creation, and agency. As Zavella describes:

> [T]he Chicana feminist project related to sexuality becomes breaking the silence – theorizing the relative absence of discourse about sexuality, naming lesbianism, bisexuality, and transgendered subjects in our communities, challenging heterosexist assumptions and homophobia, and understanding the myriad ways in which women construe pleasure. We Chicana feminists must engage in the political work of moving sexuality from the realm of silence, repression, and control toward women's autonomy, empowerment, and creativity. (248)

This argument can be extended to breaking the silence of rape and sexual assault, as well as many forms of institutional violence perpetrated by the state on women from marginalized communities. Chicanas have the opportunity to tell their own stories, to create their own narratives, and to voice their experiences of violence from their own unique social, economic and cultural perspectives. Our communities thrive on survival narratives in which the characters emerge alive, strong and even hopeful for the future, despite the struggles they have faced. In the end of the historical novel, *Forgetting the Alamo, Or, Blood Memory*, for example, the author Emma Pérez, describes the main character, Micaela, periodically returning to her home clandestinely, despite being exiled and threatened with further violence. She dreams of returning to her lover and children for good someday and remains optimistic, even counting herself lucky, for surviving. The truth is her anchor and her faith in the power of story strengthens her resolve. Her individual experience set against the backdrop of nineteenth century Tejas juxtaposes the personal with the political in the fight against violence and erasure.

Ultimately, our struggles as survivors beg to be spoken aloud. Chicana writers have documented these stories of survival by linking them with both historical injustice and contemporary discrimination. We have a right and a responsibility to rise up and speak out against violence, in all its forms, and to recognize the

links between the interpersonal and institutional types of violence as oppressive and insidious. Castañeda also writes, "Every time we remain silent and do not take a stand against these interlocking evils wherever we encounter them, we become complicitous with them and we reproduce them" (318). Holding each and every one of us culpable, she argues that we all have an obligation to do what is possible to combat oppression and hold ourselves, and others, accountable for the project. As I have previously stated, Chicana survival narratives act as a catalyst for social transformation by linking individual experiences of assault to centuries of systemic violence. Through methods of radical storytelling, these texts speak not only to survivors of violence, but to entire communities of oppressed and disempowered people.

For women of color cultural producers, art as activism has long been a driving force behind social justice movements. In her call to action to women of color, "A Litany for Survival," Audre Lorde says, "but when we are silent/ we are still afraid/ and so it is better to speak/ remembering/ we were never meant to survive" (*Collected Poems* 255-6). Her words remind us that structural oppression must be dismantled through subversive inquiry, speaking truth to power, and collective struggle. It is a matter of personal and cultural survival. Chicana survival narratives act as potential catalysts for social transformation, intervening in the anti-violence movement and serve as pointed examples of writing as resistance. Survival narratives are, in and of themselves, transformative but also point to a world in which violence can potentially be overcome and the outcomes of social justice struggles are grounded in a variety of artistic, political and academic interventions. This kind of radical storytelling is a subversive act of both self-love and social protest.

ENDNOTES

1 While "Chicano" is a politically charged term to identify people of Mexican American heritage as well as other US Latino groups, US census and other government data categorizes this group of people as "Hispanic" due in part to the shared characteristic of a Spanish-speaking heritage. Also included in this are people from Latin American, Central American, South American and other countries in which Spanish is the dominant language.

WORKS CITED

Anzaldúa, Gloria E. "Border Arte: Nepantla, el Lugar de la Frontera." *The Gloria Anzaldúa Reader*. Ed. Analouise Keating. Durham and London: Duke University Press, 2009. 176-197.

---. *Borderlands/La Frontera: The New Mestiza*. San Franciso: Aunt Lute Books, 1987.

---. "now let us shift...the path to conocimiento...inner works, public acts." *This Bridge We Call Home: Radical Visions for Transformation*. Eds. Anzaldúa, Gloria and Analouise Keating. New York and London: Routledge, 2002. 540-578.

Castañeda, Antonia I. "History and the Politics of Violence against Women." In *Living Chicana Theory*. Ed. Carla Trujillo. Berkeley, CA: Third Woman Press, 1997. 310-19.

Castillo, Ana. *So Far from God*. New York: W. W. Norton & Company, 1993.

Corpi, Lucha. *Black Widow's Wardrobe*. Houston: Arte Público Press, 1999.

Crenshaw, Kimberlé. "Mapping the Margins: Intersectionality, Identity Politics, and Violence against Women of Color." *Feminist Frontiers*. 7th Edition. Eds. Taylor, Verta, Nancy Whittier and Leila J. Rupp. New York: McGraw-Hill, 2007. 431-440.

Herrera-Sobek, María. "The Politics of Rape: Sexual Transgression in Chicana Fiction." *Chicana Creativity and Criticism: New Frontiers in American Literature*. Ed. María Herrera-Sobek and Helena María Viramontes. Second Edition. Albuquerque: University of New Mexico Press, 1996. 245-56.

INCITE! Women of Color Against Violence, eds. *Color of Violence: The INCITE! Anthology*. Cambridge, MA: South End Press, 2006.

Lima, Lázaro. "Practices of Freedom: The Body Re-Membered in Contemporary Latino Writing." *The Latino Body: Crisis Identities in American Literary and Cultural Memory*. New York and London: New York University Press, 2007. 127-62.

Lorde, Audre. "A Litany for Survival." *Sister Outsider: Essays & Speeches by Audre Lorde*. Berkeley: Crossing Press, 1984, 2007.

Méndez-Negrete, Josie. *Las Hijas De Juan: Daughters Betrayed*. Latin America Otherwise: Languages, Empires, Nations. Ed. Irene Silverblatt Walter D. Mignolo, Sonia Saldívar-Hull. Durham and London: Duke University Press, 2006.

Naples, Nancy A. "Deconstructing and Locating Survivor Discourse: Dynamics of Narrative, Empowerment, and Resistance for Survivors of Childhood Sexual Abuse." *Signs: Journal of Women in Culture and Society*, 28.4 (2003): 1151-1185.

National Coalition of Hispanic Health and Human Services Organizations. "The State of Hispanic Girls." Ed. National Coalition of Hispanic Health and Human Services Organizations. Washington, DC: COSSMHO Press, 1999.

Pérez, Emma. "Beyond the Nation's Maternal Bodies: Technologies of Decolonial Desire." *The Decolonial Imaginary: Writing Chicanas into History*. Bloomington: Indiana University Press, 1999. 101-25.

---. *Forgetting the Alamo, or, Blood Memory*. Austin: University of Texas Press, 2009.

Santos, Adrianna Michelle. "Interview with Josie Mendez-Negrete." San Antonio, TX. April 22, 2012.

Saeta, Elsa. "A Melus Interview: Ana Castillo." *MELUS* 22.3 (1997): 133-49.

Tjaden, Patricia and Nancy Thoennes. "Full Report of the Prevalence, Incidence, and Consequences of Violence Against Women." *Findings from the National Violence Against Women Survey.* Ed. US Department of Justice Office of Justice Program. Washington, DC: National Institute of Justice and the Centers for Disease Control and Prevention, 2000.

Zavella, Pat. "Talkin' Sex: Chicanas and Mexicanas Theorize About Silences and Sexual Pleasures." *Chicana Feminisms: A Critical Reader*. Ed. Aida Hurtado Gabriela F. Arrendondo, Norma Klahn, Olga Najara-Ramirez, Patricia Zavella. vols. Durham and London: Duke University Press, 2003. 228-53.

EMBODIED MAPS OF MULTICULTURAL "INTEGRATIVE SOLIDARITY": A MESTIZA (XICANA, FILIPINA, AND EUROAMERICAN) APPROACH TO CREATIVE TEXTS

CRISTINA ROSE SMITH

By creating a new mythos—that is, a change in the way we perceive reality, the way we see ourselves, and the ways we behave—la mestiza creates a new consciousness. —Gloria E. Anzaldúa, *Borderlands/ La Frontera*

Our culture is rich in myths and legends. They are an invaluable resource for recalling our collective memory, for myths and legends are said to be faithful mirrors of the existing conditions of the society that produced them...Despite the long years of colonization, in several mountain communities, indigenous religious sects still honor women's leadership and continue the babaylan tradition. —EATWOT: Women in the Philippines and Asia

La mestiza embodies a multiplicity of ancestral locations, ethnicities, and cultures. On the borders and in diaspora, she is often internally divided within a socially constructed white masculinist framework and a pervasive white masculinist mentality that would have her locate herself from one homeland and identify as either "woman of color" or "white." This dominant framework is interconnected with colonial and patriarchal epistemologies, and this study explores how it, more often invisibly, encourages racism within the *mestiza's* psyche and in multicultural women's spiritual communities.

This study seeks to heal traumas of racism by employing a transdisciplinary *mestiza* approach—bearing feminist and indigenous/decolonial lenses—to engage with the nuances "in between" white and color where the *mestiza* is situated. This study steps into *mestiza* situated space to hear stories of recovering indigeneity by recognizing, grieving, and deconstructing "whiteness," in particular, those stories of *mestizas* nurtured in colonial mentality as well as able to contextually pass or cover as white. Within these stories—particularly the Xicana and Filipina—are evidence of the old myths and legends passed on to us in word and in body by our *abuelas* or *lolas* in our families and by the *nepantleras*, transformers, and the *babaylans*, culture-bearers in our communities. These stories remain faithful mirrors of indigenous practices that celebrated and continue to celebrate women's leadership.

Also within these stories is evidence of spiritual *mestizaje,* the "sacred renewal" (Delgadillo 1) or transformation of *mestiza* selves towards what I call multicultural "integrative solidarity." The phrase signifies an integration of borderlands and diasporic consciousness within the *mestiza* and within multicultural women's communities. It means a uniting of multiple ancestral locations, ethnicities, and cultures through the necessary actions of conscious social activism to decolonize and deconstruct racism in all our relationships. This focus on "integrative solidarity" adds to the discussion of AnaLouise Keating who highlights the work of "transformational multiculturalism" in our communities (*Teaching Transformation* 9-11). I particularly found Anzaldúa's words to her, which Keating records in *Women Reading Women Writing,* "This is good, AnaLouise, but you need to include more of yourself in the writing," synergistic and encouraging with my growth toward ethnoautobiographical research (180). Indeed, my work on integrative solidarity takes the discourse on transformational multiculturalism from this meso level, the community level, into the micro level as well, within *mestizas* and their relationships within themselves. Moreover, Keating's *Women Reading Women Writing* offers me a more than worthy example of a way to integrate critical and creative literary analysis with chosen creative texts.

Organized around the literary element of character that is employed in the following creative texts, this study explores the story of *una mestiza,* myself, for integrative solidarity. Drawing upon ethnoautobiographical and literary critical methodologies, I search within my creative texts as a Xicana-Filipina-Euroamerican and turn to the "role-models" I have found in published creative texts that have influenced my journey: Caridad in (Xicana) Ana Castillo's *So Far From God* and the mother-figures in (Filipinas) Jessica Hagedorn's "*Kundiman" in Dogeaters* and Merlinda Bobis's "For Maria" in *Flight is Song on Four Winds.* The word choice of "role-model" is deliberate as I work to reclaim language from my Euroamerican cultural heritage. "Role-model" was a term employed in my

family and community to signify someone worthy of emulating. I have spent my whole life seeking this role-model and working to be a role-model in my family and community. As a young adult, this meant conforming to the socially constructed white masculinist framework. As an adult, this means transforming into a woman of multicultural integrative solidarity.

Altogether, I ultimately offer two theoretical insights from this research on characters of "integrative solidarity" within my story, this new mestiza mythology or as I call it, literary mestizaje: we are 1) challenged by indigenous-inspired healers to decolonize and embrace our ancestral roots and 2) encouraged to grieve.

MESTIZA ETHNOAUTOBIOGRAPHICAL METHODOLOGIES AND PERSONAL CREATIVE TEXT

To begin the body of my work, I first offer my creative text entitled "I Ask My Younger Sister." This poem delves into my desire to have characters is my creative texts who look like me; that is, they embody the multiplicity of ancestry, with Xicana, Filipina, and Euroamerican attributes, and they inspire me to do the same.

I ask my younger sister,
"Do you think people see you as a woman of color?"

"No," she says, "It's like this:
I've only ever had two traffic tickets.
The white policeman marked me down as 'Hispanic' on the ticket;
The Hispanic policeman marked me down as 'white.'"

"And we're really not even women of color," she says.
"We're half or less. Remember our last name is Smith
And Grammie's family is from Spain.
That's white. "

I look at her "anglo" nose and know it looks much like mine. I note her brown shoulders. I consider our pear shaped bodies. I see

Our full lips,
Our wide feet, and
Our almond eyes.

I try to tell her about the name for women like us—*mestiza*—
I try to talk about our family's unspoken shame at being made fun of as kids
Because they weren't white skinned,

how that shame passed on to us—
the shame of being people of color—
how they wanted us to be all-American—
shave that upper lip, go to school, speak English, don't be like those Mexicans—

how I feel white-washed.
Don't you feel the same, sister?

But she can't hear me.

I don't tell her about the altar for our ancestors I have set up in my apartment.
I tell her, "It's not like I'm going to start wearing traditional Mexican clothes like Frida Kahlo or name my children Filipina names, whatever those are."
I don't tell her I *want* to dress like Frida Kahlo.

But all along, what I don't tell her, is that
I really just
want
to
cry.

It is the physical attributes in my poem that I find worthy of note as I approach my creative text seeking character role models with this feminist and indigenous colonial lens. For it is with almond eyes and pear shaped bodies that I describe myself. Moreover, I admit in my internal conversation with my sister in mind, my longing for connection with both my Mexican heritage, through Frida Kahlo, and my Filipino heritage with a Filipino name. My overall desire has been to embody these characteristics. Moreover, my goal is to find or tell a story, as my sister cannot in her exchanges with law enforcement, where there

is a place between white and Hispanic as well as space to transcend those labels as well.

In Xicana scholarship, this place is "the in-between place of nepantla" and it is our "home" as *mestizas*, writes Anzaldúa ("now let us shift" 574). When *Mestizas* are agents of *nepantla*, when they embrace the bridge of borderlands and diasporic sense of self as home, they are *nepantleras*, transformers within their communities that bring healing through their creativity. In contrast, my Xicana family—with roots in New Mexico, Mexico, and Europe—has consciously or unconsciously chosen to subscribe to a whiteness framework in their reading or writing of their *Mestiza* stories (*Teaching Transformation* 85); my work at uncovering these stories is, in part, what I see happening in my poem when the narrator speaks to her desire, albeit apologetically, to dress like Frida Kahlo. Frida is perhaps one of the most popular *Mestizas*, indigenous mother and German father, known for integrating her indigenous sense of self into her artwork. What dressing like Frida means to me as the narrator is the desire to know and understand the cultural practices that were suppressed because of colonization. I see this desire manifested as well in my research on such *mestizas* as Anzaldúa, Cherríe Moraga, and *la Virgen* as well as Ana Castillo, whose work I study in depth.

In Filipina scholarship, the space where multiplicities come together in integrative solidarity is in *kapwa. Kapwa*, Filipina Indigenous scholar Elenita (Fe) Mendoza Strobel writes, is rooted in the goodness of the universe and in a "relationship to Land," ancestors, and community (Strobel 165, 176). Those who take it upon themselves to pass on *kapwa* traditions, take on, as Strobel asserts, the spirit of the indigenous Filipina healers—Earth-grounded—and culture-bearers, the *babaylans*. In my poem, I briefly mention my Filipina heritage, endeavoring to explain to my sister my hesitant desire to know and understand the Filipina culture of my grandmother. There is, in that creative text, an opportunity to return to the names, particularly the names of important female figures, from my grandmother's region in the Philippines. The indigenous honoring of *diwatas*, a word that the English word 'goddess' only begins to describe, such as Mebuyan, is like the honoring of *la Virgen*, a symbol of strength and abundance, a symbol of resistance to the white masculinist framework and the endurance of the indigenous presence. I integrate my understanding of *diwata* Mebuyan and the *babaylans* into my spirituality that honors *Mahal na Ina*, Sacred Mother; (Mananzan 230), my own sacred mother, my father's Cebuana mother (from the island of Cebu).

Like my Xicana family, my Filipina ancestors also have stories that have been colonized or "white-washed" as I write. My grandmother listed herself as Filipina on her marriage certificate to my Missouri born soldier grandfather.

Oddly enough, she lists her parents as both Spanish. A survivor of the Japanese occupation of the Philippines and, in that, a witness to her mother's death at the hands of the Japanese soldiers, when my lola came to the United States after World War II, she left her languages and most of her ethnic and cultural traditions. She assimilated to U.S. culture and specifically to Missourian culture in the 1950s when anti-miscegenation laws were still in existence. Again, I see her assimilation as evidence of her pursuit of white privilege, and I do not judge her. I cannot even imagine what her life in Missouri was like, and I hear from my older cousins that lola never believed it was safe for her to return to her homeland. It is only recently that I have learned how my lola saw visions and had premonitions. Her shamanistic spirituality may have been colonized by Catholicism and my grandfather's violence, but her indigenous gifts endured. In my work, I attempt to capture some of what has been lost in family due to colonization. My Filipina mestiza family lives in diaspora of our homeland, the Philippines (Cebu), yet even in diaspora from the homeland, my grandmother's spiritual gifts have passed down to my aunt. Their discernment of visions remains, perhaps, the only lasting ethnic and cultural practice I have from my Filipino ancestry that has come through my blood family.

It is my relationship with my *lola* that drew me to remember *Mebuyan* and the *babaylans*. With my grandmother and these sacred female-figures as guides, I have begun to see how *babaylans* and *babaylan*-inspired women I meet may not look just like me nor have my experiences or white privileges; nevertheless, we share similar characteristics, enough so that we work to, as Strobel writes, "Break the boundaries" and "Crossover" and "Write" our experiences to bring about healing (Strobel 10). The Filipinas carry certain character traits that have, like my Xicana role-models, motivated integrative solidarity in my life.

Indeed, in working to be deliberate about integrative solidarity, I cannot forget all the Euroamerican ancestry in my family and the Euroamerican role-models who have been working towards transformation in women's spirituality communities as well. Exploring my Spanish and other European ancestry can be challenging as I have mentioned before. Like the policemen in my poem that my sister identified as white and Hispanic, often parts of our ethnicity are invisible. I have encountered friends who completely dismiss my Spanish roots. In their eyes, the Spanish in me is not a part of my ancestry because they were the colonizers. As I attempt to explain to my sister in my poem, I can often feel "white-washed" already having been raised in the way that we were—as if we were white—but I want integrative solidarity, a sense of integrity that advocates for the Xicana and Filipina in me as well as embraces and compassionately challenges the Euroamerican in me as well. I seek Euroamerican female figures as role-models within a decolonial and indigenous paradigm now. In my creative

text, I speak about the altar I have set up in my apartment; particular Euroamerican role-models have a place on the altar. These include the dark madonnas in Spain.

Exploring the treasures of my ancestors is both challenging and enjoyable, and I see myself as part of the next generation of *nepantlera* and *babaylan*-inspired healing and transforming role-models who will, perhaps, be a main character in the new mythology of a younger *Mestiza's* life.

MESTIZA LITERARY CRITICAL METHODOLOGIES AND THREE CHARACTERS: CARIDAD, OUR MOTHER, AND MARIA

I have been inspired in this new mythmaking by Ana Castillo's *So Far From God* and particularly the character Caridad. Caridad's rough start as a disfigured survivor of assault and the final disappearance when she jumps off the cliff in Sky City may seem to make her a poor role-model, but her enduring and passionate character encourages creative transformation in her readers. It is, perhaps, with a multiethnic feminist and indigenous decolonial lens that her strength as a role-model becomes more apparent. Indeed, it is she, among the daughters of Sofi, who exhibits Euroamerican features; she is also the one labeled a "whore," and, finally, she is the one who becomes the symbol of the *Virgen* to the people of Tome. Her story begins tragically but becomes miraculous: Caridad returns home one day with her nipples bitten off, branded like cattle, and stabbed in the throat (Castillo 33), but soon after, Caridad enters into stages of transformation.

Like Anzaldúa's path of conocimiento, Caridad journeys through a process of new consciousness. First, she is healed by her sister La Loca and becomes a healer trained by doña Felicia, the town medicine woman. This first transformation catalyzed through doña Felicia leaves Caridad in a state to receive love. Soon after, she falls in love with a woman named Esmeralda. In a second transformation, Caridad enters a cave in the Sangre de Cristo Mountains to pray, not returning for a year. The Christian faithful of Tome see her as the virgin with a halo; however, she is simply a woman healer. Leaving the cave, Caridad enters her third transformation, now a confirmed medium, now appearing to simply be a casual friend of Esmeralda. In Caridad's final moments in the novel, she and Esmeralda are being stalked by dona Felicia's godson, who fell in love with Caridad after finding her in the cave. When Esmeralda sees her stalker waiting for them in Sky City, she runs for the cliff. Caridad takes Esmeralda's hand as Esmeralda runs, and they both jump off the *mesa*, mountain. However, they do not die; they simply disappear; "Tsichtinako was calling" (211).

I assert that from a *mestiza* literary critical perspective, Caridad's character and her role-modeling of growth are a pivotal representation of intermixed

ethnic cultural practices and stories. Her emergence as a medium and then as a bird called by the indigenous mother of humanity has native significance. In addition to the indigenous lens, a particularly woman of color feminist approach to literature lends itself to another interpretation of the text. Caridad's year in the cave becomes a nurturing of her feminist role-model attributes that bring her into greater leadership as a healer in her community. Finally, Caridad's symbolic rebirth to the indigenous mother enlivens a woman of color feminist hope in letting go of the white masculinist social structure of Tome and the welcoming of an indigenous-rooted community that nurtures and mothers women.

Ultimately, Caridad works as a role-model for a mestiza on her spiritual journey of one who embodies and creates transformative and healing spaces because she is both believable and unbelievable. Her story, like my own, involves emancipation from the dominant Western ways of knowing and being; her story is perhaps the story of many women (and men). Certainly, this is the work of Anzaldúa who offers that this emancipation is a true shift in perspective that hits an individual like an earthquake ("now let us shift" 543). Indeed, there is much magical realism in Anzaldúa's depiction of *conocimiento* as well as in Castillo's recounting of Caridad's personal history, and for this reason, Caridad as a character exists as both real and unreal, allowing readers to embrace the limitless possibilities and rebirths available to them as they heal and transform their own lives. This transformation is personal as well as political, bringing new consciousness to the individual and their community that offers a sense of wholeness and necessitates social activism. As Anzaldúa describes in "now let us shift," this wholeness involves reaching through our wounds to connect to our community and through the act of writing, call our whole selves together (574).

Filipina literature encourages me to recast stories with transformative, empowered, and empathetic characters. Hagedorn and Bobis offer mother figures in their works "*Kundiman*" and "For Maria." Hagedorn's "*Our Mother*" in "*Kundiman*" is a role-model of one who stands in the transformative space, like a culture-bearer, bearing fruit of the Philippines that reaches the United States. Even as Hagedorn points to the horrors and grief of sexism and racism —external and internal—throughout her novel, she has "*Our Mother*" bring a conclusion, albeit painful, to the story. Hagedorn's readers—many in diaspora —read the prayer-romantic love song and more fully resonate with the grief of her characters and the narrator as well. Additionally, the narrator of this prayer questions the oppressions the novel has portrayed, which now are displayed on the body of "*Our Mother.*" Hagedorn emphasizes throughout the novel in which "*Kundiman*" is situated, *Dogeaters*, that there is much to grieve: the rape of Filipinas by Christian colonizers as well as the need to "invent [their] own history," sometimes altogether because the truth of the indigenous stories has

been destroyed in the colonization of the Philippines by the Spanish and the United States (239). Hagedorn's narrator in "*Kundiman*" expresses rage and directs these emotions toward "*Our Mother,*" who is also called by many names including "*Our Blessed Virgin Mary of Most Precious Blood, menstrual, ephemeral, carnal, eternal*" (250). The narrator describes a mother figure who is a real, embodied, blood-filled woman with both temporary and infinite significance to the Filipina on her spiritual journey to reclaim all aspects of her ancestral history.

As an intermixture of the many bloods, this mother becomes a role-model to Filipinas themselves, women who cannot be codified and represents "overlapping and flexible centers" (Rustomji-Kerns, SriKanth and Strobel 7), being profoundly multiple. "Rose Mystica, Black Virgin of Rhinestone and Velvet Mystery," this Mother is an intermixture whose name is "Madonna of Volcanoes and Violence" (Hagedorn 250). Looking back at the names "Our Mother" has been given, both sacred and profane, the narrator also then is able to recognize the fruits of this multiple and integrated role-model, a very transformational multiethnic position. Hagedorn dismantles the potential for selective memory when she includes the painful names—the names used against her as a feminine, intermixture of colonized and colonizer with indigenous roots. She is the one who inhabits the multiple and liminal; hence, Hagedorn creates a new mythology with an "*Our Mother*" that looks like us and calls us to question and transform the culture we are bearing.

And, the fruits, Hagedorn offers, of this woman, "Blessed...among women," are of the Earth particular to the homeland. "Kundiman" concludes with this celebration of these fruits of the Earth: "blessed are the fruits of thy womb: guavas, mangos, santol, mangosteen, durian. Now and forever, world without end. Now and forever" (251). Although her fruits come from the Philippines and ends with a finality of "now and forever," the "amen" is missing. Although this leaves open the potential for continued transformation, Hagedorn's use of the Eurocentric Catholic words suggest that she is able to remove the white man, but not the white framework, from her literature. Retelling the old story, Hagedorn uses her voice as an empowered writer to critique the Catholic and colonial system that oppressed the Philippines and silenced Filipina indigenous voices. Interestingly enough, this same system then empowered her to write, albeit from a position of assumed white masculine power, that is, from the format of the "Lord's Prayer." Her work connects deeply with Mestiza literary critical tradition that aims to "complicate" the Filipina Mestiza mother figure and make visible in order to challenge "whiteness" and "masculinist" as normalized frameworks. "Our Mother" may not be a babaylan or able to fully step into her indigenous power; however, I argue she has that potential. Altogether, Hagedorn's prayer emerges as a sacred reincarnation of the Lord's Prayer to "Our Mother" instead

of "Our Father." Moreover, Hagedorn's mother-figure expands the characteristics of a role-model of integrative solidarity to include the reality of Filipinas and Filipina-Americans as individuals and as a community.

Like Hagedorn, Bobis's poem describes the mothering and Earth-rooted healer as a source of ancestral gifts. Together, these works, both published in 1990, work together to develop a character of the mother that are reminiscent of the *babaylans* that transform through grief and decolonization to eventually bring solidarity and reconciliation.

Bobis, as well, explores a mother figure as a main character and as role-model for life giving properties. It is perhaps no mistake that Bobis also employs allusions to Christianity's influence in the Philippines. She, like Hagedorn, writes a prayer, and yet, instead of a prayer to "*Our Mother*," she writes a letter to the woman whose name is most associated with Spanish speaking Christianity, "Maria." In "For Maria," she presents how this character is in her "bamboo forest" when she is "filled with the child by air" because of her "love for the lost." The narrator speaks as the "lost strange wind" that came into the "all-year-round feast" of Maria's "green body" and was "welcomed…with jasmine." Maria, as the Earth herself perhaps, then birthed the narrator, and "Now," the narrator writes that she is "birthing/ poetry and life" (68). In this poem, Bobis highlights this character's nurturance with suggestions of the Earth's nurturance as well. With a profound love for the lost, Maria's womb carries in it the poet herself. Sensually greeted with floral scents and music, she is held in the womb until she is able to birth her own creations. Bobis's narrator connects with her roots entrenched in motherly and earthen signifiers. The writing too moves forward into discovery while looking to her ancestry to manifest her ethnic roots as well. As Bobis appears to be the narrator poet in "Maria," this poem works as a ethnoautobiographical text. The evidence suggests that Bobis may have experienced silence when she wanted to know about her ethnic and cultural differences. Indeed, Bobis survives in order to find this mother -Maria role-model to rebirth her into the darkness often associated with "deathlessness." In the mother's earthen body, Bobis seems to have found what she needed. Motherly nurturance and a character she could emulate that had an earthen body, the narrator poet in Bobis's poem, too, becomes a "Maria" who can nurture newness. This woman can transform as she has been transformed through the Earth-like womb of this role-model. This female figure has, above all, created a space for growth. Moreover, Bobis's creative intermixture of dark and light as well as death and rebirth depicted in the Maria-mother that the poet becomes herself offers—in the language of the multiply ethnic, feminist, and tribal—an empowered *Mestiza* role-model who, like *nepantleras* and *babaylans,* ushers women into "poetry [creative expression] and life" (68). This deepened conversation, I argue, will bring transformation to

multiethnic woman as well as to women's communities who are read as white communities to stand in solidarity with the women of color in the community so that a profound integrity can be established between the women.

Altogether, these characters—Caridad, *Our Mother,* and Maria—challenge readers to stand in solidarity with our painful experiences and to transform them. They give readers examples of holistic, integrated, and empowered social activist healers.

CONCLUSION: TWO INSIGHTS

To conclude, I offer two brief insights. The first insight my study reveals is that *Mestizas* and women's spirituality communities must, in the growth toward integrative solidarity, embrace the process of knowing our indigenous roots. Of course, women's spirituality facilitates a growing awareness of our motherline; however, what this study has revealed is that the process of recovering indigenous roots cannot begin without first the work of decolonization and, similarly, without the aid of a "multiculturalization" that aims to bring integration and social activism into mestizas' lives and communities. Through the work of decolonization and multiculturalization, *Mestizas* can be transformed into deeper integrative solidarity, acknowledging their privilege, deconstructing the hierarchical dualisms that are created from racism, and learning about their indigenous heritage. I found the work of embracing our indigenous roots in order to bring equitable unification within *Mestizas* and women's communities in Castillo's description of Caridad's *Mestiza* body and in Caridad's acceptance of the call of the indigenous mother (211); in Hagedorn's depiction of the "*Black Virgin of Rhinestone and Velvet Mystery*" whose womb gives the native fruits of "*guavas, mangos, santol, mangosteen, durian*. Now and forever, world without end" (251); and, finally, in Bobis's portrayal of Maria's body in the "bamboo forest" and her love for the lost" (68).

My second insight is that we must grieve in order to come into integrative solidarity. This study has been one of fumbling, trusting, and letting go as I (re) learn how to speak to myself in ways that affirm all ancestral parts of myself. I decolonize in order to move through racism and embrace my darkness. I speak to the need to simply "cry" in conversations with my sister about my *Mestiza* sense of self. In truth, I have been drawn to these particular characters because of how they modeled this fumbling and yet emancipatory process. Moreover, like these characters as well, I have been navigating my growth while in relationships with family and community. Learning from the stories of colonization from my *abuelas* and *lolas* and letting go of old visions and languages for the future, as with the stories that Castillo, Hagedorn, and Bobis depict, I have come into integrative solidarity with profound vulnerability. I am challenged to express my

rage like Hagedorn's narrator and find solace in Maria like Bobis's narrator. At this point in my personal mythology, my literary *mestizaje*, with my search for a *Mestiza* approach to my spirituality, I have come through much grief in order to celebrate my location on the borderlands and in diaspora both within my psyche and within my women's communities.

WORKS CITED

Anzaldúa, Gloria. *Borderlands/La Frontera: The New Mestiza.* San Francisco: Aunt Lute Books, 1987. Print.

———, "now let us shift...the path of conocimiento...inner work, public acts." In *this bridge we call home: radical visions for transformation.* Eds. Gloria E. Anzaldúa and AnaLouise Keating. New York: Routledge, 2001. 540–78. Print.

Bobis, Merlinda C. *Flight Is Song On Four Winds* [Ang Lipad ay Awit Sa Apat na Hangin]. Manila: Babaylan Publishing Women's Collective, St. Scholastica's College, 1990. Print.

Castillo, Ana. *So Far From God.* New York: Plume, 1995. Print.

Delgadillo, Theresa. *Spiritual Mestizaje: Religion, Gender, Race, and Nation in Contemporary Chicana Narrative.* Durham, NC: Duke University Press, 2011. Print.

Ecumenical Association of Third World Theologians (EATWOT), Women in the Philippines and Asia. *Toward an Asian Principle of Interpretation: A Filipino Women's Experience. Patriarchy in Asia and Asian Women's Hermeneutical Principle.* Theology/Spirituality of Struggle Series. Manila: Forum for Interdisciplinary Endeavors and Studies, Institute of Women Studies, 1991. Print.

Hagedorn, Jessica. *Dogeaters.* New York: Penguin, 1990. Print.

Keating, AnaLouise. *Teaching Transformation: Transcultural Classroom Dialogues.* New York: Palgrave Macmillan, 2007. Print.

Keating, AnaLouise. *Women Reading Women Writing: Self-Invention in Paula Gunn Allen, Gloria Anzaldúa, and Audre Lorde.* Philadelphia: Temple University Press. 1996, Print.

Mananzan, St. Mary John, OSB. *Woman, Religion, and Spirituality in Asia.* Manila: Anvil and the Institute of Women's Studies, 2004. Print.

Rustomji-Kerns, Roshni with Raini SriKanth and Leny Mendoza Strobel. "Introduction." *Encounters: People of Asian Descent in the Americas.* Eds. Roshni Rustomji-Kerns, Raini SriKanth and Leny Mendoza Strobel Lanham, MD: Rowman and Littlefield Publishers, Inc, 1999. 1-12. Print.

Strobel, Leny Mendoza. *A Book of Her Own: Words and Images to the Honor the Babaylan.* San Francisco: T'Boli Publishing, 2005. Print.

APPLYING AND EXTENDING ANZALDÚAN CONCEPTS

SKA AS A BRIDGE TO PRE-MESTIZA CONSCIOUSNESS: RHYTHMIC MOVES IN ANZALDÚA'S BORDERLAND

CRYSTAL E. SERRANO

The struggle has always been inner…played out in the outer terrains. Awareness of our situation must come before inner changes…before changes in society. Nothing happens in the "real" world unless it first happens in the images in our heads. —Gloria E. Anzaldúa, *Borderlands/La Frontera*

Before Gloria Anzaldúa's work had reached me, I struggled as an adolescent to understand the reasons why I felt shame about my family, language, and culture. Although being of light complexion and American citizenship, I was born to Mexican immigrant parents who came here without documents. Despite being bilingual, I was placed in ESL courses for inexplicable reasons to me at the time. Schooling made me suspicious of the Spanish language, and forced me to advocate for my own education to become mainstreamed. However, to succeed in a normative environment, I realized that I would have to give up my Mexican ethnic identity, which entailed rejection of my language, and, more importantly, dismissing my parents and the culture they upheld. It was during my teenage years, and through my interaction with alternative forms and hybrid styles of music that I began to recover the cultural losses with which I had disidentified.[1] Having learned from a young age that I would have to fight for my own

educational success, it was in high school, being surrounded by young activists and musicians, that I began to theorize about the injustices in the world, that I started to use my education as a way to reconnect with my community and culture. Ska music became that bridge for me.

(UN)POPULAR CULTURE

We are ashamed that we need your good opinion, that we need your acceptance. We can no longer camouflage our needs, can no longer let defenses and fences sprout around us... To rage and look upon you with contempt is to rage and be contemptuous of ourselves...Here we are weaponless with open arms, with only our magic. Let's try it our way, the mestiza way, the Chicana way, the woman way. —Gloria E. Anzaldúa, *Borderlands/La Frontera*

While going through the process of coming to self, I did not have the language that Anzaldúa expresses; however, upon being introduced to her work, I could then make the connections to what had previously been my bridge towards consciousness. It was through mainstream American popular culture that I internalized oppression against my own people—distancing and disidentifying with them.[2] I equated being Mexican with poverty. My father's inability to speak English and my mother's accent were limitations to our progress, and became a source of embarrassment.

Throughout elementary school I was lumped in the classroom with the "Mexican kids." I saw the way others looked at us, the way they undermined us, judged us; our fifth grade teacher saying we were dirty because we would come back sweaty and smelly after playing soccer during recess, but I knew her comment extended to external factors beyond that. Having the determination to do well academically, I knew I had to remove myself from this image, from this group, otherwise I would remain in the shadows. Therefore, when middle school began I engaged in as much mainstream American popular culture as I could because I knew that would mark me as different from the rest. "To be close to another Chicana is like looking into the mirror. We are afraid of what we'll see there. *Pena.* Shame. Low estimation of self" (Anzaldúa 80), and for this reason I removed myself from Chicanas/os and Mexicanas/os as much as possible.

All I wanted to do was fit in: speak English, wear designer clothes, and listen to Euro-American music, those things which my family did not have access to. I spent my entire middle school years lost in ignorance, trying to be someone I was not. Then, during early high school, we moved to an urban ethnic working-class neighborhood, forcing me to rethink and examine our lives and community much differently. It was in Carson, in the South Bay of Los Angeles, California, that I was exposed to youth of color, particularly Chicanas/os who embraced their ethnic, cultural, and linguistic identity. Most were members of

Punk and Ska bands or followed similar musical genres that promoted a very strong Mexican identification. It was evident in the way they spoke, how they dressed and carried themselves—it was written all over their bodies. This music consumed their lives, but it was music unlike anything I had heard before.

Prior to our move, my mother noticed my rejection of the family, and would regularly push me to listen to Spanish music. She seemed concerned that I was only consuming mainstream American English music, but her music did not speak to me. Although, I relished traditional and regional Mexican music when I was younger because that was all I was exposed to living in an immigrant household, it was not until a hybrid style of Chicana/o Latina/o Ska music that I began to make musical connections—the lyrics were in Spanish or bilingual and it spoke about those matters I had tried to distance myself from. As I began to listen to this more urban ethnic version of Punk and Ska, and attended backyard shows, a transformation began taking over my body. I did not know how to articulate it, but I was coming into consciousness.

Soon after, I returned to speaking Spanish, feeling comfort in knowing that I had not completely lost my language as I reconnected with the beauty and depth of my Mexican heritage. But this beautiful reunion did not come without pain. Angry with myself, I felt a great disappointment to have ever allowed myself to think otherwise, to have felt ashamed of being Mexican. The music helped those feelings diminish, as I began to realize there was nothing wrong in admitting that we were poor; it became a source of strength to acknowledge how much our parents and community have endured. Instead, we found pride in reclaiming our history and cultural practices in ways that the younger generation could connect with. Whereas before I resisted my parent's music and style, we found ourselves looking to our parent's music, finding new ways to reinvent and articulate their musical expressions in a way that spoke to us.

Embracing hybridity and rasquachismo, we created a consciousness about the environment that we were living in, forcing ourselves to find ways to be creative with the limited resources that were available to us. Not having the means to go to clubs and shows all the way in Hollywood, we found alternate ways to use the spaces we had access to. We started having backyard shows and charging a fee between $1-3, allowing us to create a music scene that was not out of our reach, promoted collective community efforts, and helped families raise funds for their needs. With a backyard, we could throw a show and raise money to cope with the financial stresses around us. Most parents embraced our efforts and accepted these shows, aside from the drinking and use of minor drugs that took place, but these spaces kept us out of trouble as we skanked3 the night away, rather than becoming involved with gangs—music became a healthier path to expression.

POLITICAL ORIGINS OF SKA

Focusing on racialized and criminalized experiences, Ska music is enacted as a form of protest. Among the Chicana/o Latina/o Ska subculture, the music expresses issues about education, immigration, violence, police brutality, and access, while also celebrating our cultural heritage and national pride. It often speaks about political issues affecting younger generations, their parents, and community at large, but in the style of upbeat, fast-paced rhythms.

As a Chicana, learning the history of Ska has also provided a point of connection. Ska has Jamaican origins and stems from the cultural expression and discontent of oppressed youth on the island and those that were forced to emigrate due to economic instability after Jamaica's Independence in 1962. With political and economic origins, Ska became a medium through which they could contest the exploitation, poverty, dislocation, and racism they were experiencing, and create a call for unity and hope, as they imagined a Jamaica free from the effects of colonization and globalization. As Scott Calhoun states,

> ...the rise of ska indicates when and where social, political, and economic institutions disappoint their people and push them to reinvent the process for making meaning out of life. When a group embarks on this process, it becomes even more necessary to embrace expressive, liberating forms of art for help during the struggle. In its history as a music of freedom, ska has flowed freely to wherever people are celebrating the rhythms and sounds of hope. (Augustyn x)

And in this way, it is not surprising that Ska music has flowed and made its way to the multitude of youth around the world, becoming a transnational hybrid musical style found all over Latin America, the Caribbean, Europe, and beyond—wherever violence and colonization fester. Thus, the necessity for Ska and musical expression will always be there.

Through his research on subcultures in Great Britain, Dick Hebdige relates how Reggae and Ska music were used as mediums for identity and resistance against oppressive conditions for the African/Jamaican communities. "Sound-systems," a form of a club, sprang up all around where these immigrant communities resided:

> To a community hemmed in on all sides by discrimination, hostility, suspicion and blank incomprehension, the sound-system came to represent, particularly for the young, a precious inner sanctum, uncontaminated by alien influences, a black heart beating back to Africa on a steady pulse of dub. (Hebdige 38)

For immigrant populations coming from and living in poor and working-class communities, music becomes a method around which they can express their

culture, customs, language, and history when they are far away from home. The socio-political limitations placed on immigrants because of their lack of citizenship, race, and economic status inspire Ska music as a way to construct a sense of worth and identity, as well as a tool of conversation and educational strategy among those living in the native and host country.

Tracing the routes of Ska, Joseph Heathcott illuminates the fact that we must "pay close attention not only to the flows of people and ideas across borders but also to the urban spaces in which these ideas are generated, absorbed, reworked, and exported (187). He also reinforces how "the shantytowns reflected the spatial logic of colonial capitalist maldevelopment," and it is in these spaces that "Jamaican working-class people struggled for some amount of spatial autonomy and control over their destinies," and in this way youth subcultures forged "spaces of resistance and autonomy" (192). Ultimately, to understand Ska is to become familiar with the survival strategies of a group. It is through youth and the subcultures they form, and the ways in which they express themselves, that one can have a greater sense of their experiences, struggles, hopes, and vision for a better world. Whether singing about poverty, violence, or heartbreak, they do it with a smile on their face, hips swaying left to right, hands jerking up and down, determined to never let the music stop.

CHICANA/O CULTURAL PRODUCTION AND POLITICS: ARTICULATING A THIRD SPACE

During the 1990s when Governor Pete Wilson advocated Proposition 187, heightening the criminalization of immigrants, Los Angeles gave way to many hybrid musical styles as young Chicanas/os and Latinas/os became active in their communities and began speaking out against injustice. As part of these efforts, Chicanas/os and Latinas/os have adopted Ska and made it their own with their language and rhythms to give it a distinct style. This unique sound is attributed to the use of timbales, a horn section with trumpets, a trombone, and sometimes even a saxophone, as well as the influence of *cumbia*, *salsa,* and other styles to give it a danceable rhythm—some bands even blend a punk and hardcore style with it.

Chicana/o and Latina/o artists have a long history of musical adaption and hybridity, which allows them to not only use the dominant popular culture, but to turn it on its head, transform it into something empowering for oppressed people, and give it back and challenge the dominant class with it. These musical constructions are a form of resistance, primarily because they take all the elements of which the U.S. has tried to deny to people of color, fusing them into something new that reflects their lived experiences. They contest the dominant culture, which erases our histories and identities, and challenge imposed and sugar-coated views of American life. It focuses on a lived reality—a reality that

directly challenges the notion of assimilation and Manifest Destiny—and that heals historical wounds.

For example, Leticia Higuera Arellano's dissertation on Chicana/o and Latina/o Punk experiences discusses the creation of a Latino Punk scene in the 1990s, and what made this expression different from its White dominant counterpart. Through their unapologetic use and conscious decision to sing in Spanish, lyrics challenging imperialism and the status quo, and maintaining a community-centered focus, Latina/o Punk took on a critical and social justice emphasis based on their racialized identities and experiences. In support of this, Arellano mentions that "Making the decision to sing in Spanish in a country where segregation and discrimination was a fact of life for musicians and their loved ones was no less than solid affirmation of their identity and an act of resistance" (33). Unlike traditional (White) Punk, through which young artists sought to distance themselves from their parents, Latina/o Punk artists maintained those connections with their parents and their ethnic identities. In this case, Punk music allowed them to express their anger at the injustices confronted by their elders, as well as the exploitation, poverty, and violence surrounding them, and the colonization and criminalization of their communities both here and abroad. Martin Sorrondeguy, lead singer of the punk band *Los Crudos*, attests to this when he states,

> For us, singing punk doesn't mean letting go...of those ties that we have to our parents, to our families, or to where we're from or to our language. It [doesn't] mean breaking away from that. It means working with them to get somewhere, to get to a new level. (Sorrondeguy as cited in Okoh, as cited in Arellano 45)

With his band, Sorrondeguy was able to critique the conditions that Chicanas/os and Latinas/os face in the U.S., but through his travels in visiting and playing for youth in Latin American countries, he was better able to make connections to the transnational and global struggles of all Latinas/os.

While subcultures are rooted in resistance, they develop from youths' rebellion against the contradictions that they witness. They try to resolve some of the issues that they experience much differently than their parents do, "even where experience was shared between parents and children this experience was likely to be differently interpreted, expressed and handled by the two groups" (Hebdige 78). In that sense, while Latina/o parents may feel that their children are straying from their culture, in reality the music that they listen to is still very much influenced by their ethnic and linguistic roots, and touches upon their shared experiences, but is expressed in a different rhythm. Therefore, while it may seem that youth are trying to remove themselves from their parents and become completely independent, their shared experiences still exist, and

subcultures become a space through which they negotiate the relationships, dualities, contradictions and multiple identities that they live.

BAILANDOCONLAMESTIZACONSCIOUSNESS:AREFLECTIVECONCLUSION

As a person, I, as a people, we, Chicanos, blame ourselves, hate ourselves, terrorize ourselves. Most of this goes on unconsciously; we only know that we are hurting, we suspect that there is something wrong with us, something fundamentally "wrong."—Gloria E. Anzaldúa, *Borderlands/La Frontera*

Having access to the words of Anzaldúa much later in life, allowed me to recognize that other Chicanas/os and Latinas/os such as me were beginning to articulate a mestiza consciousness without even realizing it. Despite not possessing a decolonizing language and the theories that provide a frame of reference, we were able to understand ourselves as third space dwellers through a racialized and hybrid musical style that facilitated analyzing and understanding the world around us. For many of us, our consciousness began with a musical style that silences and negates race, class, and gender, creating the need for our own spaces, a third space where we can articulate a different experience, a different history, a different *movimiento.*

Once I had begun the process of conocimiento, I started reflecting and realizing how wounded some of the people I grew up with were. Two of my best friends from elementary through high school were Vietnamese and Filipino, and they also came from immigrant households. All of our parents migrated from their respective countries, and we each knew how to speak our native language. Despite the richness that we carried within us, we expressed a discontent toward anything having to do with our ethnic identity. Even though we would never be able to fit the White standards of beauty, we still upheld them and valued them; wanting to be like and dress like White girls, obsessing over White boys from Torrance and Redondo Beach, and adorning our folders with collages of boy bands.

Although I lost touch with these women over the years, I often think about the wounds that we carried as children and the depth of the pain that we inflicted on ourselves each day, some more than others. None of us ever felt comfortable in our own bodies. Anzaldúa's words resonate about the discomfort when she illustrates that, "In our very flesh, (r)evolution works out the clash of cultures. It makes us crazy constantly, but if the center holds, we've made some kind of evolutionary step forward" (103). The pressures of society and popular culture pushed us away from that which gave us meaning and completion, to the point that we were dismembered, *perdidas.* We were trying to affix pieces that did not belong, pieces that were foreign to our bodies, and were only making us sick.

Chicana/o Latina/o Ska music became a medium through which I could sing and dance the pain away. The image of young brown bodies everywhere,

fists in the air, expelling all their energy and rage, has done wonders for my soul, and continues to make my heart dance to this day. "Estan bailando como indios," my mother-in-law exclaimed when she saw young kids skanking in her backyard. And I thought, yes, yes they are. They are returning, making themselves whole again.

When I read Anzaldúa's work, it is like having an intimate conversation. Her words allow me to reflect on the ways I have resisted and challenged White supremacist and heteropatriarchal systems of oppression from a very young age—*perdida a veces,* but still rebelling against and navigating some type of inequality. In my process of conocimiento, I fell ill and was damaged along the way. I became lost at times, confused, taking the wrong turn. It was through rejecting the desconocimientos about who I am in relationship to self and others that I realized my family and community have always had what I needed for my recovery. Once I began this process of knowing myself in relationship to others, I realized the tools to my liberation were there all along; I was just too blind to see it then.

ENDNOTES

1 Disidentification is a term coined by José Muñoz, defined as "the survival strategies the minority subject practices in order to negotiate a phobic majoritarian public sphere that continuously elides or punishes the existence of subjects who do not conform to the phantasm of normative citizenship" (4). In this case, my engagement with Ska allowed me to work with pre-existing racial-ethnic identities, while at the same time resisting and recreating our own understanding based on our experiences. We were not only challenging American normative standards as people of color, but also Mexican and Latina/o normative practices through this subculture which became a third space for many Mexican and Latina/o youth.

2 Disidentification in this sense meant a rejection of my racial, ethnic, cultural, and linguistic identity. As a person of color, it became difficult to identify with my ethnic identity because it did not readily fit into American normativity. Thus, even disengaging becomes part of the disidentification process.

3 It is important to acknowledge that the term skank has been commonly used as a derogatory term to describe a "promiscuous" female. But within Ska and Reggae, the term has been adapted to describe the style of dancing that is done to the music. The Merriam-Webster dictionary defines it as: a rhythmic dance performed by swinging the arms while bending the knees especially to reggae or ska.

WORKS CITED

Anzaldúa, Gloria E. ***Borderlands/La Frontera: The New Mestiza.*** San Francisco: Aunt Lute Books. 2012. Print.

Arellano, Leticia Higuera. ***A Subculture of a Culture: A Hermeneutic Study of the Latina/o Chicana/o Punk Experience.*** Diss. Wright Institute Graduate School of Psychology, 2011. Retrieved from ProQuest. (UMI Number: 3475507).

Augustyn, Heather. ***Ska: The Rhythm of Liberation.*** Lanham: Scarecrow Press Inc. 2013. Print.

Heathcott, Joseph. "Urban Spaces and Working-Class Expressions Across the Black Atlantic: Tracing the Routes of Ska." ***Radical History Review,*** 87 (2003) : 183-206. Web.

Hebdige, Dick. ***Subculture: The Meaning of Style.*** New York: Routledge. 1979. Print.

Muñoz, José E. ***Disidentifications: Queers Of Color And The Performance Of Politics.*** Minneapolis: University of Minnesota Press. 1999. Print.

EXPLORING THE TENSIONS IN VISIONS OF THE FUTURE: EXAMINING TRANSSEXUAL MASCULINITY AND QUEER NATION-BUILDING IN CHERRÍE MORAGA'S *A XICANA CODEX OF CHANGING CONSCIOUSNESS*

MICHAEL LEE GARDIN

"To assert the emergence of transgender studies as a field only in the 1990s rests on a set of assumptions that permit a differentiation between one kind of work on "transgender phenomena" and another, for there had of course been a great deal of academic, scholarly, and scientific work on various forms of gender variance long before the 1990s." —Susan Stryker and Aren Z. Aizura

The changing shape of feminist, queer, and transgender discourses, theories, and concerns can be documented in various ways, and my effort in this essay is to think through continued dialogues between transgender scholars and activists and non-trans scholars, specifically women of color feminists, since the conceptualizing of the academic discipline that has come to be known as transgender studies. I would like to be immediately transparent in my outsider positions—positions of privilege—as a white queer and non-trans scholar.

Barbara Cameron asserts: it is not "only third world people [who] are responsible for speaking out against racism," and it is not just queer individuals responsible for speaking out against homophobia (51). I embark on this exploration of transgender and feminist scholarship because of my belief that it is not just transgender and transsexual people or people of color who must think through gender and sexuality at play with racialization, ethnicity, class

stratifications, and national identity, if a different and just world is a goal. While exploring trans and non-trans feminist conversations, contentions, and rifts is nothing new, investigating recent publications can illuminate successes and failures of visions of just futures.

Since the 1980s, women of color feminists have crafted multiple concepts and visions for different futures. These futures are often queer futures, even if such writings are frequently marginalized or left out of genealogies of queer theory.[1] The writings of Gloria Anzaldúa and Cherríe Moraga, co-editors of the foundational women of color feminist text *This Bridge Called My Back: Writings by Radical Women of Color*, are treated as contemporaries by many; I similarly treat the works in conversation because of the ways their writings offer visions for radical transformation. Throughout her writings, Gloria Anzaldúa articulates what she calls new tribalism. AnaLouise Keating describes new tribalism as a disruptive category that redefines previous ethnocentric forms of nationalism (5). Anzaldúa's notion deconstructs nationalism, and she even asserts her distrust in nationalism when it causes people to erect walls—delineating borders and boundaries of supposed belongings. Anzaldúa says, "we [that is, Chicanas feminists, many of us dykes], looked for something beyond just nationalism while continuing to connect to our roots... We have returned to the tribe, but our nationalism is one with a twist" (*Interviews/Entrevistas* 185). How does new tribalism translate to a radical praxis for social justice work, for radical pedagogy, or for radical interventions in university settings, in institutional disciplines and knowledge-production? Anzaldúa's conceptualizations of new tribalism relate to her notions of planetary citizenship. She understands herself not only as from a particular tribe, or ethnic or racial group, but also as a citizen of the universe, open to interacting with others, that is, with other ethnic groups and interacting with other cultures and ideas (Anzaldúa, *Interviews/Entrevistas* 185). How does this theorization of interconnectedness relate to the rifts and tensions between activist-scholarship and pedagogy within the fields of feminism and transgender studies? Can such visions of an alternative world-making provide illumination to recent works that further codify divides rather than unions in activist-scholarship and writing? I use Anzaldúa's concept of new tribalism as a point of departure from which I wish to ask new questions, especially about texts involving divisive rhetoric regarding trans people in visions for social justice. Specifically, I ask questions of Cherríe Moraga's visions of queer nation-building. I investigate Moraga's mobilizations of queer radicalism in the 2011 publication, *A Xicana Codex of Changing Consciousness: Writings, 2000-2010,* because of the ways Moraga often invokes and simultaneously redefines nationalism, a queer nationalism.

In "Queer Aztlán: the Re-formation of Chicano Tribe," Moraga proposes a re-tribalization, a new Chicano nation, not one in which Chicana lesbians

and gay men are merely included, "but [one] strong enough to embrace a full range of racial diversities, human sexualities, and expressions of gender" (164). According to Moraga, a new Chicano nationalism calls for "the integration of both the traditional and the revolutionary, the ancient and the contemporary. It requires serious reckoning with the weaknesses in our mestizo culture, and a reaffirmation of what has preserved and sustained us as a people" ("Queer Aztlán" 174).

In "Queer Aztlán," Moraga outlines this re-tribalization of Chicana/os, which includes resisting occupation of land and resources, resisting the occupation of the bodies of women and queer people, and recognizing a global community. She argues the necessity of "invent[ing] new ways of making culture, making tribe, to survive and flourish as members of the world community in the next millennium" ("Queer Aztlán" 174). At this stage of Moraga's writing trajectory, her queer nation or re-tribalization and Anzaldúa's new tribalism resemble similar visions for different futures.

Moving forward, Moraga situates her most recent text in a certain type of lineage. She names her book a codex and explains how it follows in the tradition of "the pre-Columbian manuscripts [which] offered images of flora and fauna, myth and history, genealogy, war, and ritual—from the mundane practices of daily life to ceremonies of great sacrifice" (xvi). According to Moraga, the "Mesoamercian codices" function to "create a cartography of time and place and of the divine energies animated through them" (xvi). Moraga says her text reflects "a map of [her] own journeying in the first decade of a new century – as writer, teachers, mother, daughter, and lesbian lover" (xvii). Furthermore, Moraga uses an X in chicana and chicano to "indicate a re-emerging política, especially among young people, grounded in Indigenous American belief systems and identities" (xxi). The X reflects "the Indian identity that has been robbed from us [Chicanas/os] through colonization" (Moraga xxii). According to Moraga, since "many Raza may not know their specific indigenous nation of origin, the X links us as Native people in diaspora" (xxi).

In *Xicana Codex,* Moraga continues to put forth and simultaneously disrupt a type of nationalism, and I hope to illuminate her vision of a queer nation in this text. Moraga's nation-building project becomes one that concerns trans men of color. I address how queer nation functions with regard to her generalizations and misrepresentations of black and brown trans masculinities. Finally, rather than separate and parcel out Moraga's thoughts about trans men, fragmenting her work without doing its messages justice, I question what can be gained by reading Moraga's assertions about trans men of color concurrently with how indigeneity is presented and functions in the text. I argue such a reading illuminates the limitations of her construction of a queer nation. A recognition

of these limitations can further or contribute to examinations of continuities and discontinuities of feminist, queer, and trans people, scholarship, and activism.

In an effort to trace Moraga's politicized articulation of queer in the chapter titled "Still Loving in the (Still) War Years/ 2009: on Keeping Queer Queer," I recognize it is through Moraga's premise of the threat of queer erasure that she specifies a vision of queer's potential and use. Moraga begins by looking back on her "warriorship," her past writings against the disappearance of queers, Natives, Mexicans, women (175). In fact, the chapter is structured around Moraga's framing of a threat to queerness. Within this frame, she illustrates her assertion of the political power, potential, and use of *queer.* She describes and critiques what she sees as a new lesbian arena of butch and femme "performances" that rely on and reify patriarchal and capitalist masculinities and objectifications of women as "irresistible object[s] of desire" (Moraga 177). Moreover, Moraga critiques the movement for marriage equality in the underlying desire for recognition and participation in the heterosexist, patriarchal, and racist structures of society. Moraga also correlates these critiques with her problematic discussion of the emergence of trans identities and embodiments as "technology [that] might actually afford us the opportunity to *choose* our gender" (177).[2] Significantly, Moraga associates queerness with freedom, while questioning "what happened" to it (177). She laments recent changes, ones she interprets as moving away from radicalism: "as these political and societal 'gains' present themselves to us, we have to look more deeply into what may be truly liberating about non-conformist queer identity, so as not to confuse 'progress' with progressive politics" (Moraga 177). In short, Moraga exemplifies the utility she sees in queer in the potential for radical critique and movement toward transformation.

Yet, Moraga fears "the transgender movement," which she implicitly relates to "plain ole peer pressure," and how it may "preempt young people from simply residing in that queer, gender ambivalent site for as long and as deeply as necessary" (184). Furthermore, Moraga fears that "technology" but also the lives, bodies, and identities of trans men could result in butch lesbians becoming "a dying breed, headed for extinction" (186). Finally and more generally, Moraga situates trans identities and trans people as a threat to queer resistance, equating transition with "conspiracy...[where what] were once sites of political and cultural opposition in U.S. society," are now conspiracy, "not to free our queer bodies through technology, but ultimately to have us fall in line with society's mandates about gender and desire" (188). Significantly, the direction of Moraga's fears and her deployment of queer political strategy here, that is, her queering of the nation, are not toward those promoting or perpetuating norms or hegemonic iterations of heterosexist, sexist, racist, classist ideologies, but instead toward trans men of color, who may be *queers themselves,* or nonetheless seemingly allied

with other peoples rendered non-normative by Western ideologies, institutions, and practices.

Moraga's perceived fears play out in her effort to keep queer "queer," which result in a certain type of policing of trans men and their identities and bodies. Moraga speaks of trans men as a threat to womanhood, butch lesbians, and gender ambivalence. Her argument relies on assumptions that devalue or do not acknowledge trans men's agency and assumptions that inply that radicalism can be prioritized based on gender identification and representation. First, in her fears that trans identities are dangerous in terms of their threat to radical gender ambiguity and gender variance "without the aid of surgery or hormones," Moraga fails to recognize the nuances of trans lives (Moraga 184). For example, not all trans people, including trans men, will undergo or desire to undergo medical transition, such as through hormone therapy and surgery. And those who do seek out medical transition do not have the same journeys or desired endpoints. Transitions are not homogeneous. Susan Stryker's definition of transgender as "the movement across a socially imposed boundary away from an unchosen starting place – rather than any particular destination or mode of transition" exemplifies this diversity (1). In a response to "Still Loving in the (Still) War Years," Morgan Callado says, Moraga's statements "reduc[e] the trans* experience to those just transitioning. It erases all of those trans* identified folks who are pre-op or non-op and who do exist in that space. The two are not mutually exclusive" ("On Actually Keeping Queer Queer"). Moraga also prioritizes non-op gender ambivalence as "more radical" by identifying non-transsexual gender variance as a site of resistance while generalizing and aligning transition with normalization. Moraga herself explains how there cannot be a ranking of oppression (*Loving* 46). A ranking system, whether of oppressions or of prioritized identities and bodies based on their level of perceived radicalism, obscures and halts any effort or chance for coalition building. Julia Serano calls this subversivism, which I will analyze in more depth below. In associating transition with peer pressure, as if it were a tempting fad, Moraga misconstrues transition as something monolithic and even simplistic. This ignores the variety of experiences of trans people and trans embodiments, including experiencing violence, invisibility, hostility, misgendering, and the repetitive need to defend and explain one's gender, all of which show the need to acknowledge the complexities and *specificities* of the lives of trans people. So while Moraga paints transition as tempting, alluding to her suspicion of its "tempting" connection to male privilege and heterosexuality, she in fact simplifies the nuanced realities of the lives of trans men.

Moraga assumes a decisive position. That is, Moraga's argument sets forth her presumed ability to determine whether or not trans people are queer and/or

engender queer resistance, as she decisively correlates transition with normalization. Indeed overwhelmingly, Moraga's discussion of trans people consigns them to being a threat to queer resistance. She posits: when queers "become good, law abiding, [...] legally married male citizens from whom biology lines up perfectly with social gender construction" then "'queer liberation'" ceases to exist (Moraga 188). However, in her conclusion, Moraga then assigns "queer" to transgender, declaring that "no amount of surgery or hormones really removes the 'queer' from transgender. There is no complete assimilation, no erasing of a person's queer, gender-dissonant history" (188). She seems to be the deciding agent of trans men's queerness. She reveals her presumption that she understands transition, the origins of one's decision to transition, and the journey/process itself (falsely representing it as singular) in all its manifestations, as not a matter of an individual's life and agency, but a "sell out" to mainstream ideologies. And in many ways, Moraga's findings rely heavily on what transgender writers have pointed out as a misunderstanding—the thought that transition is about *sexuality* rather than gender identity. By this I mean, Moraga seems to present transition for young men of color as something motivated by their sexual desires for women. In others words, Moraga suggests trans men transition to appear to the world as a heterosexual man—as if transition were an undertaking to fit heteronormative society's normative regimes of "coherence" between sex, gender, and desire. But time and time again trans writers delineate gender identity, gender expression, and gender roles from sexuality in being distinct even if mutually constitutive.[3] Moraga does not address trans men's agency and ability and need to self-name—which includes whether or not trans men decide to identify as queer.

I see a very real need to understand *why* Moraga senses such threat and how a reading can contribute to understanding the functions, uses, and possibilities for queer. On one level, Moraga's efforts to keep queer "queer" serves as an example of the possible pitfalls, limitations, and dangers of politicizing identity as a strategy, and that is exclusion—exclusion in the space where inclusion, alliance, and coalition would allow for greater visions of a better future. However, it is limiting to assume that strategic political representation is always already doomed to failure; instead a clear picture of *what is at stake* in Moraga's deployment of such a strategic representation can guide us to a deeper understanding. First, it seems Moraga's attempt to uphold her ideas of radical queer politics rely heavily on her effort to "preserve" womanhood. Moraga's pleas for trans men to "hold on to womanhood" because there is "something in being born female from a female in a female-hating world that still matters" (189). In "Still Loving," Moraga laments and wishes to cease to "lose" "[her] macha daughters to manhood through any cultural mandates that are not of our own making" (186). Callado explains that this line of argumentation is sadly similar

to the rhetoric used by "homophobic people of color who posit that queerness is something that belongs to whiteness" which erases and trivializes queer people of color as if they don't exist—or if they do their "queerness is imported from white culture" and their "identities shaped from cultural mandates that are not their own" ("On Actually Keeping Queer Queer"). Thus, Moraga's claim that transition is a "sell-out" to hegemonic culture reads as: transsexuality is a "white people thing."[4] To further understand her efforts to stabilize and uphold womanhood, I turn to both Moraga's discussion of indigeneity and Suzanne Bost's reading of Moraga's mestiza identity in her earlier works.

Throughout *A Xicana Codex*, Moraga anchors her politics in a remembering of and connection to indigeneity. Her *Xicana* politics highlight the specificity of the lives of women of color in the context of colonialism or neocolonialism. Her emphasizing of indigeneity and her related turn to pre-colonialization provides us with access to a layered analysis of her claims. Bost argues that "mestizaje, for Moraga and for others, reflects a simultaneously racial, sexual, national memory, an embodiment of colonization and conquest" (9). Perhaps Moraga's insistence on womanhood is an insistence on the significance of the past. Bost says, "sex at the origins of miscegenation led to [...] obsession with sex and women's bodies as the site of potential racial transgressions—which explains how race, nation, sex, and sexuality are so interwined in representation of mix-race subjects" (Bost 9). In fact, according to Bost, "bodies that are racially, culturally, and/or nationally mixed then are expected to respond to multiple different standards of what counts as male and female, masculine and feminine" (133). Reading Moraga's upholding of a stabilized notion of womanhood, then, could be representative of the complexities of sexual and racial identities, the cultural and social expectations that come along with such, and an emphasis on memory of a colonial past and its persistent effects.

Moraga's insistence on upholding "womanhood" reflects her assertion of the need to center the memory of the history of colonial oppression of women of color within feminist and women's and gender studies conversations. Moraga's text deploys a politicized stance by invoking indigeneity, even in the genre itself because by naming her work codices, Moraga acknowledges and brings into consciousness pre-colonial codices and the colonial violence of erasure. Throughout the text, Moraga exemplifies the need to prioritize remembering, that is, remembering "the Xicana Indígena story: the story of displacement, amnesia, exile, orphanhood, rape, and genocide" (42). Moraga's declaration that "womanhood matters" and her fear of "losing [her] macha daughters to manhood through any cultural mandates that are not derived of our own making," therefore, should be read with her efforts to center women of color voices, needs, and histories as significant and vital in feminist discourses and

movements (186). To use Bost's words, Moraga works to "[retain] a memory of the historical circumstances at the origins of mixture in the Americas: the violent racial and sexual oppressions" (13). In fact, even more than 20 years after the publication of *This Bridge Called My Back*, Moraga explains how "to date...few politically progressive movements in this country have fully incorporated the specificity of the woman-of-color experience into their analyses of oppression and their liberation strategies" (29). The shortcomings Moraga points out here are further exemplified and specifically related to her chapter discussing her relationship with Gloria E. Anzaldúa. She explains that when she learned the new publication of *this bridge we call home* and learned "the new collection was to include men and white women, [she] decided not to contribute to the book, not out of the politic that can be dismissed as 'exclusion,' but due to what [she] perceived as strategic in terms of the further development of U.S. women-of-color feminism" (122-123). How does this connect to Moraga's fear for queerness because of what she perceives as the threat of trans men? Moraga says: "We [women of color] had yet to effectively develop a national network of coalesced women-of-color organizing, or a women-of-color theory and practice which might incorporate a new generation of Indigenous peoples and immigrants..." (123). Therefore, for Moraga, including gay men of color, white women, trans people, etc. would work against the "need for an autonomous dialogue within" because the movement "had not arrived at a place of such inclusion" (123). According to Moraga, to center women of color within feminism is to not "diverge" and include other voices. In Moraga's effort to center the specificity of experiences of women of color, especially in terms of colonial history, and to center the transformative power of queerness, she seems to suggest trans men are "giving up on womanhood," diverging from or even trivializing the discussions of women of color and queer women of color politics.

Moraga's discussion might risk ignoring the histories and consciousness of trans men of color and their possible relations to women-of-color feminism as well as their recognition of colonization and resulting patriarchal cultural narratives. According to Callado, "numerous queer people of color organizations across the country," including trans* youth, "are attempting to define masculinity, and femininity, for themselves," such as "The Brown Boi Project," which "focuses it's framing of Black and Brown masculinity within the contexts of anti-oppression and gender justice and works towards community wellness" ("On Actually Keeping Queer Queer"). Similarly, bi-racial transgender writer, Logan Gutierrez-Mock, discusses the overlappings, intersections, and contradictions of his identity: "It was only through coming out to my family as transgender, and claiming my heritage, that I began to feel at home with my family" (229). While his light skin color often result in large racial misidentifica-

tions, Gutierrez-Mock comments on the dark skin of his sister relating to her "sell out" position in the family's eyes, echoing a historical narrative of colonialism, as his sister became "*la malinche (*the betrayer) and the fucked one" because of her "act of turning her back on her family" (230). Gutierrez-Mock explains how his transition has challenged his family's assumptions about machismo and heteronormativity, while simultaneously catalyzing his resistance to his past anglocization.[5] He says, "I've created a new male identity within my family—an identity that embraces my female past while insisting on my biracial transgender present: queer/mestizo/ trans machismo" (234-235). As a transgender man and as a writer, Gutierrez-Mock does not diverge attention or value from the specificity of women of color realities. Instead, he acknowledges them, highlights results of patriarchal oppression, and attempts to deconstruct machismo and reconstruct a different masculinity. Trans men of color have a unique and specific history, one related to the history and specificity Moraga centers within feminist discourses. White transsexual scholar Jean Bobby Noble situates many trans men *within* feminism as "sons of the movement," discussing his past feminist activism—a history he claims "quite proudly" in his text (22). Noble asserts the ability, and in fact, the unique ability, in having perspective on feminism and masculinity, to contribute to redefining masculinity in non-phallic embodiments of non-hegemonic and pro-feminist masculinities. This is of course not the perspective or stance of all trans men, but certainly one that must be in conversation with Moraga's conclusions about trans men of color's masculinities. Recognizing trans men's agency to go about participating in a society with the effects of colonialism in ways different from dominant masculinities and seeing some challenges trans men write of the roles patriarchal cultural narratives construct for men demonstrate how the concerns and experiences of trans men, such as Gutierrez-Mock's, might *not* represent a divergence from Moraga's effort. Rather, trans men of color arguably have similar stakes in decolonizing and transforming the Western ideologies about sex and gender that are enacted violently upon multiple bodies that fall outside the realm of "normal."

But there seems to be more than a centering of women of color in Moraga's queer nation-building at play. I look to one particular moment where Moraga sets up a dynamic using the image of a Two-Spirit person. Moraga connects indigeneity and queerness-as-rebellion. She explains that "three decades after the birth of the Chicano movement, indigenous belief systems—as a life practice and a radical politic—are applied with new vigor to Chicano activism" (Moraga 183). She queers this application, looking to "historical models of resistance—to pre-conquest, pre-slave trade, pre-capitalist-patriarchy worldviews" to "uncover a roadmap to being viably queer in the twenty-first century" (187). She narrates her interaction with a Two-Spirit person in Tejas:

> s/he could move from woman to man to boy, to sister, to lover. This is what it means to be "two-spirit," I thought; that literally the male and female spirits, all their genetic messages and chemical energies, reside within the same body and are made manifest. (Moraga 187-188)

She situates her definition of Two-Spirit as rebellion, and she fears "América" threatens to "defrock" queers of their "queer powers," that is, of rebellion (Moraga 188). She calls for defenders of desire because she fears disappearance. She writes as the "queer Xicana mother" that she is, she wishes to convince a younger generation "that our disappearance is at stake here: as people of color, as queer people, as Indigenous people" (Moraga 188-189). According to Moraga's assertions, potential for rebellious queerness lies in looking to an indigenous past. In other places in her text, Moraga repeats this dynamic, where she understands 1) trans men of color and 2) Two-Spirit people and/or genderqueer embodiments and expressions as mutually exclusive. Perhaps this is a result of her understanding that trans men (and to be clear, she is really speaking specially about trans men who seek medical transition) 'assimilate' and 'erase' one's "queer, gender-dissonant history" (188). For Moraga, transsexual men are mainstreaming, like gay marriage, wherein queer people are "selling out" or committing an act of betrayal to queer liberation have one's biology line up perfectly with social gender construction, therefore damaging queer liberation.

This trend is not entirely new. Stryker writes that while transgender people were organizing with and among gay and lesbian activists, "it suddenly became fashionable on the left to think of transgender people as antigay and antifeminist" ("Why the T in LGBT is Here to Stay" 200). Furthermore, what Moraga's positioning and decisions regarding trans men *does not* account for is any agency of whether trans men of color do or wish to see themselves within certain brands of queer liberation efforts. Max Wolf Valerio, transsexual American Indian and Latino writer and performer, explains in his 2006 text *The Testosterone Files: My Hormonal and Social Transformation from Female to Male,*

> Changing sex is radical because it is extreme, far-fetched, and magical, not because of any imagined alliance to any particular political ideology. Being transsexual has nothing to do with being part of a unilateral political movement, a religion, or a cult. It is not my particular job to reeducate society and change it to some utopian, or possibly dystopian, multigendered blob. (5)

So we might ask ourselves what type of political expectations and assumptions are placed onto trans people by non-trans people, individuals and groups who might seemingly be allies, but are outsiders nonetheless.

To return to the image of a Two-Spirit person that Moraga positions in the chapter as a model for queer liberation, a concept from transsexual feminist

writer, activist, and performer Julia Serano proves helpful. She names a trend she finds in queer and trans activism "subversivism." Subversivism is the "practice of celebrating and extolling certain gender and sexual expressions and identities simply because they are nonconforming" (Serano 346). In other words, subversivism occurs when certain transgressive genders are "good" because they "subvert" oppressive binary gender norms (346). Serano critically observes a popular account occurring in multiple venues, with a certain reading of recent queer theorists as its backing; she writes,

> [people read how] all forms of sexism arise from a gender binary system, and since the gender binary system is everywhere, in our thoughts, language, traditions, behaviors, etc. – the only way we can overturn it is to actively undermine the system from within. Thus, in order to challenge sexism, people must have genders that function to bend, break, and blur all the imaginary distinctions that exist between men and women, presumably leading to a system wide binary meltdown. (346)

So what happens, according to Serano, is that in queer and trans communities, there is a celebration of subversive or transgressive expressions and identities. This seems to be a way of "accommodating a seemingly infinite array of genders, but this is not quite the case because subversivism has an 'other'" (Serano 347). Serano explains that "by glorifying identities and expressions that appear to subvert or blur gender binaries, subversivism automatically creates a reciprocal category of people" whose identities and expressions "are by default inherently conservative, even 'hegemonic,' because they are seen as reinforcing or naturalizing the binary gender system" (Serano 347). And often, transsexual masculine men and feminine women, in being deemed not "subversive enough," run the risk of being called sexist.

When one type of gender identity and/or expression get valued more highly than others, even in being called "good," "cool," "bold," or "transgressive" etc., while others are deemed "bad" or conservative, a new hierarchy is created (Serano 348-349). And as Serano reminds us, resisting others placing meanings onto our gender and sexual identities and expressions is often what brings many of us to feminism and queer efforts in the first place (359-360). Serano's notion of extolling some genders over others can be useful in terms of how Moraga sets up a dynamic between her image of a Two-Spirit identity and transsexual men of color. However, I believe Serano's notion cannot just be applied to Moraga because it does not fully take race and the context of colonialism into account. In other words, for Moraga, there is more at stake than just a gender binary system. In many ways, the hierarchy Moraga sets up in this chapter is one where trans men are just consigned to be not just agents of an oppressive binary gender system, but agents of neocolonialism.

In the end, Moraga does decide to include trans men of color in her queer nation. She writes, "the young transman asks me to really see him, to not write him off so easily, to not suspect that he has abandoned me, us, his mothers, sisters" (Moraga 189). And she explains how the man opens her eyes and she interprets a "promise in this/his change" (Moraga 189). Moraga says, "I feel him oddly my queer… like I feel my own blood boy… and a member of my queer nation" (Moraga 189). Thus, further meditation on nation, on nationalism, or on tribe, on tribalism, or really the relation between them become vital. What do we make of a project of nationalism or of a queer nationalism in a time of neocolonialism? In earlier "Queer Aztlán," Moraga proposes, imagines, and at the same time subverts a type of nationalism. The Moragan visions of queer nationalism here and the Anzaldúan tribalism seem related, certainly not contradictory. But I remind us that Anzaldúa says she breaks with nationalism when walls are erected. In the conceptualization of a queer Chicano nation in the chapter of her most recent text, Moraga invokes an image of Two-Spirit identity and erects walls by casting suspicion upon trans men of color as agents of neocolonialism.

Perhaps one rationale for the suspicion has to do with how Moraga sees Two-Spirit identity and medical transition as mutually exclusive, even contradictory. Valerio might provide a more complex picture. He writes,

> changing sex is an act of subverting nature's implacable authority […] Transsexual men are real. Nature is an evolving paradigm of conflicting tendencies and escalating discoveries; transsexuals hold a fun house mirror up to nature. We reimagine identity, sexuality, biological sex, and gender. (Valerio 2)

He continues "I live my life inside an ongoing paradox. Ambiguity and peril. *Postmodernism suits me. And sorcery. A shaman has three marks to indicate that he or she has completed initiation: scars, a new name, a secret*" (3). I bring the works of Valerio and Moraga into dialogue not to proclaim anything definitive about Valerio's identity or even about Two-Spirit identity, but instead to perhaps complicate Moraga's decided binary of transsexuality and Two-Spirit being. Deborah Miranda provides an extensive tracing of Two-Spirit peoples and a description of gendercide of peoples she calls "joyas," coining a term that signifies those living in the time of pre-conquest and the time of Spanish colonialism of California (353-355). Miranda explains that through the destruction of spiritual traditions such as burials and ceremonies, through disease, violence, that is—"murder, renaming, regendering, and replacement – the *joya* gendercide was carried out" (359). Miranda argues that, still, "the joya identity did not disappear entirely," because "contemporary California Two-Spirits are the rightful descendants of joyas" (360). While Miranda does

not speak about medical transition, I hope to highlight the nature of this understanding of Two-Spirit identity. For Miranda, Two-Spirit is a name to alert others and "remind ourselves that we have a cultural and historical responsibility to the larger community" including working to attend to "a balance of energies" (360). According to Miranda, "we are still learning what this means....maybe this will be the generation to figure it out" (360). So again, while this does not provide commentary specifically with regard to transition or even the relationships between transgender identity and Two-Spirit identity, Miranda's writing illuminates some complexities surrounding Two-Spirit identity, as one that functions to urge attention to the necessities of the roles of Two-Spirit people, but also an identity with meaning still in process, in the state of becoming, which suggests and presupposes unanswered questions, including questions about embodiment.

Moraga's outlines of and reflections on her nation-building efforts display her combating of erasure and disappearance. Moraga's discussion of her—and other Xicana/os'—indigenous roots, can be understood as similar to Gloria E. Anzaldúa's coining of the term *new tribalism,* as a coalition of peoples to forge a mestiza/o nation. According to Anzaldúa, new tribalism as a social identity can "motivate subordinated communities to work together in coalition" (185). Anzaldúa recognizes how crafting and promoting new tribalism "may unwittingly contribute to the misappropriation of Native cultures, [and] that [she] (and other Chicanas) will inadvertently contribute to the cultural erasure, silencing, invisibility, racial stereotyping, and disenfranchisement of people who live in real Indian bodies"(186-187). She says she fears "unknowingly helping the dominant culture remove Indians from their specific tribal identities and histories" (187). But according to Anzaldúa, she feels the imperative of something such as new tribalism and related discussions outweighs the fear of detribalization. Emma Pérez's theoretical model of the decolonial imaginary can help to inform this reading of Moraga. Movement toward decolonization, according to Pérez, happens in a third space—a space where differential politics and social dilemmas can be negotiated. Moraga could be working within that third space, moving toward decolonization. And specifically, the importance of work toward coalition, and Moraga's work against cultural genocide, racist erasures, and the multiplicitous products of colonialism cannot be overstated.

Furthermore, Driskill, Justice, Miranda, and Tatonetti explain that "many Indigenous GLBTQ2 people define Two-Spirit identity as once a point of continuity with tribal traditions and a statement of contemporary intertribal identity and politics," thus showing that the term cannot be drawn along an analytical distinction between 'traditional' and 'nontraditional' (14). According to these authors, in addition to eschewing a clear distinction between "ancient"

and contemporary, the term also eschews a clear distinction between local intratribal specificities and something more pan-tribal. Furthermore, the authors describe how the term intended to become "an indigenously defined pan- Native North American term that bridges Native concepts of gender diversity and sexualities with those of Western cultures" (13). Contributors argue that "by disrupting colonially imposed and internalized systems of gender and sexuality, Indigenous queer and Two-spirit critiques can move decolonizing movements outside of dominant logics and narratives of "nation"' (19). The choice of the contributors of this Two-Spirit anthology in defining Two-Spirit as a *bridge* is significant and worth considering further. Anzaldúa stresses: "people who are initiating a new politics of difference and who are the carriers of difference must have boundary-crossing visions" ("The New Mestiza Nation" 209). She posits the insufficiency of inscribing traditional cultural models that "set up a we-are-right/they-are-wrong binary opposition" (Anzaldúa, "The New Mestiza Nation" 209). She repeatedly uses the image of a bridge: the bridge as the need to recognize boundary crossing, in identity and in racial separatism; the bridge as the person (including herself), that is, the initiator of and the site of possibilities for transformation; and the bridge as the process of mediation. I return to Anzaldúa to point to my attempts to think through some of Moraga's moves in queer nation-building and to inspire further consideration of visions and strategies for transformation and better futures.

The potential for Moraga's understanding of trans men of color to erect walls in her queer nation is not the only concern I would like to conclude with. As so many scholars, writers, and activists demonstrate, recognition of power and privilege have to be at the forefront of organizing and of activist-scholarship, something the women's movements, civil rights movements, gay and lesbian movements, and respectively women's and gender studies, ethnic studies, and queer studies have taught us in this century. Patricia Elliot writes, "trans and non-trans person have enormously different stakes in the debates that traverse the newly designated field of trans studies," and while this should not equate to a silencing of non-trans voices, "acknowledging those stakes is a crucial matter," when one's "personal integrity and material well-being are not affected by their outcome" (5). In taking seriously "outcomes" of visions for transformation offered by Anzaldúa, Moraga, and others, I hope to suggest further explorations of these "stakes" continue. In fact, not only does this essay attempt to suggest a thorough examination and negotiation of privilege with regard to trans identities is vital, but I also hope for my analysis to inspire further commitment to acknowledging and engaging with the diversity of theoretical and political positions about gender, sex, sexuality, and identity, while at the same time thinking through the competing and contending points, the ruptures they make, and their implica-

tions—because as Elliot states, "serious engagement is also critical engagement, which means one includes points of disagreement rather than avoiding them" (15). In sum, working through the rifts, recognizing the bridges, and critically examining the material or perceived boundaries between queer, feminist, and trans activist-scholarship could be an essential part of working toward a just future.

ENDNOTES

1 See Michael Hames-García's "Queer Theory Revisited" in *Gay Latino Studies: A Critical Reader.* Eds. Michael Hames-García and Erensto Javier Martínez. Durham: Duke University Press, 2011.

2 Moraga's representation of gender identity and especially transsexual identity as simply a choice echoes sentiments Julia Serano describes as unrecognized cissexual privilege, wherein non-transsexual identities are understood to be a complex mixture of intrinsic dispositions, social construction, social conditioning, and elements of decisions and choices, while those who medically transition are thought to have a gender identity only explained by "choice" rather than acknowledging that the same complexities affect all people living in the West within our current gender/sex system.

3 See Serano's discussion of the consistent misunderstanding of MTF transition as always motivated by a desire to be—not just heterosexual—but an object of sexual attraction of heterosexual men and her discussion of the damaging results of this misunderstanding.

4 In my reading of Moraga's assumptions about trans men in constructing transsexuality as a "white thing," I must also stop to recognize this transsexuality-as-white-import is presented in the text without a real discussion of access. By this I mean, medical transition very well might be a privilege as it is costly and requires a certain navigation through the Western medical institution, and because of the ways racism and class function, white trans people may have access to and/or seek out medical transition more frequently or with more ease. However, access is not the focus of this construction in Moraga's text.

5 In fact, Gutierrez-Mock explains how his development in terms of his gender identity and his experiences with gender transition become the moments and also means through which he is able to deal with his past white-identification, cultural erasure, etc. It is difficult not to hear the similarities between Gutierrez-Mock's description here and Moraga's telling of how coming out as and coming to terms with her lesbianism facilitated her consciousness of her anglocizing, her class, and her ability to theorize and challenge multiple and complex oppressions at multiple axes of power in her essay "La Güera."

WORKS CITED

Anzaldúa, Gloria E. and Cherríe Moraga Eds. *This Bridge Called My Back: Writings by Radical Women of Color.* New York: Kitchen Table: Women of Color Press, 1981. Print.

Anzaldúa, Gloria E. *Interviews/Entrevistas.* Ed. AnaLouise Keating. New York: Routledge, 2000. Print.

-----. *The Gloria Anzaldúa Reader.* Ed. AnaLouise Keating. Durham: Duke University Press, 2009. Print.

Bost, Suzanne. *Mulattas and Mestiza: Representing Mixed Identities in the Americas, 1850-2000.* Athens: The University of Georgia Press, 2003. Print.

Callado, Morgan. "On Actually Keeping Queer Queer: A response to Cherrie Moraga." *XQsí Magazine.* XQsí Magazine, 13 Apr. 2012. Web. 25 Apr. 2014.

Cameron, Barbara. "Gee, You Don't Seem Like an Indian from the Reservation." *This Bridge Called My Back: Writings by Radical Women of Color.* Eds. Gloria Anzaldúa and Cherríe Moraga. New York: Kitchen Table: Women of Color Press, 1981. 46-52. Print.

Driskill, Qwo-Li, Chris Finley, Brian Jospeh Gilley, and Scott Lauria Morgensen. *Queer Indigenous Studies: Critical Interventions in Theory, Politics, and Literature.* Tucson: The University of Arizona Press, 2011. Print.

Elliot, Patricia. *Debates in Transgender, Queer, and Feminist Theory: Contested Sites.* Burlington: Ashgate Publishing, 2010. Print.

Gutierrez-Mock, Logan. "F2Mestizo." *Nobody Passes: Rejecting the Rules of Gender and Conformity.* Ed. Mattilda AKA Matt Bernstein Sycamore. Emeryville: Seal Press. 228-235. Print.

Keating, AnaLouise. "Risking the Personal: An Introduction." *Interviews/Entrevistas.* Ed. AnaLouise Keating. New York: Routledge, 2000. 1-15. Print.

Miranda, Deborah A. "Extermination of the *Joyas*: Gendercide in Spanish California." *Transgender Studies Reader 2.* Eds. Susan Stryker and Aren Z. Aizura. New York: Routledge, 2013. 350-363. Print.

Moraga, Cherríe L. "La Güera." *This Bridge Called My Back: Writings by Radical Women of Color.* Eds. Gloria Anzaldúa and Cherríe Moraga. New York: Kitchen Table: Women of Color Press, 1981. 27-34. Print.

-----. *Loving in the War Years: Lo que nunca pasó por sus labios.* Expanded Second Edition. Cambridge: South End Press, 2000. Print.

-----. "Queer Aztlán: the Re-formation of Chicano Tribe." *The Last Generation: Prose and Poetry.* Boston, South End Press, 1993. 145-74. Print.

-----. *A Xicana Codex of Changing Consciousness: Writings, 2000-2010.* Durham: Duke University Press, 2011. Print.

Noble, Jean Bobby. "Sons of the Movement: Feminism, Female Masculinity and Female to Male (FTM) Transsexual Men." *Atlantis* 29.1 (2004): 21-28. Print.

Pérez, Emma. *The Decolonial Imaginary: Writing Chicanas into History.* Bloomington: Indiana University Press, 1999. Print.

Serano, Julia. *Whipping Girl: A Transsexual Woman on Sexism and the Scapegoating of Femininity.* Berkley: Seal Press, 2007. Print.

Stryker, Susan and Aren Z. Aizura. "Introduction: Transgender Studies 2.0" *Transgender Studies Reader 2.* Eds. Susan Stryker and Aren Z. Aizura. New York: Routledge, 2013. 1-12. Print.

Stryker, Susan. *Transgender History.* Berkley: Seal Press, 2008. Print.

-----. "Why the T in LGBT is Here to Stay (2007)." *Finding Out: An Introduction to LGBT Studies.* Eds. Deborah T. Meem, Michelle A. Gibson, and Jonathan F. Alexander. Los Angeles: Sage, 2010. 198-200. Print.

Valerio, Max Wolf. *The Testosterone Files: My Hormonal and Social Transformation from Female to Male.* Seal Press, 2006. Print.

"CROW IS THE LEFT-HANDED GUARDIAN WHO DOES NOT LET THE PAST EAT US UP": UTOPIAN HORIZONS, COALITIONAL MODELS, AND *RESSENTIMENT* IN KATHI WEEKS'S *THE PROBLEM WITH WORK* AND GLORIA ANZALDÚA'S *EL MUNDO ZURDO*

MAGDA GARCÍA

On May 10, 2013, Kathi Weeks, Women's Studies Associate Professor and Director of Graduate Studies at Duke, gave a keynote address, titled "Feminism, Marxism, and the Refusal of Work," as part of the Commoning Precarity: No Work, Refusal, and Autonomy conference held at the University of California, Santa Barbara. Defined as a state of life without predictability or stability, precarity has become a concept through which to recognize the increasingly permanent lack of employment and link the experiences of (former) workers. While Weeks insisted upon the importance of gender in building collectivities amongst (former) workers during her talk, she stated that she does not take into account Women of Color feminist theory, particularly Gloria Anzaldúa's scholarship, because it is too "narrow" and "replicates the very identities we need to move away from." As the only Chicana graduate student in a room overwhelmingly filled with white faculty and students, I felt silenced and my history, self, and work erased by Weeks's remarks. Thus, I undertake Anzaldúa's concept of El Mundo Zurdo as a response to claims that Chicana feminism replicates divisive identities and argue that El Mundo Zurdo not only recognizes the reality of our always already gendered and racialized bodies as it calls for an activism that enables the creation of new and as yet unknown subjectivities and

collectivities, but that it is also an anti-capitalist intervention that emerges from the materiality of a specific site, namely the Rio Grande Valley. More specifically, I examine how the concept of El Mundo Zurdo presents a utopian project that accounts for historical context and the materiality of race as it calls for the transformation of our very selves and embraces a multitude of political visions, thereby not only challenging the charge of *ressentiment* that Weeks implicitly levies in *The Problem With Work: Feminism, Marxism, Antiwork Politics, and Postwork Imaginaries* against people of color movements and intellectual thought but also resisting the traps of utopian thinking that Weeks discusses and laying bare the assumptions of whiteness as non-identity and non-race undergirding Weeks's conceptualization of utopian projects. By so doing, I assert that there is an ignored materialism and implicit material critique that undergirds Anzaldúa's El Mundo Zurdo, and indeed her broader theorization, and that such materialism and critique implicitly resists the recreation of a work ethic, thereby displaying antiwork politics and a postwork utopian horizon whose very coming into being is predicated upon harnessing the gendered, queered, and racialized identities that capitalism creates in its unending exploitative quest while working to dismantle racial essentialism.

Weeks's *The Problem with Work*, to which her talk made reference, examines and critiques how antiwork politics and postwork imaginaries have been deployed by 1970s Anglo-American feminist projects, and the lessons we can learn from such movements as part of her larger focus on shifting the conceptualization and discussions surrounding work from the ethical to political arena. Weeks is particularly concerned with the need to embrace ambiguity and willingness to undo the structures that produce our very identities and subjectivities. Weeks's concerns and hopes for current and future feminist projects come through in her chapter on utopian projects, titled "The Future is Now: Utopian Demands and the Temporalities of Hope." Because of the need to embrace ambiguity, Weeks uses the term "postwork imaginary" as a placeholder given we have yet to think of work in ways that are "postwork." Indeed, one of Weeks's main critiques of socialism is that it presumes to know too much about how the future should/will look like, which underestimates the depth to which work has been ingrained in and even constitutes us.

Throughout *The Problem with Work*, as in her talk, Weeks focuses on 1970s Anglo-American Marxist/Socialist Feminism, such as Maria Dalla Costa and Selma James' 1971 *The Power of Women and the Subversion of the Community*. Weeks explains that she focuses specifically on this feminism because it publicizes, politicizes, and transforms the Marxist understanding of work (24). Nevertheless, Weeks is critical of the projects pursued by said feminism and uses the category of the refusal of work as a tool with which to reconfigure

each of these focuses by providing correctives and additions to 1970s Marxist feminism (24). Weeks seeks to acknowledge and intervene in the ways in which this feminism has reproduced its own version of the work ethic by focusing its critique on work's organization, distribution, and valorization rather than on the ethics and morality undergirding work. She explains that 1970s feminism has done this in two specific ways: first, by establishing waged labor as the means of women's emancipation from gendered domestic labor and, second, by demanding a valorization of and wages for housework. By so doing, feminism reifies work. While Anzaldúa's scholarship is not explicitly Marxist or primarily focused on transforming the Marxist understanding of work, her concept of El Mundo Zurdo, as further discussed below in regard to El Mundo Zurdo as a model of coalition building, is shaped by the materiality of race and sees the potential for transformation as located within the very identities that are created by capital's endless pursuit of cheap labor. Most significantly, El Mundo Zurdo, which is above all a utopian project, is a prime example of how both the challenges to utopian thinking and the traps into which 1970s Anglo-American Marxist/Socialist feminist utopian projects fall identified by Weeks in 2011 are recognized, articulated, and negotiated by 1970s/80s Chicana feminists such as Anzaldúa.

One of the central reasons that Weeks focuses on Anglo-American Marxist/Socialist projects is because she believes that they exhibit a commitment to "thinking within a horizon of utopian potential" and transformation (29). In "The Future is Now," Weeks focuses on the utopian aspects of such projects and examines them from the stance of the present moment in order to ascertain what caused utopianism to be decried as incompatible with the political and consequently abandoned. In other words, she tries to understand how the utopianism that flourished during the 1960s and 1970s came to be denigrated as simple impossibility in subsequent decades. To this end, Weeks examines the work of Karl Popper and Francis Fukuyama to identify the two ways in which utopianism came to be seen as utterly unconnected with our social reality. Furthermore, she places Ernst Bloch and Friedrich Nietzsche in conversation with each other in order to flesh out the ways in which a functional utopianism necessitates particular understandings of the past, present, and future and the relationship between each. It is the challenges that Weeks's discussion of Bloch and Nietzsche bring to the fore that concern this paper since they illuminate Anzaldúa's complex understandings and negotiations of the past, present, and future in her articulation of El Mundo Zurdo, or The Left-Handed World.

Using Nietzsche's concept of *ressentiment*, which Weeks (influenced by Wendy Brown's discussion of racial melancholia) describes as "characterized by a structure of desire more backward-looking than anticipatory" and an investment

in past historical injuries, Weeks explains that utopian projects may be faced with the temptation of falling into *ressentiment*, thereby allowing historical injuries to dictate the view of the present and envisioning of the future (185). In other words, utopian projects that are too focused on the past run the risk of being reactionary rather than being generative or creative. While Weeks does not cite any examples of such projects or scholarship, she does state that projects that hinge upon or place particular significance on history tend toward being reactionary. This view, coupled with Weeks's remarks about Women of Color feminism and Anzaldúa, clearly render the work of people of color, whose concern is with historical subject formations, as always already at risk of falling into *ressentiment*. This is not to say that cases of *ressentiment* in Chicana/o scholarship do not exist, but rather that this scholarship is diverse and even contradictory to each other, as the two genealogies that can be discerned within Chicana/o Studies show: namely, the genealogy that emerges from Chicana feminism and that which emerges from the Chicano Movement. Indeed, Chicano scholarship that clearly exhibits *ressentiment*, even against the work of Chicana feminists, continues to be produced. Jorge Mariscal's 2005 *Brown-Eyed Children of the Sun: Lessons from the Chicano Movement, 1965-1975*, which revisits the Chicano Movement and criticizes Chicana feminist scholars, is an example of *ressentiment* at work as Marsical attempts to recuperate a certain masculinity and nationalism. Interestingly, Weeks quotes the late queer Latin@ performance studies scholar José Esteban Muñoz as she describes the demands of working toward utopian horizons: "Utopian fragments might require more of us; to borrow José Muñoz's description of what it might take to access queerness as a utopian horizon, 'we may indeed need to squint, to strain our vision and force it to see otherwise, beyond the limited vista of the here and now'"(213).[1] However, as Muñoz attests throughout his body of work, his work on queerness emerges from a Women of Color/Chicana genealogy that is best exemplified by *This Bridge Called My Back*, edited by Cherríe Moraga and Gloria Anzaldúa.

Nevertheless, it is Anzaldúa's work that has been at the forefront of advocating for transformation. Moreover, while Anzaldúa is clearly concerned with history and race, she has also been at the forefront of letting go of race's primacy as she works toward El Mundo Zurdo and a planetary tribalism, which leads us to the second challenge identified by Weeks. Namely, that the development of utopian projects requires that we recognize and accept that a utopian future means doing away with the very structures that constituted the subjectivities with which we are familiar, including ours. Nevertheless, Weeks, using Bloch's work, recognizes

1 The quote Weeks references is from Muñoz's chapter, titled "Queerness as Horizon: Utopian Hermeneutics in the Face of Gay Pragmatism," in A Companion to Lesbian, Gay, Bisexual, Transgender, and Queer Studies (2007). It is Weeks's only reference to Muñoz.

that the development of utopian projects requires the negotiation of a relationship between the past and future. Weeks describes this as a relationship between the "real-possible" and the "novum," the two concepts central to what Bloch sees as a "concrete utopia," or a utopia that is a necessary extension of our political practice and imagination (194). However, Weeks seems to regard this negotiation as possible only when undertaken by white feminist projects; in other words, those feminisms that are not perceived as inherently shaped by race. Of course, this assumes whiteness as a non-race and non-identity. Without addressing this issue, utopian projects will ultimately replicate colorblindness. Moreover, Weeks states, "Hoping as an exercise of concrete utopianism does not ignore the present as it has come to be; it is not inattentive to history. On the contrary, it must be cognizant of the historical forces and present potentials that might or might not produce different futures; the present is a fulcrum of latencies and tendencies" (196). Nonetheless, even though Weeks turns to terms such as "the novum," as well as "eternal return" and "overman," in the work of Bloch and Nietzsche, respectively, in order to challenge the view of utopianism as irrational, she implicitly accuses the very work that has dealt with these theoretical challenges while acknowledging the importance of the past as instances of *ressentiment* and racial melancholia simply because this work is put forth by Women of Color feminist scholars.

Weeks asserts that the label "socialism" not only obscures the fact that the Marxist and socialist feminist tradition "was willing to affirm the value of utopian speculation about a radically different future," but also assumes that said utopian horizon "could be named and its basic counters predetermined" (30). Thus, Weeks uses the label "postwork society" not to anticipate an alternative so much as to point toward a horizon of utopian understanding (30). Anzaldúa's concept of El Mundo Zurdo, as a model of coalition building, is explicitly predicated upon a utopian horizon and centered upon the coming to be of something that Anzaldúa readily embraces as yet unknown.

Identified by AnaLouise Keating as one of Anzaldúa's frequently underexplored concepts, El Mundo Zurdo appears in Anzaldúa's early works, specifically in her 1977 poem titled "The coming of el mundo surdo," as well as in her 1979 autoethnographic essay "La Prieta," her contributions to the 1983 *This Bridge Called My Back*, and the 1990 *Making Face, Making Soul/Haciendo Caras: Creative and Critical Perspectives by Feminists of Color*. What is significant about the first mention of El Mundo Zurdo is Anzaldúa's choice to spell "Zurdo" with an "S" in order to contextualize her work within the specific geo-political space that is the Rio Grande Valley, where the "Z" is pronounced softly. By so doing, Anzaldúa speaks to the material reality out of which the concept emerges. Yet, this is not a material reality that is destined to remain static and Anzaldúa refuses

to kneel before deterministic ideologies. Rather, El Mundo Zurdo is the coming to be of a different way of being. Indeed, one of the stanzas to "The coming of el mundo surdo" reads: "I am becoming-being / the questor the questing the quest / You and I have already met / We are meeting we will meet" (37). Similar to Weeks's discussion of the "not yet" in regard to Bloch's concept of "the novum," Anzaldúa embraces the ambiguity of the future through the use of the phrase "becoming being" (37). Moreover, by describing the path that forms the coming of "el mundo surdo" as a walking together "through walls by the lunar / light see our / left-handedness / with our third eye" Anzaldúa signals toward the concept as a utopian horizon that can be intuited only through the light of the moon, the hand less accustomed to use, and our inner vision, thereby recognizing that we cannot glimpse this horizon simply through our understanding of the present or past (36). The poem continues, "I am the unmoving center / Within my skin all races / sexes all trees grasses / cows and snails implode / spirals lining thought / to feeling" (36-37). Anzaldúa's assertion that all races are within her is not just metaphorical, but signals toward a critique of colonialism's and whiteness's oversimplification of race by mystifying, obscuring, and attempting to erase the historical class and racial diversity, tensions, and contradictions of what we now understand as whiteness. By so doing, Anzaldúa refuses to essentialize race, but nevertheless recognizes the force that is whiteness and seeks to dismantle it. She similarly mentions race and blood in "La Prieta," as I discuss below.

In "La Prieta," Anzaldúa acknowledges the negotiation that must take place between the past, present, and future, describing El Mundo Zurdo as, "The pull between what is and what should be" (49). She further writes, "I believe that by changing ourselves we change the world, that traveling El Mundo Zurdo path is the path of a two-way movement—a going deep into the self and an expanding out into the world, a simultaneous recreation of the self and a reconstruction of society. And yet, I am confused as how to accomplish this" (Anzaldúa 49). Anzaldúa's assertion that "by changing ourselves we change the world" is not simply a new age sentiment, but rather recognition that seeking to transform, instead of merely reform, our present social structures also means transforming ourselves since it is the very structures that we are trying to change that produce our subjectivities. Similarly, in *This Bridge Called My Back*, Anzaldúa speaks to the Third World Feminist project and recognizes how material reality shapes even our innermost selves and desires: "We must recognize the effects that our external circumstances of sex, class, race, and sexuality have on our perception of ourselves--even in our most private unspoken moments" (196). By so doing, Anzaldúa readily accepts that the development of a utopian project means desiring and working toward a future in which our current subjectivities will not be reproduced, nor should this reproduction be desirable, and pushes us to

begin practicing the necessary disidentification in the present. At the same time, Anzaldúa acknowledges that she does not know what the path to El Mundo Zurdo should look like, but is willing to embrace the ambiguity and contend with the uncertainty.

Uncertain about what the path to El Mundo Zurdo looks like, Anzaldúa delves into her multiple identities and lived experiences. Significantly, the image of blood, which undergirds the construction of race, is central. In "La Prieta," she writes, "The mixture of bloods and affinities, rather than confusing or unbalancing me, has forced me to achieve a kind of equilibrium. Both cultures deny me a place in *their* universe. Between them and among others, I build my own universe, *El Mundo Zurdo*. I belong to myself and not to any one people" (49). However, in this case blood is instead used to signal the mixtures of race and histories that are always already present in blood, but obscured and simplified by colonialism and whiteness. Moreover, Anzaldúa is clearly willing to question and, as her later work on planetary tribalism further reveals, eventually let go of race: "I was terrified because in this writing I must be hard on people of color who are the oppressed victims. I am still afraid because I will have to call us on a lot of shit like our own racism, our fear of women and sexuality" (39). Her statement disrupts any attempt to accuse her of, or read her work as an example of, racial melancholia or *ressentiment*. Rather, Anzaldúa's sense of being betrayed by her culture keeps her from romanticizing race and, indeed, from establishing race as central to the concept of El Mundo Zurdo. In other words, because of the psychical violence that Anzaldúa recognizes as having suffered at the hands of her family she knows that privileging race will not lead to a truly liberatory project.

Nevertheless, Anzaldúa does not dismiss race, but instead incorporates it into her critique of capitalist and patriarchal oppression: "I can't discount the fact of the thousands that go to bed hungry every night. The thousands that do numbing shitwork eight hours a day each day of their lives. The thousands that get beaten and killed everyday. The millions of women who have been burned at the stake, the millions who have been raped. Where is the justice to that?" ("La Prieta" 49). Anzaldúa evokes the past witch burnings in Europe alongside present-day Ciudad Juárez femicides and mundane violence against women. By so doing, Anzaldúa presents an intersectional antiwork critique that links the past and present. Moreover, Anzaldúa's linking of "numbing shitwork" with other forms of violence leads us to understand El Mundo Zurdo as a utopian project that is not likely to replicate forms of the work ethic as is the case with Anglo-American Marxist/Socialist feminism.

The charge of *ressentiment* levied against Anzaldúa is further dismantled by examining her discussion of privilege in the introduction to *Making Face, Making*

Soul, titled "Haciendo Caras, Una Entrada." In this section, Anzaldúa's understanding of the past as something that we must negotiate and history as something that can be theorized differently is explicitly made known: "Our strength lies in shifting perspectives, in our capacity to shift, in our 'seeing through' the membrane of the past superimposed on the present, in looking at our shadows and dealing with them" (xxvii). Anzaldúa then shares a medicine story about a crow fascinated with her own shadow and writes, "Crow is the Left-Handed guardian who does not let the past eat us up" (xxvii). Thus, Anzaldúa clearly understands that the past has the capacity to cloud our envisioning of a different future. By creating a new mythology, Anzaldúa is able to call forth a figure to protect us from being consumed by and with the past as we work toward the as yet unknown future that is El Mundo Zurdo and, by so doing, seeks to ward off racial melancholia and *ressentiment*. Anzaldúa further writes, "Encrucijadas, haunted by voices and images that violated us, bearing the pains of the past, we are slowly acquiring the tools to change the disabling images and memories, to replace them with self-affirming ones, to recreate our pasts and alter them—for the past can be as malleable as the present" (xxvii). Thus, she theorizes the past as something that can be changed, which shows her engagement and complication of the relationship between the past, present, and future. In "El Mundo Zurdo," a piece located in *This Bridge Called My Back*, Anzaldúa states, "The vision of our spirituality provides us with no trap door solution, no escape hatch tempting us to 'transcend' our struggle. We must act in the everyday world" (217). Thus, Anzaldúa deems it important to conceptualize history as changeable because it provides a way to keep us from being consumed by the past, which is of utmost importance because retreating into the past offers a false sense of security and liberation when in actuality no other exit or true form of liberation exists than the ambiguous path to an as yet unknown future.

Thus, Anzaldúa incorporates a diverse array of subordinated knowledges as she challenges the demarcations laid out by ethnic nationalist, feminist, and Marxist/Socialist movements. She not only embraces the ambiguity of the "becoming-being," but recognizes that, in embracing this unknown, she is unsure of what the path toward this becoming should look like and is willing to go beyond being simply and blindly reactionary against whatever insults, women, Chicanos, etc.: "That which is insulted I take as part of me, but there is something too simple about this kind of thinking. Part of the dialectic is missing. What about what I do not identify as?" ("La Prieta" 47). By so doing, Anzaldúa rejects the walls erected between race, gender, sexuality, and class differences, particularly as mobilized by different movements, while also making it clear that the utopian horizon that El Mundo Zurdo represents is not possible by ascribing wholesale to any one movement, including the feminist movement. Anzaldúa's assertions

lend nuance to the utopian horizon that Weeks envisions and, I argue, reveal that Weeks's utopian model, for all its embrace of the unknown, ultimately inhibits this unknown by seeking to stitch together class and hegemonic feminist movements without interrogating how each of these movements must actually be transformed. In other words, Weeks extends the walls of each movement over each other's perimeter and way of thinking. As Anzaldúa succinctly explains in her section on El Mundo Zurdo in *This Bridge Called My Back*, "The change evoked on these pages is material as well as psychic. Change requires a lot of heat. It requires both the alchemist and the welder, the magician and the laborer, the witch and the warrior, the myth-smasher and the myth-maker" (218).

For Weeks, the refusal of work is a model of resistance (against both the modes of work imposed upon us and their ethical defense) and a struggle for a different relationship to work (26). However, as my discussion of utopian projects reveals, there are particular assumptions regarding racial identity and coalition building undergirding the refusal of work. Weeks further states that a different relationship toward work is potentially capable of emerging from the collective autonomy that a postwork ethics and increased nonwork time would help us achieve (26). However, we must ask whether a postwork ethics that dismisses the work of women of color, work that recognizes the linkages between work and other forms of violence, is capable of being truly anti-capitalist. Most significantly, for Weeks work is not just a site of oppression and exploitation, but also a site of revolutionary potential. Yet, she overlooks the excesses and identities that emerge from capitalism when it is these very excesses and identities, according to Anzaldúa, that are the sites from which revolutionary potential and critique is capable of emerging: "The rational, the patriarchal, and the heterosexual have held sway and legal tender for too long" ("La Prieta" 50). Moreover, as Roderick Ferguson so poignantly argues in *Aberrations in Black: Toward a Queer of Color Critique*, racialization is always already gendered. For Ferguson, whose work is very much influenced by a Women of Color feminist genealogy, a critique of capitalism becomes possible through the subjects and identities that are created by capitalism's unwavering search for cheap, exploitative labor but stand in opposition to the subjects and identities desired and sanctioned by the state. Thus, Anzaldúa and Ferguson lead us to understand work as the site where capitalism's demand for cheap, exploitable labor confronts the identities and subjectivities privileged by the state. Doing otherwise means that we are not truly accounting for the depth at which work creates particular subjects and serves as a site of revolutionary potential. This is further significant considering that Weeks states, "Work is not only a site of exploitation, domination, and antagonism, but also where we might find the power to create alternatives on the basis of subordinated knowledges, resistant subjectivities, and emergent

models of organization" (29). Indeed, El Mundo Zurdo functions as a model of coalitional politics by allowing all those who do not fit into the above description (rational, patriarchal, heterosexual) to come together in solidarity. In other words, Anzaldúa presents a coalitional politics centered explicitly around difference: "We are the queer groups, the people that don't belong anywhere, not in the dominant world nor completely within our own perspective cultures. Combined we cover so many oppressions. But the overwhelming oppression is the collective fact that we do not fit in, and because we do not fit in, we are a threat" ("La Prieta" 50). Moreover, "We do not have the same ideologies nor do we derive similar solutions. Some of us are leftists. Some of us practitioners of magic. Some of us both. But these different affinities are not opposed to each other" ("La Prieta" 50). Thus, difference is not homogenized, but functions instead as a locus of power. Moreover, Anzaldúa recognizes the importance of multiplicity when it comes to working toward a utopian project. Nevertheless, Weeks regards the work of scholars who focus on unearthing and practicing subordinated knowledges as ways to re-envision the future and models of coalition building as tinged with *ressentiment.*

Though Weeks seeks to embrace the ambiguity of the future and establishes work as a site of both domination and revolutionary potential, she stops short of fully articulating a coalitional politics. While articulating a coalitional politics may not be central to her project, her dismissal of Women of Color feminist theory, and particularly a theorist such as Anzaldúa, whose work focuses on transformation and planetary citizenship, nevertheless reveals that race grounds the identity politics she sees as divisive. Thus, those with racially marked bodies enter into an antagonistic model of coalition building in which whiteness is replicated as a non-racial identity. In "La Prieta," Anzaldúa describes being pulled in different directions by the Chicano, Third World, and feminist movements. She further elaborates, "Then there's my allegiance to the Gay movement, to the socialist revolution, to the New Age, to magic and the occult. And there's my affinity to literature, to the world of the artist. What am I? A third world lesbian feminist with Marxist and Mystic leanings. They would chop me up into little pieces and tag each piece with a label" (45). Thus, Anzaldúa attempts to work through the issues regarding identity politics that Weeks discusses and, rather than oversimplify or dismiss, she instead seeks to envision a form of coalition building centered around difference.

Though Weeks's regard of Anzaldúa's work as an example of the *ressentiment* exhibited by Women of Color feminist scholars clearly shows a misreading and overlooking of Anzaldúa's sophisticated theoretical understandings of time and space, Weeks's comments nevertheless signal toward a broader issue, namely that the material critiques embedded within the work of Women of Color/Chicana

feminist scholars, work that speaks to a "politic born out of necessity," fail to be noticed and we are consequently left out of discussions that seek to decipher and meet the challenges posed by late capitalism (*This Bridge Called My Back* 21). Indeed, the fact that I was the only Chicana graduate student present at the Commoning Precarity: No Work, Refusal, and Autonomy conference speaks to this omission.

Finally, by engaging Anzaldúa's concept of El Mundo Zurdo as a utopian project in which material critiques are implicitly and not so implicitly embedded, rather than simply recuperate El Mundo Zurdo as part of Chicana feminist history I instead seek to build toward the larger project of resituating Chicana third space feminist theory within the twenty-first century Rio Grande Valley in South Texas, a site which my project seeks to loosen from strictly U.S. boundaries and to use as a tool to examine the conceptual apparatus that is third space within Chicana feminist theorization during this moment of late capitalism. The concept of third space within Chicana feminist theorization is not simply metaphorical, but emerges from a specific geo-political space. However, this has been overlooked in subsequent applications of the term. In anchoring my project in the materiality of the Rio Grande Valley, I resist abstraction and dehistoricization. I argue that looking at the Rio Grande Valley as a laboratory for modernity will guide us as to how to preserve and further the epistemological value of a third space within Chicana feminist theorization. Moreover, I situate my analysis of Chicana third space feminism within a third-world feminist studies framework and, as such, Marxist theory also informs my analysis as I strive to return, from a Chicana/o Studies standpoint, to a discussion of the material while locating the Rio Grande Valley within a hemispheric context in an effort to recognize the work of women of color and Chicanas such as Anzaldúa as forming a genealogy of decolonial thought.

WORKS CITED

Anzaldúa, Gloria. "The coming of el mundo surdo." *The Gloria Anzaldúa Reader*. Ed. Ana Louise Keating. Durham: Duke UP, 2009. 36-37. Print.

---. "El Mundo Zurdo." *This Bridge Called My Back: Writings By Radical Women of Color*. 3rd ed. Ed. Cherríe L. Moraga and Gloria E. Anzaldúa. Berkeley: Third Woman Press, 2002. 217-218. Print.

---. " La Prieta." *The Gloria Anzaldúa Reader*. Ed. Ana Louise Keating. Durham: Duke UP, 2009. 38-50. Print.

---. "Haciendo Caras, Una Entrada." *Making Face, Making Soul: Haciendo Caras*. Ed. Gloria Anzaldúa. San Francisco: Aunt Lute, 1990. xv-xxviii. Print.

Ferguson, Roderick. *Aberrations in Black: Toward a Queer of Color Critique*. Minneapolis: University of Minnesota Press, 2004. Print.

Moraga, Cherríe L. and Gloria E. Anzaldúa. *This Bridge Called My Back: Writings By Radical Women of Color.* 3rd ed. Berkeley: Third Woman Press, 2002. Print.

Weeks, Kathi. *The Problem with Work: Feminism, Marxism, Antiwork Politics, and Postwork Imaginaries*. Durham: Duke UP, 2011. Print.

MESTIZA CONSCIOUSNESS AND *LA FACULTAD* IN THE BORDERLANDS: JOSEFINA LÓPEZ'S *DETAINED IN THE DESERT*[1]

TREVOR BOFFONE

I change myself, I change the world. —Gloria Anzaldúa

INTRODUCTION

On April 23rd, 2010, the Arizona government grabbed headlines with the introduction of the controversial and unconstitutional Arizona Senate Bill 1070, officially the Support Our Law Enforcement and Safe Neighborhoods Act, better known as Arizona SB1070. At the time, it was the most severe law against undocumented immigration that had been passed in the recent history of the United States, making it illegal for all immigrants that did not possess the appropriate documentation to be in Arizona. The act required that police detain people who they suspected to be in the country without proper authorization, thereby promoting racial discrimination. This xenophobia and ethnic intolerance is what inspired Chicana playwright Josefina López to write her play *Detained in the Desert* (2010),[2] which deals with questions about the discriminatory nature and the consequences of this law. The play serves as an appeal to action in which the playwright utilizes the feminist teachings of Gloria Anzaldúa and the new Mestiza consciousness toward the development of *la facultad* with the objective

of establishing a more active Chicana Feminist Movement that will ignite a new wave of borderlands activism. One of the play's two protagonists, Sandi Belén (a fair-skinned second-generation Latina who doesn't speak Spanish), experiences racial discrimination because of Arizona SB1070 and, subsequently, decides to conceptualize a feminist ideology and a new way of thinking and self-defense, Anzaldúa's notion of *la facultad*. Sandi receives this epiphany as a consequence of having been racially profiled and consciously deciding to fight against the oppressive forces that society imposes on women of color. In ***Detained in the Desert***, Josefina López manifests the need for Chicanas to develop survival tactics such as *la facultad* in the face of social oppression by highlighting the transformation of Sandi, who acquires consciousness about her identity as a result of the injustice(s) she faces on the US/Arizona border because of Arizona SB 1070.

CHICANA FEMINISM: ANZALDÚA, LA FACULTAD, AND (BORDERLAND) IDENTITY POLITICS

In the 1970s and 80s, Chicana feminists began looking to their own experiences as a platform to theorize the multiple forms of oppression and deconstruct the systems of thought that had threatened their well-being and continue doing so. Within this search for identity, a new identity politics emerged from these internal and external struggles. In "Chicana Feminism and Postmodernist Theory," Paula Moya points out that "...just as Chicanas' political activism and struggles are often based on a certain theoretical knowledge, that knowledge is frequently produced in their experiences of political struggle" (445). This calls attention to a realist theory perspective in order to explain the conflicts that one experiences; it intends to focus on these conflicts with the goal of creating a new and more desirable social order for women.

According to a realist theory, identity, experience, and individual knowledge are inextricably connected. This theory is based on the concept that race, class, gender, and sexuality—one's social location—are relevant experiences mobilized on the formation of identity (Moya and Hames-Garcia 136-41). In other words, one's interpretation of an event depends on how it is conceptualized from one's understanding of one's relationship with the people and context of the event. By deciphering the event in such a way, one must acquire a political stance, which leads to an alteration in which the historically oppressed individual begins to imagine "the emergence of qualitatively new desires, social relations, and modes of association" (Gilroy 37). In accordance with a realist theory of identity, "identities are politically and epistemically significant because they reveal the links between individuals and groups and central organizing principles of the society" (Moya, "Chicana Feminism" 467). By theorizing the process of forming one's identity, the functions of ideology and oppression are revealed. Specifically, identity is constructed based on one's

experience as a woman and as oppressed in order to apply theories to explain society and contextualize such experience.

Gloria Anzaldúa imagines the development of a mestiza consciousness in *Borderlands/La Frontera* that makes knowledge of oneself and one's place in society possible.[3] In *Borderlands*, the border functions primarily as a metaphor in the sense that the border space as a geopolitical region converges with discourses of class, gender, sex, ethnicity, and sexual preference. The text serves as a call to action, a process to "uncover our true faces, our dignity, and self-respect" (Anzaldúa 108). She highlights the most significant dichotomy with respect to our thoughts between the subject and object. By refusing restrictions according to one's gender, race, and class, the new Mestiza establishes herself in a more powerful position in which she is capable of balancing multiple cultures and fighting oppressive forces and intolerance. According to Beth Berila, "Anzaldúa interrogates dominant conceptions of nation and identity, exploring whether and how it might be possible to develop a sense of national identity that doesn't exclude and do violence to women and men of color and those who are poor or queer" (121). Anzaldúa writes, "I seek our woman's face, our true features, the positive and the negative seen clearly, free of the tainted biases of male dominance. I seek new images of identity, new beliefs about ourselves, our humanity and worth no longer in question" (87). This conception of mestiza consciousness allows the woman to better understand the oppressive forces that surround her, making possible a dialogue about the new history of Chicana subjectivity. By formulating a gendered discourse, the text functions as a "new conceptualization of consciousness's relation to the world" (White 121). The new mestiza questions the traditional gendered dualities and the relationship that this imposes on women. The Chicana subject rejects such an established division as well as its implications with respect to self-representation (Licona 104).[4] This consciousness motivates the woman and her search for unbiased knowledge about herself and her position in the world. Such self-understanding is necessary in order to cultivate political agency and action. By imagining a better society, the Chicana feminist is capable of creating a dialogue about the indispensable efforts, directions, and actions to provoke change.

Mestiza consciousness is based on the demand to develop self-defense tactics, which Anzaldúa calls *la facultad*, a strategy that marginalized people can employ. *La facultad* marks the awakening of the individual in which she begins to exist; it represents the moment when the person loses her innocence and ignorance, producing a change in perception that adds meaning and multiple interpretations to the way the person sees society and the world. Anzaldúa posits:

> This shift in perception deepens the way we see concrete objects and people; the senses become so acute and piercing that we can see through

> things, view events in depth, a piercing that reaches the underworld (the realm of the soul). As we plunge vertically, the break, with its accompanying new seeing, makes us pay attention to the soul, and we are thus carried into awareness – an experiencing of soul (Self). (39)

By experiencing the soul and, therefore, gaining self-enlightenment, the woman obtains consciousness in order to employ a feminist agency. This consciousness and self-understanding demonstrates the paths that the Chicana takes with respect to the actions, directions, and efforts that she must experience in order to fight against oppression. Anzaldúa supplies the structural changes that enable the Chicana's liberation (Adams 26).

BORDERLANDS CHICANA ACTIVISM: SANDI BELÉN'S PSYCHOLOGICAL TRANSFORMATION

Detained parallels the stories of Sandi Belén and Lou Becker, whose lives converge in the Arizona desert. After refusing to show proof of citizenship, Sandi is sent to an immigrant detention center. Meanwhile, Lou is kidnapped by three siblings whose brother has been killed by a hate crime influenced by Lou's program, "Take Back America." While Sandi is being deported, her bus crashes and she becomes stranded in the desert. Simultaneously, Lou is freed by one of his kidnappers and meets Sandi during his journey home. By helping each other survive in the harsh desert, Sandi and Lou come to fully understand the hardships of the undocumented immigrant across the Arizona desert.

By situating her play on the border, López is able to illustrate, as Castillo and Tabuenca Cordoba posit, Anzaldúa's "gesturing toward a more heterogeneous transnational space of identity formation" (3). The border highlights a privileged site of operations in which those with light skin are given higher sociopolitical standing. To this end, Sandi, as a woman of color, must develop an oppositional consciousness and awareness of the system of oppression in the Arizona/Mexico borderlands. Therefore, the action that drives *Detained in the Desert* is Sandi's psychological transformation and acquisition of consciousness and *la facultad*, thus manifesting López's main goal: the ascent of a new dialogue towards Chicana consciousness. Through this new form of seeing the world and critical thinking, Sandi serves as an exemplary model of one intending to renegotiate the traditional power paradigm.[5] She reinforces Anzaldúa's ideology of the political and psychological situation of the Mestiza only changing through the removal of masks and disguises that hide them. It is indispensable that Sandi brings the audience (or reader) to a catharsis with the end result being the comprehension of the ways in which Josefina López theorizes and constructs Chicana experience and identity. The play details the self-exoneration that the protagonist undergoes by recognizing the oppressive dichotomies and the ways

in which she should alter herself. As a recent university graduate, Sandi is in the process of returning to her community with questions about how she will utilize her education. These issues drive the action of the play (T. López 18). With her new vision of the world, she realizes that she must embrace her true identity in order to make a change become reality.

La facultad functions as a survival tactic for Chicanas, allowing her to adjust to threatening circumstances that surround her. According to Paula Moya, "With origins in experiences of pain and trauma, *la facultad* involves a loss of innocence and an initiation into an awareness of discrimination, fear, depression, illness, and death" ("Chicana Feminism" 469). Moreover, Chela Sandoval explains the development of *la facultad* as a process marked by constant shifting and changing:

> In order for this survival skill to provide the basis for a differential and unifying methodology, it must be remembered that la facultad is a process. Answers may be only temporarily effective, so that wedded to the process of la facultad is a flexibility that continually woos change. ("U.S. Third World Feminism" 23)

Sandi's behavior in *Detained* represents a wide panorama: at the beginning of the play she is seen as innocent, but, through her understanding of the world, she abruptly loses her innocence in the process of developing an oppositional consciousness. Sandi realizes that the world does not change by itself, but that we are the ones that provoke change. Anzaldúa claims, "The struggle has always been inner, and is played out in the outer terrains. Awareness of our situation must come before inner changes, which in turn come before change to society. Nothing happens in the 'real' world unless it first happens in the images of our heads" (87). The individual must experience a psychological shift, crossing an emotional borderland, before a legitimate change can occur in the outside world. After her experience with the police, Sandi will be ready to give voice to her political agenda and begin the process of becoming a political agent. Crossing the psychological border seems to provide a more distanced reflection that allows her to better evaluate the oppression that people of color, specifically those appearing to be of Mexican descent, face on a daily basis in the Arizona borderlands under the current political climate.

Nevertheless, the principal transformation that drives the play is not her first. While she is imprisoned, Sandi explains the shame that she has carried with her with respect to denying her origin. She tells of the first time she understood discrimination when she attended a primarily Anglo elementary school. A White student had lice and the school examined all of the Latina/o students, an event that implied that the White teachers believed that Mexican students were the primary carriers of lice. Sandi states, "When we were all returned to our classes,

everyone laughed at us. Nobody wanted to be our friend because they thought they would get lice from us" (J. López 51). This event elevated her consciousness, but, showing her need to survive she decided to change her identity with the goal of integrating into the Anglo community. Just like Cherríe Moraga explains in "La Güera," Sandi realized that "White was right. Period" (31). Sandi learned to be White and assimilate to the school's dominant culture in order to survive this difficult period of her adolescence; this day represented her acceptance into the dominant ring of society. Her recognition of the school's existing class system, essentially a microcosm of the United States, functions as the catalyst of her first transformation, the mere intent to survive. Anzaldúa reinforces this notion, speaking to the violent othering of Chicanos and other people who do not adhere to dominant Anglo-American culture. Anzaldúa declares:

> Gringos in the U.S. Southwest consider the inhabitants of the borderlands transgressors, aliens – whether they possess documents or not, whether they're Chicanos, Indians or Blacks. Do not enter, trespassers will be raped, maimed, strangled, gassed, shot. The only "legitimate" inhabitants are those in power, the whites and those who align themselves with whites. (3-4)

She understands that race impacts her social position and is able to utilize her light skin as privilege. Sandi continues assimilating to the oppressor class until her confrontation with the law when she is detained, the moment in which her Chicana consciousness is awakened. She is able to see the world as it truly is, possibly, for the first time, thus laying the necessary foundation for a feminist politic.

Nevertheless, this decision to unite herself with the oppressing community is not sufficient. Sandi had to prove her loyalty to the majority in order for them to genuinely accept her. She tells of how the students were calling her and another Latina student pejorative names such as "Beaner" and "Wetback" and how she joined the dominant class by calling the girl, Milagros, a "Beaner." This day represented her acceptance into the predominant ring of her school. Sandi explains:

> After that day, I was no longer seen as one of them. I was accepted, and nobody ever called me a "Beaner" or a "Wetback." I stopped speaking Spanish and stopped calling myself Sandra and started calling myself "Sandi." As Sandi, I would fit in better. Then Courtney and Britney and Brianna made an exception for me and became my friends. I was treated like I was different...and I liked it... (J. López 52)

By recognizing the existing class system in her school, essentially a microcosm of the United States, this event functions as the catalyst of her first transfor-

mation, the mere intent to survive. Anzaldúa argues in *Borderlands* that "The only 'legitimate' inhabitants are those in power, the whites and those who align themselves with whites" (3-4). Similar to Anzaldúan thought, Sandi understands that race impacts her social position and, therefore, can utilize her light skin as privilege in order to reject her chicanidad. By transforming into an Anglo girl, Sandi avoids discrimination until adulthood.

The central confrontation with the police marks the first time Sandi experiences discrimination as an adult. She is mistaken for an undocumented immigrant solely due to her skin color and physical location in the borderlands and consequently begins to feel the plight of *la mujer indocumentada*, a woman that Anzaldúa describes as:

> ...doubly threatened in this country. Not only does she have to contend with sexual violence, but like all women, she is prey to a sense of physical helplessness. As a refugee, she leaves the familiar and safe homeground to venture into unknown and possibly dangerous terrain. (12-13)

Sandi's experience of the multiplicity of oppression that women of color face in the Arizona borderlands leads to analyzing her own identity. This metaphysical crossroads is the moment in which she starts to question the hierarchy of color and gender. According to Temperance David, "The Subject's experience of rejection from the dominant culture, allows (forces) her to perceive, at least unconsciously, those repressive and ideological State apparatuses that create her as Other" (338). Sandi decides to ignite a revolution through movement and consciousness-raising instead of waiting for another woman to do so; she realizes that the more she transforms, the more realistic the possibility of a fundamental change will become. Her decision to fight represents the comprehension that she should develop a self-defense tactic such as *la facultad* in order to achieve self-approval; her determination to resist against an unjust law such as Arizona SB1070 functions as an integral part of her becoming Chicana.

As I previously discussed, Sandi continues assimilating successfully to the oppressor class until her confrontation with the law seen in *Detained in the Desert*, the moment in which her Chicana consciousness emerges. Due to her personal struggle, she begins to create the indispensable foundation for a feminist politicization. Above all, it is necessary to examine and question the oppressive restrictions that are a burden to women of color in the United States borderlands, a geopolitical zone in which women, according to Sonia Saldívar-Hull, are dehumanized to such a high degree that they fully lose their value (61). In order to understand the transition that Sandi experiences, one must comprehend her education within the racist systems and structures at work in the United States, a supposedly free nation but, on the other hand, marked by what Rodolfo Acuña has called a legacy of hate, the result of not upholding the various

stipulations proposed in the Treaty of Guadalupe Hidalgo in 1848 (56-9). This hierarchically organized world (class, race, gender, etc.) manifests the unjustified fear of a nation saturated in the middle of a fresh wave of nativism and hostility towards immigrants, both documented and undocumented. The popular myth in United States history is that the nation has welcomed immigrants, forming the famous "melting pot." Nevertheless, the cruel reality is that the only immigrants who are truly accepted are those that can pass as WASPs. Nativism is a form of xenophobia that reemerges during difficult times in our history; historically, when the economy prospers, expressions of nativism remain submerged (Acuña 165-6, 208-11). In other words, Arizona SB1070 is the result of these nativist fears. Arizona blames the current recession on undocumented immigrants ; among other things, immigrants serve as an easy scapegoat to justify current governmental problems.

Josefina López highlights the racist nature of SB1070 in *Detained in the Desert* through the character Matt, Sandi's boyfriend, an undocumented White Canadian immigrant. The geographical location of Arizona on the border is key to understanding the injustices directed towards minorities, in this case towards Sandi, and the free pass that Matt receives thanks to his White skin. The police officer tells Sandi: "You are six miles from the border and you look – I mean... you have given me reason to suspect your status " (J. López 32). The officer realizes that his justification is solely based on Sandi's skin color and rectifies his declaration. He himself is aware that this law should have nothing to do with race or ethnicity, but it appears inevitable to separate the multiple indoctrinated stereotypes and the law. As an agent of the law, he believes that undocumented immigrants should look like Sandi. He does not even question Matt's citizenship, something that enrages Sandi. Of course, she has the easy option of avoiding further discrimination and detention; she simply has to show some form of identification to continue her journey uninterrupted.

The borderlands "have historically been spaces of colonization where powerful forces have imposed, (mis)interpreted, and (mis)represented historical truths" (Licona 113). Even though these lands were originally part of Mexico, popular opinion is that Mexican-Americans are mostly undocumented immigrants. Therefore, regardless of his undocumented status, Matt does not suffer the discrimination that Sandi is subject to because he does not fit within the confines of the culturally accepted model of an undocumented immigrant. López is able to demonstrate the bias of a law that allows the undocumented to remain in the country as long as their physical appearance is stereotypically North American. The irony of the abduction scene manifests the need to question a system that in reality has found an undocumented immigrant but,

due to the government's indoctrinated racism, believes that the person of color is at fault. It is precisely this racial profiling that assists Sandi's development of *la facultad* and the adoption of a politicized agency. As it is "an emotional and intellectual skill which is developed amidst hegemonic powers", the police effectively reiterate the power of the White man (Sandoval, "U.S. Third World Feminism" 22).

As Josefina López establishes in the scene with Milagros, Sandi avoids racial discrimination by passing as a White girl in her youth, but the confrontation with the police marks the first time that she experiences it as an adult. This metaphysical crossroads is the moment in which she begins to question the gender and color hierarchy that predominates in the United States. Sandi consciously decides to initiate change instead of waiting for another woman to do so; she realizes that the more she transforms, the more realistic the possibility becomes of a fundamental change (O'Sullivan 70-86). She recognizes that she does not control the oppressive culture even though she holds the tools at her disposition to end the confrontation. Mary Louise Pratt notes, "While subjugated peoples cannot readily control what the dominant culture visits upon them, they do determine to varying extents what they absorb into their own, how they use it, and what they make it mean" (6). Her decision to fight represents the understanding that she should develop self-defense tactics such as *la facultad* in order to achieve self-approval; her determination to fight against such an unjust law functions as an integral part in becoming Chicana.[6]

From this moment, the protagonist endures the collective experience(s) of the oppressed. These feelings of fear are crucial to the manifestation of *la facultad*. In order to transform her consciousness with the intent of embracing her true identity, Sandi must better understand her political, economic, and social situation. Nevertheless, this understanding of the social world is not enough; it is necessary to examine the multiple conditions that lead to conceptualizing *la facultad*. In other words, it is essential that the woman suffers from multiple forms of oppression in order to cultivate it (Moya, "Chicana Feminism" 471). According to Paula Moya, the following realist theories can be applied to one's development of *la facultad*:

> (1) As long as our world is hierarchically organized along enduring relations of domination, people occupying different social locations will tend to experience the world in systematically different ways; and (2) not everyone who has the same kind of experience will react in the same way or come to the same conclusions about that experience. ("Chicana Feminism" 472-3)

In light of these realist premises, there are people better situated to cultivate *la facultad*. Being a woman of color is not enough; it is obligatory that Sandi decide to fight against

the law. By reacting to the police in such a way, she decides to combat nativism. She elects to search for possible ways of navigating the decisive modalities of the dominant consciousness (Sandoval, *Methodology of the Oppressed* 105).

Similar to Cherríe Moraga in "La Güera," Sandi understands her differences from privileged Anglo women. Moraga explains in the preface to *This Bridge Called My Back: Writings by Radical Women of Color*: "My growing consciousness as a woman of color is surely seeming to transform my experience. How could it be that the more I feel with other women of color, the more I feel myself Chicana, the more susceptible I am to racist attack!" (xv). She must recognize the differences between herself and her Anglo counterparts. Sandi's dispute with the Arizona police serves as the point of departure in her awakening as a woman of color. Instead of showing documentation and continuing her trip, she decides to continue her confrontation with the law. She yells at the police: "No! I am not showing you no stinking badges, cabrón!" (J. López 33). Furthermore, in the detainment center she understands that as soon as she shows some form of identification she will be free, but she realizes that nothing will change unless she initiates it. She is required to cultivate a methodology in order to decipher the borderlands from a feminist perspective. Only after understanding *la facultad* and her new politicized agenda, is she able to give voice to the Chicana community by igniting a movement against Arizona SB1070. Her boyfriend Matt tries to convince her to end her fight, but she responds to his lack of understanding: "... you will never know what it's like to be me. You don't have dark skin. Nobody ever questions your right to exist or succeed. You have no clue how hard it is to be an American when you look like me!" (J. López 43). As a White male, Matt is not discriminated against and does not understand how it feels to be objectified or dehumanized even though he is the one in the play that represents the undocumented community. Neither does he understand why nor how the Chicana is seen as equal to an undocumented immigrant according to Arizona legislation. Sandi conceptualizes the relationships between power and domination and how it affects her own existence, giving her the opportunity to search for new methods of self-defense and development in addition to her ideologies. Sandi possesses the essential tools that make possible her search towards a redefinition of her self-consciousness beginning from the moment in which she realizes the reasons behind the discrimination. Her identity as a woman subject to double discrimination influences her interpretation of the experience. After analyzing, deciphering, and deconstructing the oppressive ideologies, Sandi comprehends the dominant structure that positions women of color as illegitimate citizens. After having recognized the pain and anguish of her Otherness, she begins to explore the ways in which the Other, in this case the woman of color, expresses her identity and resistance.

Sandi's intuitions are necessary to acquire political knowledge. Her borderlands consciousness provokes a new revolutionary theory about politics, overrun with feminist ideologies representative of Chicana pioneers Anzaldúa and Moraga. Just as Moraga describes in "La Güera," considering Sandi's conceptualization of consciousness from a realist perspective demonstrates "that her changing political commitments are tied to her evolving conception of what her place in society is versus what it should be" (Moya, "Chicana Feminism" 475). Effectively, the shift in ideology and identity is a source of motivation in her search for truth and the desire to create a better society.

Her ideological metamorphosis successfully ends when she is lost in the desert; Sandi experiences symbolically and literally the experience of those who cross the border daily. This dangerous and difficult situation acts as the spark that fires her recently discovered political agenda. In the last scene of *Detained*, López incorporates two subtle lines of dialogue that contrast with the beginning of the play in reference to music and her name. In the second scene, Sandi expresses her dislike for Mexican-American music: "*(SANDI turns on the radio. She dials it. A Ranchera song comes on.)* God, I hate Rancheras. Not another Ranchera station" (J. López 27). Sandi is clearly bothered by this type of music, but instead of simply changing the station, she feels the need to voice her opinion. Moreover, she reveals in the scene with Milagros, the adult ghost of the girl who Sandi called offensive names at her elementary school, that she decided to call herself "Sandi" instead of her birth name, "Sandra." Without a Hispanic name, it would be easier to pass and be accepted. However, in the last scene, she presents herself as Sandra Sánchez, declares that she loves Rancheras, and commits to helping in the fight against the injustices that occur in the Borderlands (J. López 65). Sandi highlights her new thought process, possibly for the first time in her life; she is going to adopt her culture and Chicanidad. These two subtle changes represent her new strategy of acquiring her identity in an attempt to fight against the society that has classified her as a second-class citizen.

By means of implementing a feminist agenda and arriving at agreement with Chicana culture, Sandi serves as the ideal woman to join the fight for borderlands equality. Conscious or not, her actions express the reformation of Aztlán "from a male nation state to a feminist site of resistance" (Saldívar-Hull 61). This represents "a conscious rupture with [...] oppressive traditions" (Anzaldúa 82) in which she is capable of reinterpreting culture and history and, ultimately, new structures of cultural myth such as Aztlán, La Malinche, La Virgen de Guadalupe, and La Llorona. This alludes to the canonical feminist declaration of Combahee River Collective: "We realize that the only people who care enough about us to work consistently for our liberation is us . . . This focusing on our own oppression is embodied in the concept of identity politics.

We believe that the most profound and potentially the most radical politics come out of our own identity, as opposed to working to end somebody else's oppression" (212).

At the end of the play, Sandi decides to dedicate her future to social justice. She tells Ernesto: "...I want to help. Next time you go deliver water, I want to join you" (J. López 64). An enormous weight is lifted from her shoulders when she decides to join the Cause. This draws attention to the metaphor that Anzaldúa uses of a person that is revising a box, removing what no longer holds value and keeping what is useful; she declares that the new Mestiza "bota lo que no vale, los desimentos, los desencuentos, el embrutacimiento. Aguarda el juicio, hondo y enraizado, de la gente antigua" (82). After having revised her metaphorical box, Sandi is ready to give up everything with the goal of starting over, liberating herself, and embracing her new identity. In order to successfully fight against racial oppression, Chicanas must come to consciousness about race, gender, and sexuality to challenge the predominant narratives of the majority (heterosexual, Anglo, and middle-class women) who do not typically take into consideration the interests and needs of women of color. Just as the Combahee River Collective states, the only woman capable of ending social oppression is the one who suffers said oppression: Sandi in the case of *Detained.*

CONCLUSION

In *Detained in the Desert,* Josefina López highlights the injustice(s) of Arizona SB1070, legislature that promotes racial discrimination towards marginalized groups, in particular, Chicanas and other women of color. She questions anti-immigration activity and the political climate of not only Arizona, but also the United States. Through the protagonist Sandi, López is able to demonstrate the need for Chicanas to cultivate a new consciousness and survival tactics such as Anzaldúa's *la facultad.* Sandi's identity transformation is motivated by means of an authentic desire to better understand her surroundings and the aim to create a more inclusive world. As a new Chicana living without borders and boundaries, she acquires a better perspective to confront the oppressive effects of the racially and socially privileged. To this end, *Detained in the Desert* serves as the point of departure towards a new Chicana feminist movement in which López urges other Chicanas to create a dialogue towards Chicana consciousness and have a higher degree of seriousness towards political and social change, thereby embracing the words of Gloria Anzaldúa, "I change myself, I change the world" (70).

ENDNOTES

1 An earlier version of this article was published in Spanish in *Label Me Latina/o: Journal of Twentieth & Twenty-First Centuries Latino Literary Production.* See "Detenida en la frontera: La conciencia de la mestiza en Detained in the Desert de Josefina López." *Label Me Latina/o.* Spring 3 (2013).

2 Detained in the Desert received its world premiere in 2010 (October 1st - November 21st) in Los Angeles, California at CASA 0101, the theater founded by Josefina López herself.

3 This awakening of consciousness draws attention to Cherríe Moraga, who also decides to embrace her mestizaje and chicanidad. This decision to self-identify as a woman of color is precisely what manifests the understanding that one's best tool to create a society truly free of the oppression of women just like the author. Moraga explains the importance of developing a consciousness of her authentic identity. She explains in *Loving in the War Years* what she calls "Conscientización...a consciousness born of a body that has a shade, a language, a sex, a sexuality, a geography and a history. And that sometimes changes everything, including with whom you love and lay" (203).

4 In *Borderlands/La Frontera,* Anzaldúa explains: "The work of mestiza consciousness is to break down the subject-object duality that keeps her a prisoner and to show in the flesh the emergence and thought in her work how duality is transcended" (80).

5 As Emma Pérez indicates, feminism is used as a methodological tool to liberate oneself from the restrictions that have historically limited Chicana women (22).

6 Thanks to her implementing of *la facultad,* Sandi supplies the structural entities of the reformation of a feminist Aztlán in which women have both agency and voice. Given that the Chicano Nation traditionally is manifested through Aztlán, the mythical homeland, the feminist Aztlán becomes an intangible space in which contemporary Chicanas have the tools to participate in the construction of a multiplicity of meanings of this mythical land (Pérez 59-72).

WORKS CITED

Acuña, Rodolfo. *Occupied America: A History of Chicanos*. 5th ed. New York: Pearson Longman, 2004. Print.

Adams, Mary Louise. "There's No Place like Home: On the Place of Identity in Feminist Politics." *Feminist Review* 31 (1989): 22-33. Print.

Anzaldúa, Gloria. *Borderlands/La Frontera: The New Mestiza*. San Francisco: Aunt Lute, 1987. Print.

Berila, Beth. "Reading National Identities: The Radical Disruption of *Borderlands/La Frontera*." *Entre Mundos/Among Worlds: New Perspectives on Gloria E. Anzaldúa*. Ed. AnaLouise Keating. New York, NY: Palgrave Macmillan, 2008. 121-28. Print.

Castillo, Debra A., and Córdoba María Socorro Tabuenca. *Border Women: Writing from La Frontera*. Minneapolis: University of Minnesota Press, 2002. Print.

Combahee River Collective. "A Black Feminist Statement." *This Bridge Called My Back: Writings by Radical Women of Color*. Ed. Cherríe Moraga and Gloria Anzaldúa. New York: Kitchen Table, Women of Color, 1983. 210-18. Print.

David, Temperance K. "Killing to Create: Gloria Anzaldúa's Artistic Solution to 'Cervicide.'" *intersections* 10.1 (2009): 330-40. Print.

Gilroy, Paul. *The Black Atlantic: Modernity and Double Consciousness*. Cambridge: Harvard University Press, 1993. Print.

Licona, Adela C. "(B)orderlands' Rhetorics and Representations: The Transformative Potential of Feminist Third-Space Scholarship and Zines." *NWSA Journal* 17.2 (2005): 104-29. Print.

López, Josefina. *Detained in the Desert & Other Plays*. Carlsbad, CA: WPR: Latino Insights, 2011. Print.

López, Tiffany A. Introduction. *Detained in the Desert & Other Plays*. By Josefina López. Carlsbad, CA: WPR: Latino Insights, 2011. 17-18. Print.

Moraga, Cherríe. "La Güera." *This Bridge Called My Back: Writings by Radical Women of Color*. Ed. Gloria Anzaldúa and Cherríe Moraga. New York: Kitchen Table, Women of Color, 1983. 27-34. Print.

--- . *Loving in the War Years: Lo Que Nunca Pasó Por Sus Labios*. Boston, MA: South End, 1983. Print.

Moya, Paula M. L., and Michael R. Hames-Garcia. *Reclaiming Identity: Realist Theory and the Predicament of Postmodernism*. Berkeley, CA: University of California, 2000. Print.

Moya, Paula M. L. "Chicana Feminism and Postmodernist Theory." *Signs: Journal of Women in Culture and Society* 26.2 (2001): 441-83. Print.

O'Sullivan, Sue. "Passionate Beginnings: Ideological Politics 1969-1972." *Feminist Review* 11 (1982): 70-86. Print.

Pérez, Emma. *The Decolonial Imaginary: Writing Chicanas into History*. Bloomington: Indiana University Press, 1999. Print.

Pratt, Mary Louise. *Imperial Eyes: Travel Writing and Transculturation.* London: Routledge, 1992. Print.

Saldívar-Hull, Sonia. *Feminism on the Border: Chicana Gender Politics and Literature.* Berkeley: University of California Press, 2000. Print.

Sandoval, Chela. *Methodology of the Oppressed.* Minneapolis, MN: University of Minnesota Press, 2000. Print.

--- . "U.S. Third World Feminism: The Theory and Method of the Oppositional Consciousness in the Postmodern World." *Genders* 10 (1991: Spring): 1-24. Print.

White, Hayden V. *The Content of the Form: Narrative Discourse and Historical Representation.* Baltimore: Johns Hopkins University Press, 1990. Print.

THE CORPOREALITIES OF POLITICS: A MEDITATION ON THEORY IN THE FLESH

TALA KHANMALEK

When we refuse to consider the value of knowledge that is rooted in the body, in the psyche, in paralogical experience, we fail to challenge colonialist, post-Renaissance, Euro-Western conceptions of reality. We need to move beyond the facile dichotomy of "essentialism" and "constructionism" to embrace other theoretical paradigms inclusive of embodied and in-spirited knowledge. —Gloria E. Anzaldúa, "Foreword" to *Cassell's Encyclopedia of Queer Myth, Symbol and Spirit*

Traditions of radically theorizing and narrating the self have been historic to women of color feminisms from the 1960s to the present. The following meditation begins with a review of the formulation "theory in the flesh," first introduced by Cherríe Moraga and Gloria Anzaldúa in the groundbreaking 1981 anthology *This Bridge Called My Back* (*Bridge* for short). As a contemporary philosophy of corporeality, theory in the flesh submits the body's relationship to the world anew. Next, I conduct a brief reading of the formulation by way of Audre Lorde's *The Cancer Journals* (1980), in which she scrutinizes the meaning of breast cancer in her life and in society. Finally, I end with a few reflections that may be useful to our speculative visions.

In "A Black Feminist Statement," the Combahee River Collective argues that racism is a feminist issue because for black women, multiple oppressions

are simultaneous and interlocking. Rather than applying a categorical analysis of domination that disconnects axes of difference and therefore erases the experiences as well as existence of black women, the Collective advances an understanding of race, class, gender, sexuality and ability as co-constitutive. "The synthesis of these oppressions," they state, "creates the conditions of our lives" (Hull, Bell Scott, and Smith 13). In other words, categories of identification are mutually inclusive and informed by the same system of domination.

Dated April 1977, the statement was published both in *Bridge* and in the later anthology *All the Women Are White, All the Blacks Are Men, But Some of Us Are Brave* (1982). The contributors of both canonical texts, many of whom are the same, further expand an analysis of oppression as embodied and literally mutational, arguably pioneering the more critical turn in the present-day field of epigenetics, the study of changes in gene expression caused by social factors. In *Bridge*, an equally embodied politics of identity ingeniously un-thinks and rethinks the relationship between politics, biology, and race. On the one hand, *Bridge* confirms that race is a social construct. On the other hand, it subverts racism and other social inequalities without denying their *material* impacts. We must foreground critique in the discursive *and* the material; failure to ground discourse in materiality, they argue, is to privilege the position of those whose subjectivities have never been subjugated. Here is the ingenious part: as a result of these material impacts, our ways of knowing are also materially conditioned. The body (not just the abstract self) is a social site of domination that materializes and consequently senses injustices viscerally. Because the personal, including the structure of our very anatomy, is political, politics must emerge from specific corpo*realities*.

According to theory in the flesh, theorizing is, of necessity, based on the multiplicity of our particular experiences (Moraga and Anzaldúa 23). The flesh is more than an ideological location. Rather, *Bridge* centralizes how the body knows against the grain of theory itself as bodiless and the un-locatable knowledge claims of universal Man. "How do we deal with the ways in which this diseased society has infused our very blood systems?" they ask (62). "We are interested in pursuing a society that uses flesh and blood experiences to concretize a vision that can begin to heal," they respond, the bridges connecting us being our very backs (23). Theory in the flesh is thus neither a reinscription of biological determinism nor an essentialist identity politics. It is a total reconceptualization of "nature"—regimes of Truth that fix alterities in essences—that at once leverages the particularities our selves *and* widens the consciousness of the self to ultimately include all others, what Anzaldúa later calls "conocimiento."[1]

Bridging is not simply a metaphor, but an intentional and multi-directional/dimensional movement that invites transformation, indeed, transmutation even

though the stakes of physical vulnerability may be as high as death. In a kind of ontological queering, theory in the flesh emphasizes difference, not subsumed in unity but in favor of heterogeneous and contradictory identity formations. Similar to the recent "affective turn," the body is relational and in motion—without allegiance to its own boundaries or those of time, space, and nations.[2] Although the body is sensorially open, it nevertheless sustains a tactical and strategic relationship to its matter. As such, theory in the flesh does not forego every consideration of the biological in an effort to transcend identity; the body can affect and be affected while remaining situated. It is only through the flesh that we truly become intersubjective, actualizing an *erotic* metaphysic. However, this radical openness is far from a romantic potentiality. If, according to *Bridge*, our indeterminatedness is measured by how sensorially open we are then border crossers always risk being wounded again. Acting *through* the body means acting through the wounds of oppression and facing the real question of pain.

Here I would like to stress the relevance of theory being in the *flesh* rather than in the body. Although integrity is crucial to women of color feminisms, flesh challenges paradigms of recovery and ideas of an always already whole body for one that has experienced dismemberment. In her seminal essay "Mama's Baby, Papa's Maybe: An American Grammar Book," Hortense J. Spillers explains that "before the 'body' there is the 'flesh,' that zero degree of social conceptualization that does not escape concealment under the brush of discourse, or the reflexes of iconography" (67). "If we think of the 'flesh' as a primary narrative," she continues, "then we mean its seared, divided, ripped-apartness, riveted to the ship's hole, fallen, or 'escaped' overboard" (67). Moraga and Anzaldúa correspondingly distinguish the body from the flesh, and insist that we theorize in the latter precisely because it has yet to be thought in the discourse of recognition. The absence of a subject position, excluded from the conditions of human intelligibility, paradoxically allows the flesh to raise the question of ethics in a way that critiques the very conditions of what it means to be human *and* the biologisms of earlier centuries that secure it.

As an analytical framework, theory in the flesh provides a way of understanding the intersectional relationship between difference and disease that highlights the racialized and gendered dimensions of biopolitics. Reading Audre Lorde's *The Cancer Journals*, a collection of writings following the six months after her masectomy, through the lens of theory in the flesh forces us to reconsider the causes and effects of sickness. "Is this pain and despair that surround me a result of cancer, or has it just been released by cancer?" she provokes (11). Lorde concludes that her body is a barometer, the pain within an echo of "abominations outside" (11). She states that her struggle with breast cancer cannot be separated from "[her] fury at the outside world's viciousness, the stupid brutal

lack of consciousness or concern that passes for the way things are" (12). "The blood of black women sloshes from coast to coast," she asserts, "and [Mary] Daly says race is of no concern to women. So that means we are either immortal or born to die and no note taken, un-women" (12). Lorde maintains that breast cancer is preventable but not prevented because it functions within a profit economy. In other words, there is only profit in its treatment, so possible prevention is unfunded and threatens the medical industrial complex. She refers to cancer as a "Cancer Establishment" or as "Cancer Inc.,"[3] describing it and the plastic surgery industry that forces prosthesis in terms of a corporation. Most importantly, she maintains that breast cancer is preventable but not prevented because it is a symptom of a malignant society. Social factors of disease, which are not just economic, actively produce sickness. Breast cancer is a systemic disease with distinct causes that positively correlate to global histories of racial slavery and colonialism.

Through her narration of breast cancer as "a Black Lesbian Feminist Experience," Lorde unnaturalizes cancer by explaining that her body is overexposed to disease and health disparities (73). In the hierarchy of being, she is not intelligible as a person, but an inhuman target of death. Lorde says that she has been in training to resist cancer for a long time, for "growing up Fat Black Female and almost blind in america requires so much surviving that you have to learn from it or die" (40). In the earlier quote she alludes to the transatlantic slave trade—another kind of profit economy that controlled mortality by regulating the bodies, specifically the reproduction, of enslaved black women. Through her particular experiences, Lorde reveals the continuities of biopolitics' raced and gendered dimensions. She situates the historical antecedents of her diagnosis and the violence that stitches her everyday survival squarely within the dehumanizing organization of politics, biology, and race that founds modernity, the nation, and science itself. To survive its fatal legacy and contemporary re-inventions, Lorde contends that "we have had to learn this first and most vital lesson—that we were never meant to survive. Not as human beings" (21). "I am an anachronism," she declares, "a sport, like the bee that was never meant to fly. Science said so. I am not supposed to exist. I carry death around in my body like a condemnation" (13).

However, for Lorde and the authors of *Bridge*, this death sentence is also a source of powerful insight, the seemingly ironic antidote to oppression if you will. It is an important reminder that identity is always a complexly embodied representational category despite a subject-less ideal of self-determination. Survival thus entails what it always has, namely, other ways of knowing away from common sense, for as Lorde famously quipped, "the master's tools will never dismantle the master's house."[4] For women of color feminisms, this

has meant turning to the particularities of flesh, not a free-floating signifier abstracted from the material histories that have produced it nor a treatment of difference as additive or normalized into a kind of universalism. For women of color feminisms, enacting a new world in the present means reimaging the body. An epistemological mutation is therefore always already a mutation in the structure of one's own genes and, simultaneously, in the structure of society. Even as it renders us more vulnerable than we already are, survival entails "a disciplined attention to the true meaning of 'it feels right to me' (*Sister Outsider: Essays and Speeches* 37). In their attention to the prediscursive perception of domination and intuitive sensiblities, what Anzaldúa calls "la facultad," women of color feminisms continue to offer us indispensable tools for ongoing speculation as well as a speculative aesthetic—that of poetics. I will close with lines from the final pages of Lorde's journals: "The only really happy people I have ever met are those of us who work against these deaths with all the energy of our living, recognizing the deep and fundamental unhappiness with which we are surrounded, at the same time as we fight to keep from being submerged by it" (*The Cancer Journals* 75).

WORKS CITED

Anzalduá, Gloria E. "Foreword." Cassell's Encyclopedia of Queer Myth, Symbol and Spirit. Connor, Randy P. London; Herndon, VA: Cassell, 1997. Print.

Anzalduá, Gloria E, and AnaLouise Keating, eds. "now let us shift...the path of conocimiento...inner work, public acts." *This Bridge We Call Home: Radical Visions for Transformation.* New York: Routledge, 2002. 540–576. Print.

Clough, Patricia Ticineto, and Jean O'Malley Halley. *The Affective Turn: Theorizing the Social.* Durham: Duke University Press, 2007. Print.

Hull, Gloria T., Patricia. Bell-Scott, and Barbara Smith. *All the Women Are White, All the Blacks Are Men, but Some of Us Are Brave: Black Women's Studies.* Old Westbury, N.Y.: Feminist Press, 1982. Print.

Lorde, Audre. *The Cancer Journals.* San Francisco: Aunt Lute Books, 1980. Print.

---. *Sister Outsider: Essays and Speeches.* Trumansburg, NY: Crossing Press, 1984. Print.

Moraga, Cherríe, and Gloria Anzaldúa. *This Bridge Called My Back: Writings by Radical Women of Color.* Watertown, Mass: Persephone, 1981. Print.

Spillers, Hortense J. "Mama's Baby, Papa's Maybe: An American Grammar Book." *Diacritics* 17.2 (1987): 64.

ENDNOTES

1 See Gloria E. Anzaldúa's essay "now let us shift...the path of conocimiento...inner work, public acts" in *This Bridge We Call Home: Radical Visions for Transformation*, eds. Gloria Anzaldúa and AnaLouise Keating (New York, NY: Routledge, 2000).

2 In *The Affective Turn* the editors describe the "affective turn" in the Humanities and the Social Sciences as a fairly new interdisciplinary way of theorizing the social. Beginning with the premise that the body's matter is to a certain extent, incorporeal, affect theory considers how the material body coevolves with its environment. In other words, how it can affect and be affected, producing a continuously renewed ontology irrespective of identity. See Patricia Ticineto Clough and Jean Halley, ed., *The Affective Turn: Theorizing the Social* (Durham and London: Duke University Press, 2007).

3 See Lorde 55-77.

4 See "The Master's Tools Will Never Dismantle the Master's House" in *Sister Outsider.*

TOWARD POETIC HEALINGS

POETRY

IRE'NE LARA SILVA

DIETA INDIGENA

what would we be if we were still
what our ancestors ate
there were no cows no pigs no chickens here
there were no domesticated animals
animals fattened beyond their ability
to survive in the wild
bred to feeble-mindedness

there were javelinas serpents turtles fish pheasants
and further north buffalo moose deer
none of them raised in captivity misery
none of them pumped with hormones
no Oestradiol Progesterone Testosterone
no Zeranol Trenbolone Melengestrol

no meat injected with ammonia dioxin
no cloned meat no poisoned meat

500 years and our bodies
cannot adjust to this foreign diet
and not just we but all humans
cannot thrive on a diet of chemicals
and preservatives
sulfur dioxide sodium benzoate sodium nitrate
propyl gallate BHA BHT
food prepared food poisoned with
partially hydrogenated oils trans fats saturated fats

and what have they done to maize
our first food
the corporations have created maize
which bears no viable seed
they would have us eating maize
born infertile born artificial born dead

what is a food that is not fertile
we are the eaters of fruit and seed
the eaters of that which has eaten fruit and seed
sustenance of fertility of blooming of gestating
our lives fed by what is alive

but if we listen to the ancestors
there is still food we can eat
food which can renew our health
food we can grow with our own hands
food which has grown in fields close to us
chiles frijoles tomates aguacate calabaza
nopales chayote cacao amaranth quinoa
food we should eat
food we must eat

sustenance our bodies have craved
all these centuries
let us eat what our ancestors ate
decolonize your diet mi raza
it is time to regain our strength

BLOOD·SUGAR·CANTO

this is what they will not tell you
and this is what you must know
if you hear nothing else i say
hear this
you cannot live in fear
you cannot heal in fear
fear will never make you stronger

fear is the language many doctors speak
they'll say this is going to kill you
your organs are being bathed in acid
amputation dialysis coma death

and when the body does not obey
as the doctor demands
more pills
more insulin
more syringes
more often

and it will wear on you
the constant battle of
necessity versus necessity

a box of syringes
vs
gas money

the price of sufficient insulin
against
the cost of groceries

testing strips and lancets
vs
the light bill

the cost of one healthy meal
vs
the cost of three fast food meals

another co-pay
and another co-pay
vs
the cost of not seeing the doctor

they will say there are no choices
but there are always choices
though the choices
we make out of fear
are not choices

fear is a prison
fear is worse
than the disease
fear
takes
everything

some will say this is war
war raging within us
blood turned against itself
our bodies falling in battle
the enemy everywhere
within and without

but the word *war*
turns us against ourselves

and the word *disease*
renders us victims
and the war is unending
and a war always claims
casualties

in a war
there is no room
for dreaming oneself well
and the first part of the dream
is learning to listen
to *your body* and to *your blood*

it is not as simple
as
eat this not that eat that not this
take this not that take that not this
do this not that do that not this

you learn to listen
until you are the one writing the song
and the daily challenges
are the discordant notes
you must work into the score
making something more beautiful
than what there was before
not planned not wanted
but more powerful
because it is truth

but the music
will not come
if you are afraid
music like most things in life
enters in only one of two ways

el amor o el dolor
through love or through pain

i know
no one said
we were worthy of love
no one said
we were precious
or that our lives were gifts
no one said
let us learn to love ourselves
heal ourselves
care for ourselves
care for each other
teach each other
how to begin
with this essential task
of
loving ourselves

i will begin here
with these words
learning love
one utterance at a time

i will not
live
in fear

i will make song

THE WORLD IS MEDICINE

let it in
the sunshine the rain the wind the lightning
eat the raw
eat the stones and eat the marrow
eat the warmth on your skin
and the words the sun is writing
eat the scent of the earth after rain
eat the storm the thunder rumbling inside

this is how you grow strong
be the roar be the keening
be the screaming be the running
be louder
be the wind be the trees growing tall
be the word be the day be the knife
be the hot rush of blood
be the clouds
be the electric spill of blooming
flowers in the desert
begin
and end with water
never forget
the ocean lives inside us
the rivers take us
where our ancestors walked
our bodies still ebb and flow
with the tides
there is no joy like the joy of the body
suspended in water weightless and fierce
water is life
drink it in
touch the world eat the world be the world
the world is medicine

let
it in

CONTRIBUTORS

Trevor Boffone is a PhD student in Hispanic Studies with a focus on US Latin@ Literature at the University of Houston. His research centers on Contemporary Latin@ Theatre, Chicana Feminism, Queer Theory, Feminist Theory, Women and Gender Studies, and Borderland Studies. He has published academic articles on the theatre of Josefina López, Nilo Cruz, Carmen Peláez, and Ramón del Valle-Inclán.

Jody A. Briones is an Assistant Professor of English at Texas A&M University-Kingsville where she serves as Coordinator of Freshman and Sophomore English. Her specializations include Chican@ Studies and Composition Studies, with special interests in class issues, Millennial Mexican American identity, conjunto music, and service-learning projects.

Deborah Cole (University of Arizona, PhD Linguistics and Anthropology) is Associate Professor of linguistics at the University of Texas-Pan American, where she also directs the Center for Teaching Excellence. Her research interests include language ideologies, institutional discourses, standardization and variation, and ethnolinguistic identity in the U.S. and Indonesia.

Rufina Cortez received her Ph.D. in Education Policy, Organization and Leadership from the University of Illinois in 2013. Her research examines the educational trajectory of Chicanas/Latinas in doctoral-granting institutions, with specific focus on the importance of community in their perseverance and graduation rates. Rufina is originally from Oxnard, California and the youngest of ten siblings. She is also the first in her family to earn a PhD. Throughout her life, Rufina has been involved with Latino youth leadership organizations, mentoring, tutoring and working with undergraduate and graduate students, parents, and the greater community.

Cindy Cruz is an assistant professor in the Department of Education at UC Santa Cruz. She is a critical ethnographer and her work with LGBTQIA street youth is grounded by her use of *testimonio* methodologies, US Third World feminisms, and critical pedagogy. She received her doctorate from UCLA in 2006, was a postdoctoral fellow at Cornell University through 2008, and is a member of the Decolonial Feminisms Research Group at UC Berkely and the Human Rights and Decolonial Feminisms Research Cluster at UC-Santa Cruz.

T. Jackie Cuevas teaches in the Department of English at UTSA. Prior to UTSA, Cuevas taught Women's and Gender Studies at Syracuse University, where she was also a member of the Democratizing Knowledge project founded by Chandra Talpade Mohanty. Cuevas' research engages the intersections of Latina/o literature, women of color feminisms, and queer theory. Cuevas is also a creative writer, member of the Macondo creative writing workshop founded by Sandra Cisneros, and co-founder of Evelyn Street Press.

Natalia Deeb-Sossa is an Associate Professor in Chicana/o Studies Department at the University of California, Davis. Her current work examines, using a feminist Chicana perspective, how immigrants, as cultural citizens, are negotiating power, resisting practices and policies of inequity in their local community, and claiming identity, space, and rights. Her work highlights how "cultural production" and addressing "social rights" is transmitted from one generation to the next through language, material objects, ritual, institutions, and art.

Yvette G. Flores, clinical psychologist and professor of Chicana and Chicano Studies has over 30 years experience as an academic, researcher, and practitioner; her areas of research interest include gender and social violence, trauma and mental health, and the challenges migration and its sequelae create for Latinas. Her writings bridge Chicana/Latina/Feminist studies. She is the current president of the section 8 {Hispanic/Latinas} of Division 35 {Society for Women in Psychology} of the American Psychological Association.

Magda García earned her BA and MA in English at the University of Texas at San Antonio, where she focused on Chicana feminist writings and theorization. She has served as part of the Society for the Study of Gloria Anzaldúa coordinating committee, as well as assisted with the efforts to revitalize Third Women Press. She is currently a graduate student in the University of California, Santa Barbara's Department of Chicana/o Studies, where she holds a UC Regents Pre-Doctoral Fellowship. Her research interests include theorizations of Empire, Chicana third space feminist theory, Chicana/o and U.S. Latina/o literature, Gender and Sexuality, oppositional consciousness, and decolonial thought.

Michael Lee Gardin is a Texan, a doctoral candidate in the department of English at the University of Texas at San Antonio, and an instructor of Women's Studies and English. Her research areas include queer studies, queer theory, feminisms, Chicana lesbian literature and theory, and transgender studies.

Ines Hernandez-Avila (Nez Perce and Tejana) is Professor and former Chair of Native American Studies, and one of the six founders of the Native American

and Indigenous Studies Association (NAISA). She is Co-Director of the three-year UCD Social Justice Initiative funded by the Mellon Foundation: http://socialjusticeinitiative.ucdavis.edu/, and lead Director for 2014-2015. She is also a poet and visual artist.

Rob Johnson is the author The Lost Years of William S. Burroughs: Beats in South Texas (Texas A and M University 2006), the editor of Fantasmas: Supernatural Stories by Mexican-American Writers (Bilingual Press, 2001), and co-editor of New Border Voices (Texas A and M University Press, 2014) and "The Beatest State in the Union": Texas and the Beat Generation of Writers (Lamar University Press, 2015). He is a Professor of English at the University of Texas Rio Grande Valley, where he teaches courses on south Texas literature and "Beat Generation" writers. He is married to the poet Erika Garza-Johnson.

AnaLouise Keating is a professor of women's studies at Texas Woman's University and the author of *Teaching Transformation: Transcultural Classroom Dialogues* and other books.

Tala Khanmalek is a Ph.D. Candidate in the Department of Ethnic Studies at UC Berkeley with designated emphases in Critical Theory and Women, Gender, and Sexuality Studies. As the former Executive Editor of *nineteen sixty nine: an ethnic studies journal,* she edited the issue on "Healing Justice" featuring the works of Aurora Levíns Morales.

Larissa M. Mercado-López is Assistant Professor of Women's Studies at California State University, Fresno, where she has taught and developed courses on Latina health, size, and women of color feminisms for Women's Studies and the Department of Chicano and Latin American Studies. Her research areas include Chicana feminism, maternal studies, borderlands studies, and feminist epistemology. Mercado-López co-edited *El Mundo Zurdo 3*; her current publications in progress include an edited collection of feminist approaches to women of color fitness and a co-edited collection of critical essays on Latina/o literature.

April Michels is pursuing a doctoral degree in Women's Studies at Texas Woman's University, where she currently serves as a Graduate Teaching Assistant. April received her Master's Degree in English Literature from Duquesne University in Pennsylvania. Her current research interests include spiritual activism, Anzaldúan theories, Womanism, Feminism and Religion and Ecological Justice.

Cynthia Paccacerqua is an Assistant Professor of Philosophy and Affiliate Faculty of Mexican American Studies at The University of Texas - Pan American. Her

current research interests are in Chicana and Latina Feminist Theory, Women of Color and Feminist Philosophy, and Philosophy of Culture and Coloniality. She completed her PhD in Philosophy at SUNY at Stony Brook and MA in Latin American Studies at Stanford University. Coauthor with Stephanie Alvarez of "De conciencia mestiza a conocimiento. La evolution teorética fronteriza de Gloria Anzaldúa" in Notices del deluvio: Textos latinoamericanos de las últimas décadas.

Anita Tijerina Revilla is an activist scholar, Associate Professor and Director of Women's Studies at the University of Nevada- Las Vegas. She loves art and has painted weekly since 2011. Her research and teaching focuses on student movements and social justice education, specifically in the areas of Chicana/ Latina, immigrant, feminist and queer rights activism. Her expertise is in the areas of Jotería Studies, Chicana/o Education, Chicana/Women of Color Feminism, and Critical Race/Ethnic Studies.

Gloria M. Rodriguez is an Associate Professor in the School of Education at UC Davis. As a researcher, she specializes in educational resource allocation and leadership from a critical, social justice perspective. Rodriguez also enjoys mentoring several undergraduate and graduate students of color, as well as junior faculty of color at UCD and across the country, drawing upon the wisdom of Anzaldúa, Freire, and Yosso in the process.

Sonia Saldívar-Hull is a Professor of English and Women's Studies and the founding Director of the Women's Studies Institute at University of Texas, San Antonio, which houses the Society for the Study of Gloria Anzaldúa. Her publications include *Feminism on the Border: Chicana Politics and Literature,* numerous book chapters, articles and introductory essays on Chicana literature, feminism, and the cultural intersections of borderland studies. Saldívar-Hull co-edited *El Mundo Zurdo 2* and *El Mundo Zurdo 3*. She is received a Distinguished Achievement Award for Literary and Cultural Criticism from the Western Literature Association and has served as co-editor of *Latin America Otherwise: Languages, Empires, Nations,* a book series with Duke University Press, since 1997.

Adrianna Michelle Santos is recent graduate of the doctoral program in Chicana/o Studies, with an emphasis in Feminist Studies, at the University of California, Santa Barbara. She also worked as a counselor and member of the speaker's bureau at the Santa Barbara Rape Crisis Center, and on the programming team at the UCSB Women's Center, where she was a co-founder

of the Women of Color in Academia Symposium. She currently teaches Multiethnic and American Literature and Writing at Texas A&M University – San Antonio.

Crystal E. Serrano is a graduate student at the University of Texas at San Antonio. Born and raised in Los Angeles, California, her work focuses on the Chicana/o Latina/o Ska music subculture. She expects to have her thesis completed by Summer 2014, titled: *Skalifornia: Identity Resistance and Empowerment in the Chicana/o Latina/o Ska(core) Music Scene in Los Angeles.*

ire'ne lara silva lives in Austin, TX, and is the author of *furia* (poetry, Mouthfeel Press, 2010) and *flesh to bone* (short stories, Aunt Lute Books, 2013). ire'ne is the Fiction Finalist for AROHO's 2013 Gift of Freedom Award, the 2008 recipient of the Gloria Anzaldua Milagro Award, a Macondo Workshop member, and a CantoMundo Inaugural Fellow. She and Moises S. L. Lara are currently co-coordinators for the Flor De Nopal Literary Festival.

Cristina Rose Smith is the daughter of Debra of Los Angeles and grand-daughter of Priscilla of New Mexico and Concepcion of the Philippines. Cristina is a PhD candidate at the California Institute of Integral Studies. Born in LA, she has sought out her motherlands while studying women's literature, teaching writing, and working in farm communities. She aspires towards *nepantla* and *babaylan* endeavors, the first of which, is to finish her dissertation on *mestiza*-indigenous auto-ethnographic creative texts.

Aunt Lute Books is a multicultural women's press that has been committed to publishing high quality, culturally diverse literature since 1982. In 1990, the Aunt Lute Foundation was formed as a non-profit corporation to publish and distribute books that reflect the complex truths of women's lives and to present voices that are underrepresented in mainstream publishing. We seek work that explores the specificities of the very different histories from which we come, and the possibilities for personal and social change.

Please contact us if you would like a catalog of our books or if you wish to be on our mailing list for news of future titles. You may buy books from our website, by phoning in a credit card order, or by mailing a check with the catalog order form.

Aunt Lute Books
P.O. Box 410687
San Francisco, CA 94141
415.826.1300

www.auntlute.com
books@auntlute.com

This book would not have been possible without the kind contributions of the Aunt Lute Founding Friends:

Anonymous Donor

Anonymous Donor

Rusty Barcelo

Marian Bremer

Marta Drury

Diana Harris

Phoebe Robins Hunter

Diane Mosbacher, M.D., Ph.D.

Sara Paretsky

William Preston, Jr